INTERNATIONAL PERSPECTIVES ON PROFITABILITY AND ACCUMULATION

NEW DIRECTIONS IN MODERN ECONOMICS
Series Editor: Malcolm C. Sawyer, Professor of Economics, University of York

New Directions in Modern Economics presents a challenge to orthodox economic thinking. It focuses on new ideas emanating from radical traditions including post-Keynesian, Kaleckian, neo-Ricardian and Marxian. The books in the series do not adhere rigidly to any single school of thought but share in common an attempt to present a positive alternative to the conventional wisdom.

The main emphasis of the series is on the development and application of new ideas to current problems in economic theory and economic policy. It includes new original contributions to theory, overviews of work in the radical tradition and the evaluation of alternative economic policies. Some books are monographs whilst others are suitable for adoption as texts. The series highlights theoretical and policy issues common to all modern economies and is designed to appeal to economists throughout the world regardless of their country of origin.

Post Keynesian Monetary Economics:
New Approaches to Financial Modelling
Edited by Philip Arestis

Keynes's Principle of Effective Demand
Edward J. Amadeo

New Directions in Post-Keynesian Economics
Edited by John Pheby

Theory and Policy in Political Economy:
Essays in Pricing, Distribution and Growth
Edited by Philip Arestis and Yiannis Kitromilides

Keynes's Third Alternative?
The Neo-Ricardian Keynesians and the Post Keynesians
Amitava K. Dutt and Edward J. Amadeo

Wages and Profits in the Capitalist Economy
The Impact of Monopolistic Power on Macroeconomic
Performance in the USA and UK
Andrew Henley

Prices, Profits and Financial Structures
A Post-Keynesian Approach to Competition
Gökhan Çapoğlu

INTERNATIONAL PERSPECTIVES ON PROFITABILITY AND ACCUMULATION

Edited by

FRED MOSELEY

Associate Professor of Economics, Mount Holyoke College, Massachusetts

and

EDWARD N. WOLFF

Professor of Economics, New York University

1992

cf. Duménil & Lévy 1993

Edward Elgar

© Fred Moseley and Edward N. Wolff 1992

Published by
Edward Elgar Publishing Limited
The Lypiatts
15 Lansdown Road
Cheltenham
Glos GL50 2JA
UK

Edward Elgar Publishing, Inc.
William Pratt House
9 Dewey Court
Northampton
Massachusetts 01060
USA

This book has been printed on demand to keep the title in print.

A catalogue record for this book
is available from the British Library

Library of Congress Cataloguing in Publication Data
International perspectives on profitability and accumulation/edited
by Fred Moseley and Edward N. Wolff.
p. cm. – (New directions in modern economics series)
Includes index.
1. Profit. 2. Saving and investment. I. Moseley, Fred, 1946–
II. Wolff, Edward N. III. Series.
HC79.P7158 1992   91–27762
338.5' 16–dc20   CIP

ISBN 978 1 85278 557 4

Printed and bound in Great Britain by
Marston Book Services Limited, Didcot

Contents

Figures

viii   *Figures*

Tables

Contributors

James R. Crotty, University of Massachusetts–Amherst, USA
Gérard Duménil, CNRS, LAREA-CEDRA, Universite de Paris, X-Nanterre, France
Mark Glick, University of Utah, USA
Jonathan P. Goldstein, Bowdoin College, USA
Michel Juillard, New School for Social Research, USA
Dominique Lévy, CNRS and CEPREMAP, France
John A. Miller, Wheaton College, USA
Fred Moseley, Mount Holyoke College, USA
Eduardo M. Ochoa, California State University–Los Angeles, USA
Jean-Luc Rosinger, Universidade de Brasilia, Brazil
Ednaldo Araquém da Silva, New School for Social Research, USA
Thomas E. Weisskopf, University of Michigan, USA
Edward N. Wolff, New York University, USA

1. Introduction

Fred Moseley and Edward N. Wolff

Has the rate of profit been falling in the USA or other industrialized countries? What are the factors that are directly responsible for its increase over time and what factors account for its decline? The rate of profit is one of the most important economic variables. It directly affects the rate of growth of an economy, both as a source of funds for new investment and as an inducement for new investment. It also has a direct bearing on the distribution of income within an economy, particularly between wage earners and owners of capital. Its movement over time is thus a major source of concern for the business community, the working population and public policy. The present volume fills an important gap in the literature on this important economic and policy issue.

This collection undertakes a rigorous statistical analysis of both profitability trends in the USA and other advanced economies and of the factors that affect its movement over time. Data collected for the USA indicates that the rate of profit generally fell from the 1860s until the First World War, and then moved upwards until the 1950s, when it again underwent a secular decline. The results also show that the postwar decline in the rate of profit also occurred in most other industrialized economies as well. However, even for the postwar period, the trend has been far from uniform, with profitability on the rise during the 1980s in many advanced economies. The authors also find that several factors have played key roles in causing changes in profitability. Among the most important are capital accumulation (investment), technology change, movements in the real wage, turnover rates, the growth of unproductive labour, raw material prices, international competition, structural change in the economy, work effort, labour–capital relations and public policy.

The first part of the book consists of four chapters on trends in profitability in major industrialized countries. They are concerned with two central questions. First, has the rate of profit been rising or falling? Second, what are the factors responsible for the observed trends in profitability? In these papers, the rate of profit, π, is typically defined as the ratio of total profits, P, to total capital, K:

$$\pi = P/K \tag{1.1}$$

By simple algebraic manipulation, this can be rewritten as:

$$\pi = (P/Y)\cdot(Y/K) \tag{1.2}$$

where Y is total national income or product. Most of the analysis concentrates on these two ratios. The first, P/Y, is the share of profits or capital income in total national income. Changes in the profit share, and correspondingly the wage share, are often interpreted as a result of a conflict between workers and capitalists. In Marxian terminology, a decline in the profit share is often referred to as the 'profit squeeze'. The second, Y/K, is the output–capital ratio, which is also referred to as 'capital productivity', since it shows the output produced per unit of capital. This ratio is also directly related to the 'organic composition of capital', a term used in Marxian analysis; and a decline in the output–capital ratio is often referred to as a 'rising composition of capital' effect. In Marxian theory, a rise in the composition of capital is viewed as the primary cause of a declining rate of profit.

With some further algebraic manipulation, movements in the profit share can be decomposed into two components:

$$P/Y = (Y - wL)/Y = 1 - w\cdot(L/Y) \tag{1.3}$$

where L is total employment, w is the wage rate, and wL is the total wage bill. Movements in the profit share are thus negatively related to increases in the wage rate and positively related to increases in labour productivity, which is the inverse of the ratio L/Y. Several analyses concentrate on the offsetting effects of a rising wage and rising labour productivity on the movement in the rate of profit.

In Chapter 2, Thomas Weisskopf analyses the trends in the after-tax rate of profit in the manufacturing sector of eight advanced capitalist countries (Canada, France, Federal Republic of Germany, Italy, Japan, Sweden, the United Kingdom and the United States) from 1951 to 1985. He finds that, with the exception of Italy, the rate of profit declined significantly in all eight countries. His analysis is based on an innovative technique which he calls a 'distribution frontier' to determine the extent to which the decline in the rate of profit in these countries was due to gains by labour and the extent to which it was due to changes in the general economic environment. Labour gains are measured by the rate of growth of after-tax real wages and are interpreted as part of the distributional conflict with capital. General economic variables include changes in the output–capital ratio, increases in the productivity of labour, movements in the relative prices of capital goods, material goods and wage goods, and changes in the tax rate. Weisskopf's results show that in Canada, France and the USA the decline in the rate of profit was due almost entirely to general environmental factors, while in the other countries distributional conflict played a significant, although usually minor, role.

Weisskopf further analyses the sources of the deterioration of the general economic environment in these countries and concludes that the most important factor was a decline in the output–capital ratio, thus lending support to the falling rate of profit variant of Marxian crisis theory which emphasizes a rising composition of capital. Finally Weisskopf hypothesizes that the outcomes of the distributional conflict depend primarily on the balance of power between capitalists and workers, which in turn depends on such factors as the rate of unemployment, the extent of unemployment insurance and the strength of unions. Using two different measures of the power of labour, Weisskopf finds that these measures are negatively and significantly related to the rate of growth of real wages, a result that is consistent with the 'profit squeeze' variant of Marxian crisis theory.

In Chapter 3, Gérard Duménil, Mark Glick and Dominique Lévy analyse the long-run trends of the rate of profit and its proximate determinants in the US economy from the Civil War to the present time. Spliced together from a variety of sources, the resulting series represents the longest continuous set of estimates of the rate of profit and related variables for the US economy that has been developed to date. These estimates show three distinct phases in the evolution of the rate of profit: a downward trend from the 1860s until the First World War, an upward trend from the First World War to the 1950s, and a downward trend since the 1950s. Estimates of the proximate determinants of the rate of profit show that the evolution of the rate of profit is due almost entirely to similar movements in the productivity of capital (or the output–capital ratio). This result is consistent with the composition of capital effect in Marxian crisis theory. The profit share showed very little variation over this entire period because the trends in the productivity of labour and the real wage remained more or less in concert (see equation 1.3). The authors emphasize that the first and third phases are very similar in many respects.

The final chapter in this first part investigates another factor affecting movements in the rate of profit, the rise of unproductive labour. In Moseley's study, unproductive labour is defined as labour which performs the functions of circulation and supervision, which Marx assumed to be unproductive of value and surplus-value. Moseley argues that a relative increase of unproductive labour requires that a greater portion of surplus-value be reserved to pay the costs of unproductive labour, thus leaving a smaller portion of surplus-value in the hands of the capitalists. In terms of equation (1.2), changes in unproductive labour affect the profit share of national income.

Moseley finds a very significant increase in the ratio of unproductive labour to productive labour (indeed a doubling) during the postwar period in the USA, which he views as the proximate cause of the decline of the rate of profit during this period. According to Moseley's estimates, the relative increase of unproductive labour accounted for approximately twice as much of the decline of the rate of profit as the increase in the composition of capital (see equation 1.2). Moseley analyses the underlying causes of the relative increase of unproductive labour. His main conclusion is that the most significant cause of the increase was the slower productivity growth of circulation labour, compared to productive labour, which seems to be inherent in the nature of the two activities. This conclusion suggests that a recovery in the rate of profit in the US economy is not very likely in the years ahead and thus that the stagflation of the last two decades is likely to persist into the future and perhaps end in a deep depression.

The second part of the book consists of four chapters which investigate the effects of structural change on movements in profitability. Structural change generally refers to shifts in the industrial composition of either employment or output. For example, in most industrialized countries, employment has grown considerably faster in service industries than in manufacturing over the postwar period. Structural shifts can affect the rate of profit in three ways. First, and most directly, it can affect movements in the output–capital ratio (see equation 1.2). The major reason is that sectors differ in their degree of capital intensity. Thus shifts in output from more capital-intensive sectors to less capital-intensive ones can lower the *overall* capital–output ratio (raise the output–capital ratio). Second, sectors also differ in their rate of labour productivity growth. Shifts in employment from higher productivity growth sectors (typically, manufacturing) to lower productivity growth sectors (typically, service industries) can lower *overall* productivity growth. This 'unbalanced growth' process has a direct bearing on the overall profit share (see equation 1.3). Third, shifts of capital from less profitable sectors to more profitable ones can raise the *overall* profit rate.

In the opening chapter of this part, Edward Wolff analyses the trends in the organic composition of capital, the share of profits and the rate of profit in the postwar US economy. Wolff estimates these variables using 85-sector input–output tables for six selected years covering the period from 1947 to

1977 and the corresponding labour and capital coefficients, using a methodology which he pioneered in earlier work. Additional estimates are provided for 1981 on the basis of national accounts data.

Wolff's estimates, like those of the other authors, show that the rate of profit declined significantly during the postwar period. The main reason was a roughly proportional decline in the share of profits; the organic composition of capital remained essentially constant. Wolff analyses the effect of 'uneven development' of different sectors (one of Marx's 'counteracting tendencies' to the falling rate of profit) on the overall organic composition of capital and thus on the rate of profit. He finds that there was a shift in the distribution of employment from sectors with a relatively high organic composition of capital to sectors with a relatively low organic composition of capital. This structural shift had a significant negative effect on the aggregate organic composition of capital and thus a significant positive effect on the general rate of profit. In other words, if this type of structural change had not occurred, the rate of profit would have declined even more than it did. According to his estimates, the rate of profit would have declined by 56 per cent, with no structural change in employment composition over the 1947–77 period, instead of the actual 37 per cent. Wolff suggests that the cause of this uneven development was the slower rate of technological change in the service sector, compared to the goods sector. His analysis demonstrates the significance of the offsetting effects of uneven development on the decline of profitability.

In Chapter 6, Eduardo Ochoa employs 71-sector input–output tables for six years during the postwar period to estimate the labour values, prices of production and wage-profit curves for the US economy. His results provide new empirical evidence related to two important theoretical controversies in Marxian and Cambridge capital theory. First, in Marxian theory, labour values and prices of production represent two sets of relative output prices for the sectors in an economy. The transformation of labour values to prices of production (the so-called 'transformation problem') depends mainly on differences in the organic composition (or capital intensity) among sectors.

In theory, prices of production can 'deviate' considerably from labour values. Ochoa's estimates show that labour values are very highly correlated with prices of production, both for a given year and, more importantly, over time. These results suggest that the 'transformation problem' in Marxian theory, about which so much has been written, is of very limited empirical significance, at least for the postwar US economy.

Second, in Cambridge capital theory, the overall trade-off in an economy between the wage rate and the rate of profit can be summarized in the so-called 'wage–profit frontier'. The shape of this curve depends in large measure on differences in capital intensity among the sectors of an economy. If this frontier is non-linear, it is possible that a given technique of production may be the most profitable at both high and low wage rates, whereas another technique of production can be the most profitable one at an intermediate range of wage rates. This is the so-called 'reswitching' phenomenon. Ochoa's estimates of the wage–profit curves (an approximation of the wage–profit frontiers) are almost linear, owing to the high correlation of values and prices of production. This linearity suggests that the theoretical possibility of 'reswitching' is also of limited empirical significance for the postwar US economy and thus that the Marxian analysis of choice of technique in terms of labour values remains valid. An important question is the extent to which Ochoa's strong results are generalizable to other countries.

Ednaldo da Silva and Jean-Luc Rosinger use a similar input–output methodology to estimate prices of production and the wage–profit curve for Brazil. They use a 20-sector input–output table for 1975, which includes circulating capital but does not include fixed capital stock, since the relevant data do not exist. Though they do not estimate individual labour values and compare these to prices of production, as did Ochoa, they do compute the overall wage–profit curve. They find, as Ochoa did, that the curve is close to linearity, suggesting that Ochoa's conclusion regarding the empirical insignificance of 'reswitching' may be generalizable to developing countries as well. Da Silva and Rosinger also analyse the effects of an increase in the wage share on prices of production. They find that in some sectors (mainly primary sectors) prices of production increase; in others (mainly modern industrial sectors) prices decline; and in a third group (mainly traditional industrial sectors) there is little effect.

In Chapter 8, Michel Juillard analyses the evolution of the postwar US economy in terms of the 'regime of accumulation' framework of the French Regulation school, which emphasizes the relation between technological change, income distribution and consumption. Juillard argues that the early postwar period was one of 'intensive' accumulation, characterized by rapid productivity growth and rapid real wage growth. This 'golden age' ended in the mid-1960s as a result of the sharp decline in productivity growth, which eventually led to a corresponding decline in real wage growth in the early 1970s. However the lag in the slow-down of real wage growth (which trailed productivity growth for about 7 or 8 years) resulted in a sharp decline in the rate of profit (see equation 1.3) and a less sharp decline in investment. Juillard argues that, in the 1980s, the US economy reverted to a regime of 'extensive' accumulation, characterized by slow productivity growth, declining real wages and strong employment growth.

Although a major crisis has been avoided so far, Juillard argues that this regime of 'extensive' accumulation has created two major problems which may result in future difficulties: increased social tensions due to growing poverty and economic inequality and a loss of international competitiveness. Juillard provides estimates of all these variables for the two main 'departments' in the economy (that producing investment goods and that producing consumer goods). In general the trends described above were more pronounced in Department II (consumer goods).

Whereas several of the previous chapters in this volume investigate the effects of investment on profitability, the first chapter of Part III analyses the effects of profitability on investment behaviour. Crotty and Goldstein first extend the traditional Marxian theory of investment by incorporating important insights from Keynesian theory. The traditional Marxian theory emphasizes competition and expected profitability as the key determinants of investment decisions. Crotty and Goldstein add the degree of 'financial fragility', mainly as reflected in the debt–equity ratio of a firm, as an important determinant of investment. They argue that an increase in financial fragility has a negative effect on investment, since it makes firms less willing to take on new risk. However they also argue that increased competition will force capitalists to continue to invest even when profitability is declining and financial fragility is rising. Such competition-induced investment requires greater financing from external funds, thus resulting in greater financial fragility and also, possibly, creating conditions for a crisis in the future.

The authors provide an econometric analysis of this theory of investment, using data for the manufacturing sector of the US economy from 1947 to 1986. Their results strongly support the enhanced Marxian theory of investment. Competition (measured by the import penetration ratio) and the rate of profit both have positive and statistically significant effects on investment, while financial fragility (measured by the debt–equity ratio) has a significant negative effect on investment. Crotty and Goldstein conclude that this theory provides an explanation of continuing strong investment in the postwar US economy despite declining profitability and increasing financial fragility.

In Chapter 10, Gérard Duménil and Dominique Lévy consider a related but more general aspect than that of the preceding paper, which is the effects of profitability on the stability of capitalism (that is, why and how profitability matters). They first consider the relevance of Marx's theory of the falling rate of profit to the evolution of the rate of profit in the USA and conclude that it is quite relevant for the periods when the rate of profit declined (the latter part of the nineteenth century and the post-war period) but not very relevant for times when it increased (the interwar years). They develop a dynamic model in which firms react to disequilibrium conditions in order to demonstrate the significance of the rate of profit for the stability of capitalism. According to this model, the rate of profit affects stability primarily through its effects on the reaction of firms to excess capacity and excess inventories.

Duménil and Lévy present a general interpretation of the economic history of the USA since the Civil War, which may be briefly summarized as follows: the long-run decline of the rate of profit in the late nineteenth century resulted in a revolution in firm management, which was characterized by stronger reactions to excess capacity and excess inventories. The managerial revolution increased the instability of the economy and eventually contributed to the severity of the Great Depression. The Great Depression in turn resulted in the restoration of profitability and greater state intervention in the economy, which created the conditions for the postwar expansion and prosperity. However the rate of profit again declined, which has resulted in the recent stagflation observed in the US economy. Duménil and Lévy conclude with three possible scenarios for the future: (1) a continuation of stagflation, (2) a new technological revolution which will restore the rate of profit, or (3) a new stage of capitalism characterized by even greater state control of the economy. They do not speculate about whether another severe depression will be required in order to raise the rate of profit sufficiently to make possible another period of expansion and prosperity, as occurred during the interwar years.

In the final chapter, John Miller investigates the role of the state in the determination of the wage and profit share. His main concern is whether the distributional effects of US government policy have increased or decreased the net earnings of labour. The key concept which is estimated is the 'net social wage', or the difference between government spending for workers and the tax burden of workers. Miller finds that the net social wage was negative throughout most of the postwar period; that is, workers paid more in taxes than they received in the form of government benefits. The net social wage became less negative in the 1960s and still less negative in the 1970s, and then became sharply more negative in the 1980s. Miller argues that, although this growing negative social wage did not result in a 'profit squeeze' crisis (as some other authors have argued), this trend may ultimately pose problems for the US economy by endangering the supply of a well-trained and well-educated labour force.

PART I
TRENDS IN PROFITABILITY
IN INDUSTRIALIZED
COUNTRIES

2. A Comparative Analysis of Profitability Trends in the Advanced Capitalist Economies*

Thomas E. Weisskopf

INTRODUCTION

The purpose of this chapter is to explore long-run trends in profitability in the advanced capitalist economies since the Second World War. It is primarily empirical in content; I will present and analyse time series data on profitability and some related variables for the manufacturing sector of eight advanced capitalist economies – the 'Big 7' plus Sweden.

The theoretical framework that informs my empirical analysis is that of Marxian crisis theory, which focuses on the rate of profit as the most critical variable reflecting and affecting the vitality of a capitalist macroeconomy. Alternative variants of Marxian crisis theory may usefully be distinguished according to whether or not they attribute a primary role to the degree of capitalist class power in the determination of overall profitability. On the one hand, the 'neo-Marxian' variant emphasizes the balance of power between capitalist and non-capitalist classes as an essential determinant of the distribution of income and the rate of profit in a capitalist economy; profitability is modelled as a positive function of capitalist class power.[1] On the other hand, alternative variants of Marxian crisis theory – for example, the theory of a falling rate of profit due to a rising organic composition of capital, and theories based on underconsumption or other forms of realization failure – focus on economic–structural

13

forces that may depress profitability even when (and some-times because) the capitalist class is powerful.[2] To contribute to our understanding of the actual behaviour of profit rates in capitalist economies, as well as to assess the applicability of alternative variants of Marxian crisis theory, it would there-fore appear useful to develop a way of determining the extent to which profitability changes are attributable to overall econ-omic–structural changes as opposed to distributional changes that may be linked to the balance of class power.

In this chapter I will propose and implement an analytical device for assessing the extent to which profitability changes can be attributed to (1) changes in the overall economic environment and (2) changes in the outcome of distributional conflict between the capitalist class and the working class. This project thus involves an accounting decomposition of profitability trends; but I believe that the present accounting analysis enables one to isolate more accurately the locus of distributional conflict in capitalist enonomies than did my earlier work along the same lines. Weisskopf (1979) character-ized distributional conflict simply in terms of a struggle over pre-tax factor shares in income; the present analysis improves upon this effort both in taking account of the after-tax distri-bution of income and in defining the distributional objectives of capitalists and workers in terms of the rate of profit and the growth of real wages. Moreover, as I suggest in the latter part of the chapter, the accounting analysis undertaken here can be extended to shed greater light on the underlying forces at work and can provide a useful basis for subsequent causal–empiri-cal analysis of some of those forces.

This study is divided into four sections. Section 1 presents time series evidence on profitability trends from the early 1950s to the mid-1980s in the manufacturing sector of each of the eight countries under study. Section 2 graphically juxta-poses trends in profitability with trends in real wage growth, so as to depict the extent to which capital and labour have participated in the gains or losses afforded by overall econ-omic change. Section 3 develops an algebraic method of decomposing changes in profitability into parts attributable to (1) changes in the overall economic environment and (2) changes in the state of the distributional conflict between capital and labour; and the results of that decomposition analysis are presented in graphical and tabular form. In the final section, ways of determining the underlying sources of change in the economic environment and in the distributional conflict, respectively, are explored, and the results of some preliminary quantitative research along the lines suggested are reported.

1 POSTWAR TRENDS IN MANUFACTURING PROFIT RATES

I have compiled annual time series data from 1951 to 1985 for the before-tax and the after-tax net rate of profit in the manufacturing sector of each of the eight countries under study.[3] For the purposes of this study the net rate of profit is defined as the ratio of a measure of net capital income to a measure of net capital stock (both in nominal terms); net profitability is preferred to gross profitability because it better reflects the true economic rate of return to capital investment. Net capital income is defined as gross value added minus fixed capital consumption and minus total labour compensation; the latter includes all contributions to social insurance and private pension plans. Net capital stock is derived from estimates of the replacement cost of gross capital stock, adjusted for annual depreciation. The after-tax profit rate is simply the before-tax rate multiplied by one minus an estimate of the rate of direct taxes on net capital income.

The estimated profit rate series are presented in graphical form in Figure 2.1. The following observations can be made on the basis of these figures.

1. In all eight countries except Italy there is evidence of a pronounced downward trend in both before-tax and after-tax profitability from the mid- to late-1960s to the early 1980s.
2. The long-term downward trend in profitability starts from the early 1950s in the case of the UK, West Germany and

Canada, and from the late 1950s in the case of Sweden; in the USA there is some evidence of declining before-tax profitability starting in the early 1950s, but no such trend in after-tax profitability before the mid-1960s.

3. Only in Japan is there evidence of a significant upward trend in profitability, which is true of the period from the early 1950s to the early 1960s.

4. In every country except Italy and Japan there has been a

Figure 2.1   Manufacturing sector profit rates

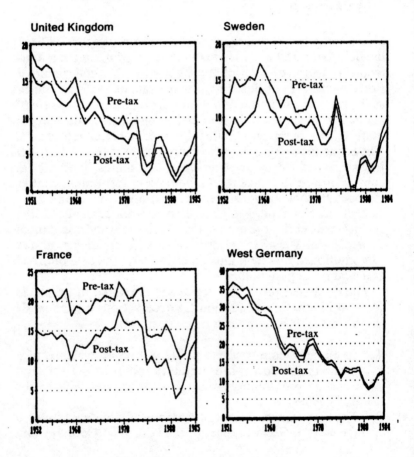

marked recovery of both before-tax and after-tax profitability in the 1980s, although in no case has it proceeded far enough to offset the prior downward trend.

5. Only in Canada and the USA is there a significant difference between the behaviour of before-tax and after-tax profitability; in each case the effective profit tax rate has diminished considerably over time, thus mitigating consi-

Figure 2.1   continued

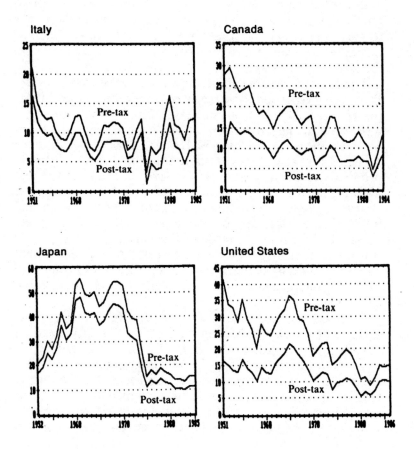

derably the long-run downward trend in before-tax profitability.

2 PROFITABILITY V. REAL WAGE GROWTH

Neo-Marxian economic analysis depicts the capitalist economy as an arena in which conflicting classes compete for
economic gains. The two most fundamental Marxian economic classes are of course capital and labour; these two classes
enter into distributive conflict as capital seeks higher profits
and workers seek higher wages. In the case of capital it seems
reasonable to suggest that the primary economic objective is
to maximize the after-tax rate of profit; in the case of labour,
an important – but not so exclusive – objective is to maximize
the after-tax real wage.

The extent to which capital is attaining its economic objectives is well represented by the *level* of the after-tax profit rate
(to be denoted by r); an increase/decrease over time in r
represents an improvement/deterioration in capital's economic position. In the case of labour, however, it is to be
expected that real wages will rise over time with the general
productivity of the economy; the level of the after-tax real
wage is therefore not an adequate indicator of how successful
labour has been in attaining its economic objectives. Instead
it would seem more appropriate to measure labour's success
in terms of the *rate of change* of the after-tax real wage rate
(to be denoted by g); an increase/decrease in g means that
workers are doing better/worse than previously in respect to
the economic benefits they derive from participation in the
economy.

To begin to address the role of distributive conflict and the
exercise of power in affecting postwar profitability trends, I
present in Figure 2.2 scatter plots of r and g for each of the
eight countries under study. To make the plots more intelli-
gible, and to reduce the effects of short-term fluctuations in
the rate of capacity utilization, I have grouped the annual time
series observations on r and g from the early 1950s to the mid-
1980s into 12 consecutive three-year averages, beginning with

the three-year period centred in 1952 and ending with the one centred in 1985.[4] Here *g* is defined as the average annual rate of growth of the hourly real wage rate (exclusive of employer-provided pension and welfare benefits) in manufacturing, from the previous to the current period, after the deduction of an estimate of direct income taxes as well as all contributions to social insurance. Figure 2.2 shows a total of 11 obser-vations for each country (beginning with 1955 so as to permit the calculation of *g* from the previous to the current three-year period), connected in sequential order by straight lines.

The graphs in Figure 2.2 permit one to assess the relative success with which capital and labour have achieved their presumed economic objectives over time. A move to the north/south represents a gain/loss for capital while labour holds its ground; a move to the east/west represents a gain/loss for labour while capital holds its ground. Movement in a northeasterly or southwesterly direction represents a harmo-nious situation in which capital and labour share gains/losses, while movement in a northwesterly or southeasterly direction represents a sharply conflictual change in which capital gains at the expense of labour or vice versa. In the case of the UK, for example, the movement from 1955 to 1964 reflects losses for both capital and labour; the movement from 1964 to 1967 represents a loss for capital while labour holds its ground; and the movement from 1967 to 1973 reflects a substantial gain for labour at the expense of capital.

The plots of *r* v. *g* in Figure 2.2 display some interesting inter-country variation in patterns. Let us focus first on the periods of declining profitability (in all countries but Italy) from the 1960s up to 1982. In the UK, Canada and the USA there is a virtually vertical drop from 1964 to 1982, indicating that, as *r* fell, *g* remained constant (with some variation in intermediate years). In Sweden, West Germany and Japan the predominant movement from the early 1960s to 1982 is in a southwesterly direction, indicating that, as *r* fell, so did *g*. In France the decline in *r* began only in 1970; the drop is more or less vertical up to 1976, and then southwesterly to 1982. In Italy there is very little variation in profitability at all (with the exception of a drop in *r* in 1976); the movement from the early

1960s to early 1982 is essentially westward, indicating simply a long-term decline in *g*.

Turning now to the (partial) recovery of profitability from 1982 to 1985, we find that the movement is northwesterly in the cases of France, Italy and Canada, vertical in the cases of the UK and the USA, and northeasterly in the cases of Sweden, West Germany and Japan. In the latter three countries we find *r* and *g* again moving in the same direction (in this case upward rather than downward), while in the first five countries *g* either stays constant or actually falls as *r* rises.

Figure 2.2   Profitability v. real wage growth

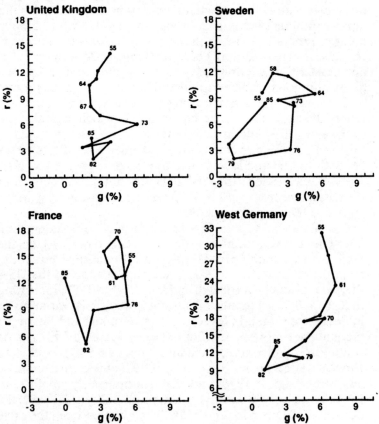

In general we find Sweden, West Germany and Japan distinctive in the extent to which improvement or deterioration in the overall economic environment is shared between capital and labour (movement along a northeast/southwest axis). In the UK and the USA – and, to a lesser extent, Canada – there is a general tendency for *r* to decline in bad times and to increase in good times more than *g* (movement along a vertical axis). In Italy there is little variation in *r* at all, but considerable variation in *g* (movement along a horizontal axis). In France there are three distinctive sub-periods of different

Figure 2.2   continued

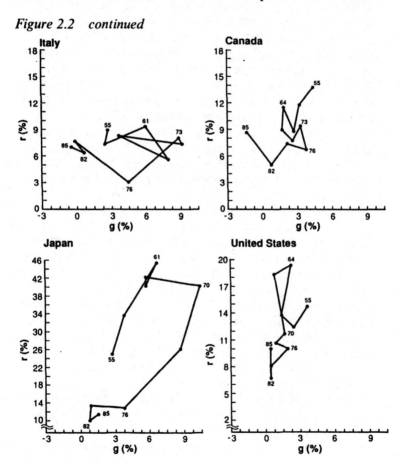

behaviour: little variation of either r or g until 1970; a sharp decline in r until 1976, and then a sharp decline in g into the 1980s.

3   DECOMPOSITION OF PROFITABILITY CHANGE

Study of the plots in Figure 2.2 suggests a potentially fruitful way to decompose changes in after-tax profit rates from one period to another. Consider the change in r from 1955 to 1958 in Canada or in the USA, shown in each case as southwesterly moves. Evidently the overall economic environment in each of the two manufacturing sectors deteriorated during this period, for in 1958 lower levels of both r and g were achieved than in 1955. Had r remained in 1958 as high as it had been in 1955, then presumably g would have been even lower in 1958 than its actual value; and had g remained in 1958 at its 1955 level, then r would have been even lower than its actual value in 1958. In effect, we may envisage a 'distribution frontier' for 1958 in r–g space which slopes downward from the northwest to the southeast, passing through the actually attained value of (r_{58}, g_{58}).

A pair of such distribution frontiers (DF_0 and DF_1) – for consecutive time periods 0 and 1 – is drawn for the general case in Figure 2.3, corresponding to actually observed r and g points (r_0, g_0) in period 0 and (r_1, g_1) in period 1. In principle we can characterize shifts in the position of the distribution frontier from one period to the next as a change in the overall economic environment, and we can characterize movements along a given distribution frontier as a conflictual change in the distribution of economic benefits from a given environment. The problem then becomes how to allocate a given overall change from (r_0, g_0) to (r_1, g_1) between environmental and conflictual components.

Clearly a movement in a northeasterly or southwesterly direction mainly involves a change in the overall economic environment, and a movement in a northwesterly or southeasterly direction mainly involves a change associated with distributional conflict; but we require a method of distinguishing the two possibilities more precisely. To accomplish this we need to define a 'conflict-neutral' point (r^*_1, g^*_1) on the new distribution frontier DF_1, which represents the values of r and g that would obtain in period 1 in the absence of any change in the state of distributional conflict between capital and labour. A reasonable way in which to define the conflict-neutral point is to locate r^*_1 halfway between r_0 and r^{**}_1, and g^*_1 halfway between g_0 and g^{**}_1, where r^{**}_1 and g^{**}_1 denote the values of r and g on the distribution frontier DF_1 corresponding to g_0 and r_0 respectively. The point (r^*_1, g^*_1) is duly indicated on

Figure 2.3   Distribution frontiers and profitability change

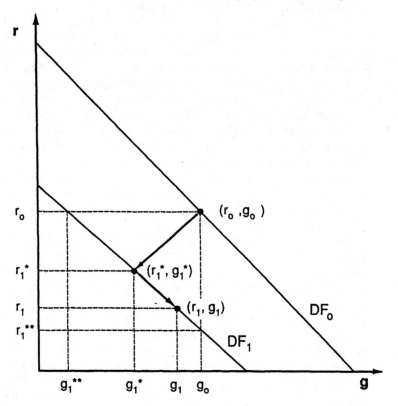

Figure 2.3; it falls on the distribution frontier DF_1 if that frontier is linear.[5]

We may now decompose the movement from (r_0,g_0) to (r_1,g_1) into two steps: (1) an 'environmental' move from (r_0,g_0) to (r^*_1,g^*_1) which measures the shift in the distribution frontier from DF_0 in the period 0 to DF_1 in period 1; and (2) a 'conflictual' move from (r^*_1,g^*_1) to (r_1,g_1), which measures the movement along the distribution frontier DF_1. In the example depicted in Figure 2.3, we have both an environmental deterioration and a further decline in r (and rise in g) associated with a conflictual movement in favour of labour. This method allows us to decompose the actual change in profitability (r_1-r_0) into one component of environmental change (r^*_1-r_0) and another component of conflictual change (r_1-r^*_1).

To apply this method to concrete cases of profitability change over time, it is necessary to generate an equation for the distribution frontier in each time period under analysis. Beginning with a macroeconomic distributional identity expressing total income in the economy (or sector) under investigation as the sum of after-tax wages, after-tax net profits, direct taxes (on both wages and profits), capital consumption allowances and external material inputs, it is possible to derive an expression for the after-tax net rate of profit, r, as a function of the rate of change (from the previous period) of the real after-tax wage rate, g.[6] The derivative of r with respect to g yields the slope of the distribution frontier, and this can be used in conjunction with the one actually observed value on the frontier to derive the frontier itself.

Using the above-described method for determining the locus of distribution frontiers and allocating changes in r to environmental and conflictual components, I have decomposed changes in the after-tax rate of profit r from 1955 to 1985 in each of the eight manufacturing sectors under study.[7] The results of this exercise are displayed in Figure 2.4. Each time series graph in these tables shows (1) the level of the after-tax profit rate in the initial 1955 period (r_o), (2) the level of the after-tax profit rate that would have obtained in subsequent periods if there had been only environmental and no conflictual changes since 1955 (r_e), and (3) the actual level of the after-tax profit rate (r). Thus the distance between r_e and r_o in any period represents the cumulative effect of environmental changes on the after-tax profit rate since 1955, and the distance between r and r_e represents the cumulative effect of conflictual changes on the after-tax profit rate since 1955.

In all the countries under consideration there was a decline in the after-tax rate of profit in manufacturing from 1955 to 1985; in every case but Sweden and Italy the lowest level of r over this period was attained in 1982. Consider then the extent to which the generalized profitability declines from 1955 to 1982 were attributable to environmental vs. conflictual changes. In most cases the overall decline in r could be attributed both to a decline in the profitability environment (a fall in r_e) and to a further decline in r associated with a distributional shift against capital since 1955 (a fall in r relative to r_e). In Italy, however, the cumulative distributional shift from 1955 to 1982 favoured capital; and in the USA there was virtually no cumulative distributional shift from 1955 to 1982, with the result that the entire decline in the after-tax rate of profit could be attributed to environmental deterioration.

To highlight the direction of distributional effects, I have darkened in Figure 2.4 the space between the r and r_e plots whenever the former exceeds the latter (indicating a cumulative distributional shift in favour of capital). In most cases the distributional shift since 1955 has favoured labour; but it is noteworthy that throughout the period 1955–85 the cumulative impact of distributional shifts on US manufacturing profitability was in favour of capital (or negligible, as in 1982). The fact that in most countries the cumulative effect of conflictual changes after 1955 has favoured labour does not imply that in some sense labour has been 'stronger' than capital, but only that labour has improved its distributional position *vis-à-vis* capital *relative* to where it stood in 1955.

The choice of the initial year 1955, from which to measure cumulative effects of environmental and conflictual changes on profitability, is of course rather arbitrary. The methodology developed here can be utilized to determine the extent to which environmental and conflictual changes have accounted for the overall change in r between any two years. To understand more clearly the sources of change in manufacturing profitability during the post-Second-World-War period it may be instructive to concentrate on key sub-periods in each country. Accordingly, I have identified for each country four separate sub-periods (spanning the whole 1955–85 period) for which different directions of profitability change, or different primary sources of profitability change, can be distinguished.

Table 2.1 displays the overall change in the after-tax manu-

Figure 2.4   Decomposition for profitability changes

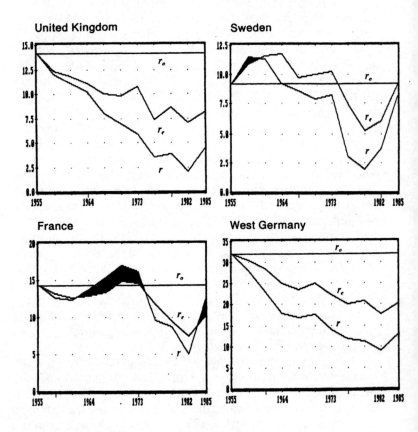

facturing profit rate (*Dr*), as well as the components attributable to changes in the profitability environment (*Dre*) and changes in distributional conflict (*Drc*), for each of the four sub-periods in each of the eight countries under study. To highlight different sources of profitability change, I have added signs within parentheses to indicate whether *Dre* or *Drc* accounts for the largest share of the overall change in *Dr*. Thus, for example, the long-run decline in the after-tax profit

Figure 2.4   continued

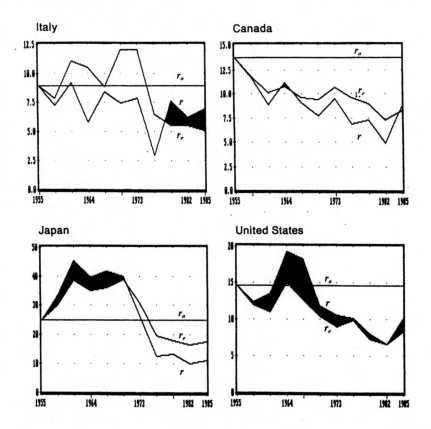

Table 2.1   Components of manufacturing profitability change

Country	Sub-period	Dr	Dre	Drc
United Kingdom	1955–64	− 3.9	− 3.1 (−)	− 0.8
	1964–73	+ 4.4	− 0.2	− 4.2 (−)
	1973–82	− 3.8	− 3.7 (−)	− 0.1
	1982–85	+ 2.4	+ 1.1	+ 1.3 (+)
France	1955–70	+ 2.7	+ 0.6	+ 2.1 (+)
	1970–76	− 7.5	− 3.2	− 4.3 (−)
	1976–82	− 4.5	− 4.4 (−)	− 0.1
	1982–85	+ 7.3	+ 2.7	+ 4.6 (+)
Sweden	1955–58	+ 2.3	+ 1.7 (+)	+ 0.6
	1958–64	− 2.3	+ 0.8	− 3.1 (−)
	1964–79	− 7.3	− 6.5 (−)	− 0.8
	1979–85	+ 6.2	+ 3.9 (+)	+ 2.3
West Germany	1955–61	− 8.9	− 3.5	− 5.4 (−)
	1961–70	− 5.5	− 3.3 (−)	− 2.2
	1970–82	− 8.7	− 7.6 (−)	− 1.1
	1982–85	+ 3.9	+ 2.6 (+)	+ 1.3
Italy	1955–73	− 1.0	+ 3.1	− 4.1 (−)
	1973–76	− 5.0	− 5.5 (−)	+ 0.5
	1976–82	+ 3.3	− 1.0	+ 4.3 (+)
	1982–85	+ 0.7	− 0.4	+ 1.1 (+)
Japan	1955–61	+20.5	+13.7 (+)	+ 6.8
	1961–70	− 5.3	+ 0.3	− 5.6 (−)
	1970–82	−30.1	−22.9 (−)	− 7.2
	1982–85	+ 1.1	+ 1.1 (+)	+ 0.0
Canada	1955–64	− 2.6	− 3.0 (−)	+ 0.4
	1964–76	− 4.4	− 1.2	− 3.2 (−)
	1976–82	− 1.9	− 2.3 (−)	+ 0.4
	1982–85	+ 3.7	+ 0.9	+ 2.8 (+)
United States	1955–64	+ 4.7	+ 0.5	+ 4.2 (+)
	1964–76	− 9.2	− 5.3 (−)	− 3.9
	1976–82	− 3.6	− 3.3 (−)	− 0.3
	1982–85	+ 3.5	+ 1.7	+ 1.8 (+)

Note: Dr measures the overall percentage-point change in the after-tax rate of profit in the manufacturing sector; Dre and Drc are the components attributable to environmental and distributional factors, respectively. The sign in parentheses indicates the predominant component in the overall change, as well as its direction.

rate in manufacturing in the UK from 1955 to 1982 was primarily accounted for by environmental deterioration from 1955 to 1964 and from 1973 to 1982, but between 1964 and 1973 it was almost entirely due to a distributional shift in favour of labour; the (modest) recovery of r from 1982 to 1985 was associated with a (modest) improvement in the profitability environment, slightly greater than the simultaneous distributional shift in favour of capital.

It is difficult to generalize about the results shown in Table 2.1, since the experience of each country has been somewhat different. But there are certain common features that do emerge. Not surprisingly, in every country there is evidence of significant environmental deterioration in sub-periods covering the 1970s; this reflects the diminished opportunities for profit making and real wage growth afforded by a world capitalist economy in crisis. Each country (except for Italy) also shows improvement in this respect in the 1980s. In each country there have been times when distributional shifts favoured capital and others when distributional shifts favoured labour; in every country except Sweden and West Germany the most significant distributional shifts in favour of labour occurred in sub-periods covering part or all of the time span from the mid-1960s to the mid-1970s.

There are also a few interesting patterns that are common to sub-groups of countries among the eight under study. In Sweden, West Germany and Japan, environmental conditions play a considerably more important role than distributional conflict in accounting for changes in profitability (in each case playing a dominant role in three out of the four sub-periods). This finding confirms the impression obtained in Section 2 that improvement or deterioration in the overall economic environment tends to be shared between capital and labour in these countries, rather than benefiting or burdening just one of the two classes. In France and Italy the opposite is true: in only one of four sub-periods are environmental factors predominant in accounting for profitability change, while distributional changes (twice in favour of capital, once in favour of labour) are most important in three sub-periods. In the UK, Canada and the USA there is no sub-period in which the profitability environment improves significantly; in those few sub-periods when the after-tax manufacturing profit rate does rise, this is always primarily the result of distributional shifts in favour of capital.

4   SOURCES OF CHANGE IN THE ECONOMIC ENVIRONMENT AND THE DISTRIBUTIONAL CONFLICT

The decomposition analysis carried out in the previous section is a useful first step in analysing sources of change in manufacturing profitability, but a full understanding of the forces governing the behaviour of profitability requires exploration of (1) reasons why the overall economic environment changes and (2) reasons why the distributional conflict moves in favour of capital or labour. These two issues are best approached in two different ways.

To analyse the sources of change in the overall economic environment as it affects profitability, I first used algebraic expressions for the actual rate of profit, r, and the conflict-neutral rate of profit, r^*, to derive an equation for the environmental component Dre of profit rate change Dr.[8] This equation implies that Dre is a function of changes in the following economic–environmental variables (with the preceding sign indicating the direction of the effect on Dre of a change in the variable):

1.   (+) the output/capital ratio (real output/real gross capital stock);
2.   (+) average labour productivity (real output/labour hour input);[9]
3.   (−) relative capital good prices (capital good price index/ gross output price index);
4.   (−) relative material input prices (external material input price index/gross output price index);
5.   (−) relative wage good prices (wage good price index/ gross output price index);
6.   (−) the overall tax rate (direct taxes on labour and capital income/gross value added).

It is possible to utilize the *Dre* equation to determine the extent to which changes in each of these six variables have contributed to the overall *Dre* change in any given time period. By this means one can determine the extent to which the observed *Dre* is due to (1) productivity changes, (2) terms of trade effects (relative price changes) and (3) tax changes. The observed productivity changes can in turn be decomposed into effects attributable to (a) changes in the rate of capacity utilization (which has a direct positive effect on the output–capital ratio and an indirect positive effect on average labour productivity) and (b) changes in underlying productivity (independent of utilization effects).

Analysis of the manufacturing sector data compiled for this study suggests the following conclusions:

1. In most countries variations in the rate of capacity utilization in the manufacturing sector account for only a relatively small fraction of observed changes in the overall economic environment (*Dre*) from one three-year period to the next. Canada and the USA represent partial exceptions to this rule, for in these two countries business cycle fluctuations are considerably greater in amplitude than elsewhere and can have a significant impact on *Dre* from one three-year period to the next – but not over longer periods of time (as upward and downward movements of utilization rates tend to cancel each other out).

2. In each country over the post-Second-World-War period there has been a secular trend of increasing taxes (including social security contributions as well as direct taxes on labour and capital income) as a proportion of gross value added; this trend has made a consistently negative contribution to *Dre*, but during country-periods when the economic environment has significantly deteriorated the growth in the tax share has been responsible for a relatively small fraction of that deterioration.

3. During most of the country-periods under study relative price trends have moved against manufacturing sector output; like the secular trend of increasing tax rates (but not so consistently) this secular trend in the terms of trade

has contributed negatively to *Dre*. The adverse effect was most significant following the energy price shocks of 1973 and 1979, which significantly raised the relative price of external raw materials in most countries; by the same token, there was a smaller positive effect on *Dre* in some countries in the 1980s, associated with the more recent decline in relative energy prices.

4. Much of the variation in *Dre* between countries and over time is accounted for by the remaining underlying source of change in the economic environment – changes in productivity (the output–capital ratio and/or labour productivity), adjusted for utilization effects. Significantly positive or negative values for *Dre* are most often accounted for largely by corresponding changes in the ratio of real output to (utilized) gross capital stock.

Unlike changes in the economic environment, changes in the distributional conflict between capital and labour over the after-tax profit rate and the after-tax real wage growth rate – as reflected in the variable *Drc* – cannot be illuminated by a decomposition analysis based on macroeconomic accounting identities. To investigate the determinants of *Drc* we must examine the exogenous forces which push the economy in one direction or the other along a given distribution frontier.

An appealing theoretical framework for analysing the outcome of distributional conflict is the neo-Marxian approach, which focuses on the balance of power between capital and labour as the critical determinant of distributional outcomes. To apply this framework we require an independent measure of the power of capital *vis-à-vis* labour – which will be denoted by P_K; neo-Marxian theory would predict that *Drc* is a positive function of P_K.

· In practice it is very difficult to derive satisfactory empirical measures of P_K. In theory P_K should vary positively with the rate of unemployment and other such measures of labour market slack – on the argument (which goes back to Marx's reserve-army-of-labour analysis of capitalist business cycles) that workers' bargaining power *vis-à-vis* capitalists increases when greater job opportunities protect them from the consequences of the sack. But P_K should also vary negatively with the extent to which socioeconomic institutions are supportive of working class interests – for example, with the strength of trade union organization, with the extent of unemployment compensation and other forms of social welfare legislation, and with the degree to which the political system is responsive to the working class. Sociologists and political scientists (for example, Cameron (1982) and Crouch (1986)) have done a substantial amount of work to derive cross-country measures related to P_K, based on such indicators as extent of trade unionization, the representation of worker-based political parties in government and so on, but consistent time series measures of P_K for any given country are very hard to find or to construct. Perhaps the best effort along these lines has been the construction of annual time series estimates of the 'cost of job loss' (an indicator of employer power over employees) for the USA by Schor and Bowles (1987) and for the UK by Schor (1987).

In a preliminary analysis of sources of variation in *Drc*, I have compiled time series for each of the eight countries under study of two possible indicators of P_L – the power of labour *vis-à-vis* capital, which is of course an inverse measure of P_K. The first indicator is the average rate of civilian employment (1 minus the unemployment rate) for each three-year period. The second indicator is an alternative measure of labour market tightness: the rate of growth of the ratio of the aggregate capital stock to the working-age population between each successive pair of three-year periods. These are both very imperfect indicators of the balance of power between labour and capital, for they are based only on labour market conditions and do not capture the larger socioeconomic institutional context.

The limited number of observations available on *Drc* for each country (11 observations, given 12 three-year time periods in all) prevents the testing of a fully-specified econometric model. Some light may be shed on the determinants of *Drc*, however, by correlation analyses of the relationship between *Drc* and P_L. I have computed for each country simple correlation coefficients between *Drc* (measured from the previous to the current period) and (1) the average rate of employment (in the previous period) as well as (2) the growth in the capital stock/working-age population ratio (from the previous to the current period). Because in some countries there is a considerable degree of short-run cyclicality in most macroeconomic variables, I have also computed for each country simple correlation coefficients between *Drc* and (3) the coterminous change in the rate of capacity utilization, to be denoted by *Dcu*; and I have computed partial correlation coefficients (controlling for *Dcu*) between *Drc* and each of the two P_L indicators. Finally, to test whether the results are specifically applicable to the distributional-conflict component of profitability change, rather than to profitability change in general, I have computed all the correlation coefficients not only with respect to *Drc* but also with respect to *Dre*.

The findings from this analysis may be summarized as follows:

1. Only in two countries – Canada and the USA, where the rate of capacity utilization is relatively volatile in the short run – is *Drc* positively and significantly (at 5 per cent or better) correlated with *Dcu*, but in almost all of the countries *Dre* is positively and significantly correlated with *Dcu*. In other words, increases/decreases in capacity utilization are generally associated with improvement/deterioration in the overall economic environment; but only in a few cases are they associated with movements in favour of capital/labour along the distribution frontier, and in these cases the phenomenon is essentially a short-run cyclical one.

2. In most countries *Drc* is negatively and significantly correlated with one or both of the P_L indicators; this statement holds both for simple correlations and for partial correlations (controlling for *Dcu*). On the other hand, only in a few countries does one observe significant negative simple or partial correlations between *Dre* and either of the two P_L indicators. In other words, there is considerable evidence that tighter labour markets (in the recent past) are associated with movement along the distribution

frontier in favour of labour; while there is much less evidence that tighter labour markets are associated with any change in the overall economic environment. These findings are quite consistent with the neo-Marxian prediction that tighter labour markets will tend to strengthen the bargaining power of labour *vis-à-vis* capital. Moreover the fact that the evidence is much stronger for *Drc* than for *Dre* suggests that the method used here to decompose overall profitability change into environmental and conflictual components has indeed succeeded in distinguishing basically different sources of profitability change.

NOTES

*   Earlier versions of this paper were presented at the Conference on International Perspectives on Profitability and Accumulation at New York University, September 1988, and at the Winter meetings of the Union for Radical Political Economics in New York City, December 1988. I am grateful to participants at both conferences for their helpful suggestions, but I am solely responsible for this final version.

1.   See Weisskopf (1988) for a presentation of the neo-Marxian approach to Marxian crisis theory, with references to the relevant literature; and see Bowles, Gordon and Weisskopf (1986) for an application of this approach to the postwar US economy. Theories of the 'high-employment profit squeeze', as well as theories associated with a capitalist power-based concept of the 'social structure of accumulation', are representative of what I have termed the neo-Marxian approach.

2.   See Weisskopf (1979) for a comparative discussion of alternative variants of Marxian crisis theory.

3.   The data were compiled with Andrew Glyn; in a few cases we lacked observations for the year 1951 or 1985. Our estimates of before-tax profit rates are based primarily on published OECD figures for capital stock, value added and factor shares (adjusted to remove the estimated labour income of self-employed persons from the 'operating surplus' as a measure of profits); but in the case of France and Italy we have relied mainly on Eurostat figures, and in all cases we have supplemented the data available from international agencies with data from national sources (especially to extend the series back into the 1950s, for which internationally compiled data are very scanty). The estimates of after-tax profit rates vary considerably in their reliability: in the case of four countries (France, Sweden, Canada and the United States) we were able to make use of national estimates of profit tax rates in the manufacturing sector; but in the case of the other four (the UK, West Germany,

Italy and Japan) we had to rely on OECD figures on profit tax rates in the entire corporate sector. A complete accounting of sources and methodology used to compile all of the data used in this study is available on request from the author.

4. From here on I will refer to particular years (for example, 1952, 1955) with the understanding that they represent centred three-year periods. In some cases the three-year averaging procedure required that the underlying annual time series be extended at one end or the other; this was achieved where necessary by extrapolation of nearby observations.

5. In the appendix of this chapter, it is shown that the distribution frontier is indeed linear under reasonable assumptions about the structure of the economy.

6. This derivation requires that real magnitudes can be distinguished from price magnitudes, and that new variables such as average labour productivity, the real wage and the real output/capital stock ratio be substituted into the original (nominal) distributional identity; for details, see the appendix.

7. The earliest change in r that can be analysed in this way is from 1955 to 1958, since one needs to know the rate of growth of after-tax real wages from 1952 to 1955 in order to locate the distribution frontier for 1958.

8. See the appendix for details of this derivation.

9. In this case there must be a rate of increase in average labour productivity greater than the previous period's increase in real wage growth in order for average labour productivity change to contribute positively to *Dre*.

REFERENCES

Bowles, S., D. M. Gordon and T. E. Weisskopf (1986), 'Power and Profits: The Social Structure of Accumulation and the Profitability of the Postwar US Economy', *Review of Radical Political Economics*, **18**, (1–2), Spring and Summer.

Cameron, D. R. (1982), 'Social Democracy, Corporatism, and Labor Quiescence: The Representation of Economic Interest in Advanced Capitalist Society', paper presented at the conference on Governability and Legitimacy in Western European Social Democracies, Stanford University.

Crouch, C. (1986), 'The Conditions for Trade Union Wage Restraint', in L. Lindberg and C. Maier (eds), *The Politics and Sociology of Global Inflation*, Washington: Brookings Institution.

Schor, J. B. (1987), 'Does Work Intensity Respond to Macroeconomic Variables?: Evidence from British Manufacturing 1970–1986', unpublished working paper, Harvard University.

Schor, J. B. and S. Bowles (1987), 'Employment Rents and the Incidence of Strikes', *Review of Economics and Statistics*, **69**, (4), November.

Weisskopf, T. E. (1979), 'Marxian Crisis Theory and the Rate of Profit in the Postwar US Economy', *Cambridge Journal of Economics*, **3**, (1), March.

Weisskopf, T. E. (1988), 'The Analytics of Neo-Marxian Crisis Theory; An Illustrative Model', *Keizai Kenkyu (The Economic Review)*, **39**, July.

APPENDIX

We begin with the following macroeconomic distributional identity:

$$G = W + R + T + C + X \qquad (2.1)$$

where W denotes the after-tax wage bill, R is after-tax net profits, T is direct taxes (on both wages and profits), C is capital consumption allowances, X is the external material input bill, and G is total income (gross of both C and M) – all measured in current prices. We define gross value added Y as follows:

$$Y = G - X = R + W + T + C. \qquad (2.2)$$

Direct taxes are related to gross value added by:

$$T = t * Y, \qquad (2.3)$$

where t is the overall direct tax rate. Total income (or output) can be expressed as:

$$G = p_g * Q, \qquad (2.4)$$

where p_g is the total output price deflator and Q is real output at constant prices. Similarly the external material input bill can be expressed as:

$$X = p_x * M, \qquad (2.5)$$

where p_x and M are price and real quantity indexes, respectively, for external material inputs. We can then write:

$$X/G = p_{xg} * m, \qquad (2.6)$$

where p_{xg} is the relative price index for external material inputs and m is the material input requirement per unit of output (M/Q). It follows from equations (2.2) and (2.6) that:

$$T/G = (T/Y) * (1 - X/G) = t * (1 - p_{xg}m). \qquad (2.7)$$

Dividing equation (2.1) by G, substituting in equations (2.6) and (2.7), and re-arranging terms, we get:

$$(1 - p_{xg}m) * (1 - t) = C/G + R/G + W/G. \qquad (2.8)$$

C, R and W may be decomposed as follows:

$$C = d * K = d * P_k * J, \qquad (2.9)$$

$$R = r * K_N = r * n * K = r * n * p_k * J, \qquad (2.10)$$

$$W = w * L = p_w * v * L, \qquad (2.11)$$

where d is the rate of depreciation, K and J are the nominal and real values of gross capital stock, r is the net (after-tax) rate of profit, K_N is net capital stock, n is the ratio of net to gross capital stock, w and v are the nominal and real (after-tax) wage rates, L is labour input, and p_k and p_w are the price deflators for capital and wage goods, respectively. Average labour productivity q and the real output/capital stock ratio z are defined as follows:

$$q = Q/L, \qquad (2.12)$$

$$z = Q/J. \qquad (2.13)$$

Substituting equations (2.4) and (2.9)–(2.13) into equation (2.8), we arrive at the following:

$$(1 - p_{xg}m) * (1 - t) = p_{kg}d/z + p_{kg}rn/z + p_{wg}v/q, \qquad (2.14)$$

where p_{kg} and p_{wg} are the relative price indexes for capital and wage goods, respectively. Re-arranging terms, we can use equation (2.14) to derive an expression for the net (after-tax) rate of profit:

$$r = [p_{gk}z/n] * [(1 - p_{xg}m)(1 - t) - p_{wg}(v/q)] - [d/n], \qquad (2.15)$$

where p_{gk} is the inverse of p_{kg}.

Defining the rate of growth of the (after-tax) real wage rate as:

$$g = (v - v_{-1})/v_{-1}), \tag{2.16}$$

we may generate the equation for a distribution frontier by expressing r as a function of g as follows:

$$r(g) = [p_{gk}z/n] * [(1 - p_{xg}m)(1 - t) - p_{wg}(v_{-1}/q)(1 + g)] - [d/n]. \tag{2.17}$$

The slope of the distribution frontier is then given by:

$$\delta r/\delta g = -[p_{wk}(z/qn)](v_{-1}) = -[p_{wk}/nj)](v_{-1}), \tag{2.18}$$

where j denotes the ratio of real gross capital stock to labour input (J/L). This slope will be constant (and the distribution frontier will hence be linear) provided that the variables p_{wk}, n and j do not vary with changes in the ratio of r/g itself. This is surely a very reasonable assumption for p_{wk} and n; and it would seem quite acceptable for j as well in the relevant short-run context.

Using the distribution frontier equation (2.17) we can derive an expression for the particular value of r – denoted by r^{**} – that would obtain if g were maintained at its level of the previous period:

$$r^{**} = [p_{gk}z/n] * [(1 - p_{xg}m)(1 - t) - p_{wg}(v_{-1}/q)(1 + g_{-1})] - [d/n]. \tag{2.19}$$

The 'conflict-neutral' value of r – denoted by r^* – is then defined as the point halfway between the previous year's r and the current r^{**}:

$$r^* = (1/2) * (r^{**} + r_{-1}). \tag{2.20}$$

The profitability change terms are in turn defined as follows:

$$Dr = r - r_{-1}, \tag{2.21}$$

$$Dre = r^* - r_{-1} = (1/2) * (r^{**} - r_{-1}), \qquad (2.22)$$

$$Drc = r - r^* = Dr - Dre. \qquad (2.23)$$

Assuming (reasonably) that d and n do not vary from the previous to the current period, and substituting the equation (2.17) (for r_{-1}) and equation (2.19) into equation (2.22), we can express Dre as:

$$r^* = (1/2n) * [(A - A_{-1}) - (B^* - B_{-1}) * v_{-1}], \qquad (2.24)$$

where $A = (1 - p_{xg}m)*(1 - t)*(p_{gk}z)$,
$\qquad B = p_{wg}*(1/q) \quad B^* = p_{wg}*(1 + g_{-1})/q$.

It follows that Dre is a positive function of $(z - z_{-1})$, $(p_{gk} - p_{gk-1})$, and $(q - [1 + g_{-1}]q_{-1})$; and it follows that Dre is a negative function of $(p_{xg} - p_{xg-1})$, $(m - m_{-1})$, $(t - t_{-1})$, and $(p_{wg} - p_{wg-1})$. It is possible to use more or less readily available data to generate time series for all of the underlying variables whose changes contribute to movement in Dre, with the sole exception of $(m - m_{-1})$; but it is not unreasonable to assume that m (material input per unit of output) does not in any case vary much over time.

3. Stages in the Development of US Capitalism: Trends in Profitability and Technology since the Civil War*

Gérard Duménil, Mark Glick and Dominique Lévy

INTRODUCTION

This study has a twofold purpose. Initially we will describe the historical profile of the profit rate in the United States since the Civil War and the accompanying transformations of wages and technology. We then derive from the examination of these variables a periodization of the historical transformation of US capitalism into three stages.

The profit rate is estimated for the total private economy, before all taxes, from 1869 to 1989, that is a period of 121 years. The definition considered is the accounting rate of profit on the stock of fixed capital. A naive examination of the resulting general profile (Figure 3.1) would lead to the observation that three trends, interrupted by two sudden breaks in the 1880s and 1940s, characterize the long-term evolution of the profit rate: upward, horizontal and downward. A more careful analysis of these movements, however – taking account of the impact of the business cycle and the movements of other variables – suggests a more refined interpretation (Figure 3.8). The more in-depth investigation reveals three stages, in which the trends are continuously modified, and no severe breaks are apparent: (1) up to the First World War, downward; (2) from the First World War to the 1950s, upward; (3) since the 1950s, downward. The productivity of capital follows the same profile as the profit rate (cf.Figure 3.4).

The two other variables considered in this study, labour cost and labour productivity, grew rather steadily from 1869 to 1989, but three stages can also be distinguished in their growth rates. A difference between these latter variables and the profit rate and productivity of capital is that no trend can be established in the third stage for labour cost and labour productivity. Their growth rates appear to continue to diminish. Thus, in the third stage, we distinguish two sub-periods in which the rates of growth are, first, still large and then small.

We use the value of the average growth rate over the entire period as a criterion to separate periods of rapid and slower growth. To this first criterion we add the variation of the growth rate which can be increasing or diminishing, and obtain the following periodization: (1) up to to the First World War, slow growth; (2) from the First World War to the 1950s, rapid growth, accelerating; (3) since the 1950s, rapid growth up to 1967 and slow growth after 1967, decelerating.

The movements of labour cost and labour productivity did not significantly affect the strong similarity exhibited between the profit rate and the productivity of capital, since the trends in the labour cost and labour productivity variables remained parallel and, consequently, the profit share (cf.Figure 3.10) was approximately constant.

The nineteenth century and the period after the late 1960s appear similar in many respects: the profit rate and the productivity of capital declined and labour productivity and labour cost increased slowly.

It is probably not fruitful to interpret these observations in terms of 'long waves', or 'Kondratieff cycles', since over the period of more than a century covered by this study the observed pattern was never repeated. Only one period of growth of capital productivity and acceleration of labour cost and labour productivity is evident (the intermediate period). The above observations suggest rather that historically specific stages in the history of capitalism exist.

The present study describes only the historical evolution of the variables and does not consider the causal relationships involved. The interpretation of these phenomena, in relation to Marx's thesis on the falling profit rate, are discussed in Duménil and Lévy in Chapter 10. There we consider, not only technology and distribution, but also stability analysis and concrete history. We also abstract totally from any consideration of the technology embodied in each new vintage of fixed capital, instead of the average technology. This is addressed in Duménil and Lévy (1991a). This latter analysis adds precision to the periodization described above. In the context of a vintage model, other profit rates, such as the economic rate of profit on investment and the economic rate of return on the stock of capital are considered.

Section 1 below is devoted to a discussion of the secular profile of the profit rate. In Section 2, we determine the trends of the three variables involved in the computation of the profit rate: capital productivity, labour cost and labour productivity. In Section 3, we reconstruct the trend of the profit rate (as well as the capital–labour ratio and profit share) on the basis of those trends obtained for the three above variables. Finally we determine the periodization, dividing the variables into two groups, 'capital variables' (capital productivity and profit rate) and 'labour variables' (labour cost and productivity). An appendix is devoted to the discussion of the major empirical studies in which these same variables are considered.

1 THE PROFIT RATE

In this section the definitions and sources used in the computation of the profit rate are introduced; the results for the total private economy are presented; and we demonstrate the robustness of the puzzling recovery of the profit rate around the period of the Second World War by considering the profit rate for the corporate sector over the period 1929–89, for which better data are available and more adequate definitions can be used.

Definitions and Sources

The unit of analysis studied below is the total private economy. Since our primary interest concerns the investigation of the impact of technological change (the combination of capital and labour) on the profit rate, we use a broad definition of profits as net product minus labour remuneration and a narrow definition of capital as the net stock of fixed capital. More precisely:

1. The product in each year is defined as gross national product (GNP) minus: (a) depreciation and (b) income created by the government. Other components which should also be deducted from GNP, such as rental income of persons, are still included, since the necessary information is not available prior to 1929. A more accurate definition is used in the computation of the profit rate for the corporate sector after 1929 (see below).
2. From this measure of the yearly national product we further deduct a measure of labour compensation to obtain an estimate of profits. This measure is determined by multiplying total private employment (employees + self-employed) by the average compensation per employee. Thus a wage-equivalent for self-employed is included within labour compensation.
3. The stock of fixed capital is net of depreciation. Residential capital is not considered as a component of the productive system, and is excluded. Thus the capital stock is limited to equipment and structures. Government owned and privately operated capital is also included.

Capital stock and depreciation since 1925 are obtained from the Bureau of Economic Analysis (BEA). GNP, employment and total compensation since 1929 are provided by the National Income and Product Accounts (NIPA). Prior to 1929 (or 1925), historical studies necessarily must be utilized: Balke and Gordon (1989) for GNP[1], Goldsmith (1952) for the capital stock, Kendrick (1961) for employment, and Lebergott (1964) for compensation. A detailed account of the construction of the series is presented in Duménil and Lévy (1991c).

It is obvious that the reliability of the data depends on the period considered, and is superior for the more recent years. Data prior to 1929 are particularly suspect and, of course, very recent years are still subject to revision.

Trends and Breaks : a Naive Examination

The results of the estimation of the profit rate are presented in Figure 3.1. A straightforward examination of this figure reveals a succession of three distinct stages: (1) from 1869 to 1883, a sharp trend upward; (2) a long plateau from 1885 to 1939; and (3) a decline since the Second World War. The breaks appear sudden : a fall from 38.3 per cent in 1883 to 24.2 per cent, the average value of the 1885–1939 plateau, then a leap to 34.3 per cent, the average value in the 1950s.

However this interpretation is misleading, since it ignores the important effects of business cycle fluctuations, which are responsible for the variations around basic trends. From what we know about business fluctuations, we can infer that the most dramatic corrections would affect the following segments of the series: (1) the high points around 1880 (a peak in

Figure 3.1   The profit rate in the total private sector (1869–1989)

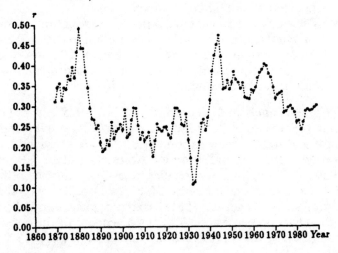

the net or gross product); (2) the low points around 1890 (a lengthy period of stagnating growth); (3) the fall into the Great Depression; (4) the sudden rise during the Second World War corresponding to the hectic activity during the war; and (5) the 1960s bulge which coincides with the exceptional levels of utilization of capacity during these years.

In the next two sections of this study we will propose an alternative reading of the historical profile of the profit rate. Since no capacity utilization rate is available for the total economy and for the period considered, it is not possible to correct for business cycle fluctuations. Instead we will reconstruct the trend of the profit rate (Section 3), from the analysis of those of the variables involved in its computation (Section 2).

Corporate Profitability since 1929

By limiting the investigation to the corporate sector and the period 1929–89, we can utilize more reliable data, and it is possible to test for the robustness of the most puzzling aspect of the profile of the profit rate displayed in Figure 3.1, the rise in the intermediate period.

As we begin the estimate of the profit rate in 1929, all series are available from the BEA, and the limitation of the unit of analysis to the corporate sector allows for a finer definition of the variables. For example, the definition of the net product can be made more rigorous, and there is no need for an estimate of the wage-equivalent of self-employed. It is also possible to include in the denominator the fraction of residential capital owned by the corporate sector. The computation is, thus, quite reliable.

The result obtained is displayed in Figure 3.2 (●). We find that the general profile is very similar to that shown in Figure 3.1. The profit rate in 1929 is equal to 17.5 per cent and rises to the average of 25.5 per cent for the 1950s.[2] These findings fully confirm the results of the earlier computation.

Parenthetically one notices that the entire benefit of this increased profitability was transferred to the state through taxation (indirect business taxes and corporate profits taxes). This is shown in Figure 3.2 (○). The average profit rate in the

*Figure 3.2   The profit rate in the corporate sector before (●)
           and after (○) all taxes (1929–1989)*

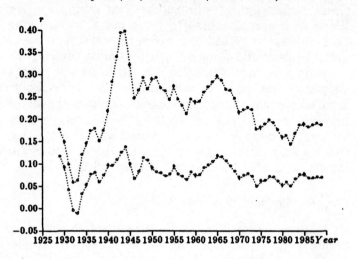

1950s is equal to 7.7 per cent; that is, even smaller than in 1929
(11.7 per cent).[3] This transfer contributed significantly to the
rise of public expenditures after the Second World War.[4]

2   PRODUCTIVITIES AND LABOUR COST

In this section we analyse the profiles of the three variables
selected as primary 'determinants' of the profit rate: the productivity of capital, labour cost and the productivity of
labour. First the general methodology used in the determination of the trend values of these variables is considered. This
is followed by the analysis of capital productivity and an
examination of the two labour variables, labour cost and
labour productivity.

Notation and Methodology

The profit rate in each year reflects the current state of technology, labour cost and the utilization of productive capacity. It
is not possible to correct for the impact of the utilization of
capacities, since no capacity utilization rate is available for

total economy and for the period covered in this study. Therefore we abstract from the 'short-term' fluctuation of the variables and focus on historical trends of technology and distribution.

The profit rate can be related to technology and labour remuneration in different ways. We have chosen to focus on three 'basic' variables. Capital productivity, denoted P_K, is the ratio of the net national product (NNP) in current dollars to the net stock of fixed capital also in current dollars. Labour productivity, denoted P_L, is the ratio of NNP in constant dollars to the number of hours worked. Labour cost, denoted w, is the ratio of the hourly wage in current dollars to the NNP deflator.

Since profits = NNP − total labour cost, total labour cost = hourly labour cost × number of hours worked and profit rate = profits / capital stock, the value of the profit rate, r, can be rewritten using these variables, as follows:

$$r = P_K\left(1 - \frac{w}{P_L}\right) \tag{3.1}$$

In a similar manner, the capital/labour ratio can be re-expressed as P_L/pP_K (with p denoting the price of fixed capital deflated by the NNP deflator) and the profit share as $1 - w/P_L$.[5]

In order to test for the hypothesis of a pattern of variation in three stages, we use the following methodology, illustrated in Figure 3.3. We assume that the profile of the logarithm of the variable considered can be interpreted as linear in the first and third periods, possibly with different slopes. In the second period, the transition is represented by a logistic curve. The model produced is the following:

$$ln\ Variable = (a + bt) + (c + dt)\ \frac{exp\left(\frac{t-\bar{t}}{\Delta}\right) - 1}{exp\left(\frac{t-\bar{t}}{\Delta}\right) + 1} \tag{3.2}$$

with $t = Date - 1900$

The logistic function increases from -1 for $t \to -\infty$, to $+1$

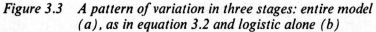

Figure 3.3   A pattern of variation in three stages: entire model (a), as in equation 3.2 and logistic alone (b)

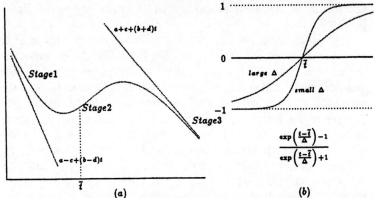

for $t \to \infty$, with any maximum slope in between (obtained for $t = \bar{t}$), depending on the value of Δ. As shown in Figure 3.3(b), it can account for a slow transition (a large Δ) as well as for a sudden leap (a small Δ). Nearly half of the transition as modelled by the logistic alone is concentrated between $\bar{t} - 1.1\Delta$ and $\bar{t} + 1.1\Delta$. Because of the factor $(c + dt)$, the maximum slope for the entire function does not coincide with $\bar{t}$ (significantly, if d and Δ are large, and only to a lesser extent if these parameters are small). The direction of the shift depends on the sign of d. In equation (3.2), the linear trends are given by $(a - c) + (b - d)t$ for the first period, and $(a + c) + (b + d)t$ for the third period, and the logistic represents the transition from the earlier to the later trend (see Figure 3.3(a)).

The Productivity of Capital

Figure 3.4 presents the productivity of capital. The profile obtained is, in many respects, reminiscent of that of the profit rate in Figure 3.1, and it is clear that this variable plays a crucial role in the explanation of the movement of the profit rate. A similar leap can be observed at the end of the Great Depression and the onset of the Second World War. From an average of 0.741 for the period 1885–1929, the productivity of

Figure 3.4 The productivity of capital (1869–1989)

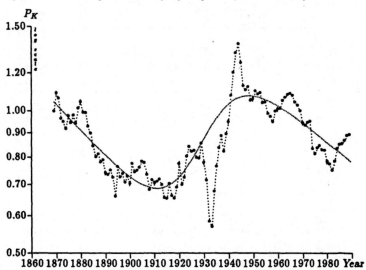

capital soars to 1.026 in the 1950s (an increase of nearly 40 per cent)!

The results of the regression using equation (3.2) are displayed in Table 3.1.[6] The trend line in Figure 3.4 corresponds to line (1) in the table, for which the years 1930–45 have been omitted, and capital productivity is defined as the ratio of NNP to the net stock of capital, both measured in current dollars. Concerning the two linear trends, one should notice that they differ only slightly (parameter d is small in comparison to b). The early trend downward is slightly stronger than that observed from the 1950s onward. The maximum slope in the logistic is obtained in 1928 (parameter $\bar{T}$), and half of the transition was realized between 1919 and 1937. The maximum slope of the trend is reached in 1929; that is, approximately the same date as for the logistic alone, since the two linear trends are not very different.

It is evident from Figure 3.4 that the distance from the first trend becomes apparent at the turn of the century, and that the trend reaches its minimum in 1911. The rise in the intermediate years begins to unravel in the 1940s and a maximum is

Table 3.1   The trend capital productivity (ln P_K) (1869–1989)

	a	b	c	d	T	Δ	R^2
(1) Net current $, 1930–45 omitted	0.141 ($t=2.9$)	−0.0112 ($t=8.9$)	0.493 ($t=7.3$)	0.00141 ($t=2.0$)	28.1 ($t=19.4$)	8.28 ($t=5.9$)	0.846
(2) Net current $	0.161 ($t=4.4$)	−0.00718 ($t=11.2$)	0.397 ($t=10.7$)	−0.00176 ($t=2.9$)	38.2 ($t=69.1$)	1.74 ($t=3.7$)	0.734
(3) Net constant $, 1930–45 omitted	−0.0836 ($t=2.8$)	−0.00810 ($t=8.8$)	0.555 ($t=12.5$)		33.0 ($t=43.9$)	7.6 ($t=8.3$)	0.947
(4) Gross constant $, 1930–45 omitted	−0.484 ($t=10.7$)	−0.0102 ($t=7.9$)	0.697 ($t=9.6$)		36.4 ($t=55.4$)	11.2 ($t=10.4$)	0.996

attained in 1948. These observations clearly define a periodization into three stages of comparable duration, with diminishing, increasing and diminishing trends, respectively. If one abstracts from the small difference in trends between the first and third period, the image is even simpler : an historical trend downward was interrupted by a rather lengthy period of restoration.

The downward trends prior to the First World War and subsequent to the 1950s are clearly apparent: the actual series is parallel to these two trends for a considerable time span. During the first stage one can recognize the effects of the peak in activity in the 1880s and the depression years in the 1890s. After the Second World War, it is easy to identify the impact of the 1958 recession, the 1960s bulge and the 1974 and 1981–82 recessions, as well as the recent recovery.

The use of econometrics is misleading in the interpretation of the (much troubled) period 1930–45. If all years are retained in the regression, as in line (2) of Table 3.1, the results are significantly different, in particular for the logistic. The maximum slope is detected in 1938 and half of the rise is concentrated between 1936 and 1940. Instead of a progressive transition, a leap is observed.

In order to shed some light on this observation, Figure 3.5 enlarges the central years of Figure 3.4. The dotted lines represent the two alternative trends. The first one, (1), corresponds to a regression with the years 1930–45 omitted. The second, (2), was obtained by using the complete series. The results are easy to interpret:

1. The 1920s are on the trend line (1). As expected, the trend passes above the series during the Great Depression and then below during the Second World War.
2. The trend line (2) is well below the observations during the 1920s, as it is 'pulled' downward by the depression years. To the contrary, it closely tracks the recovery in the Second World War.

We believe that the first interpretation, that of a progressive transition, is superior and, for this reason, in the remainder of this chapter we will continue to omit the period 1930–45 from the regressions.

Figure 3.5   Two views of the transition in the productivity of capital (1920–1960)

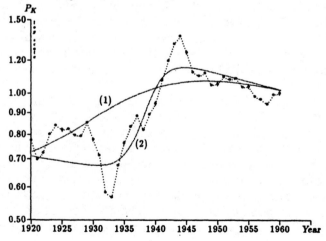

A similar type of computation can be repeated for various definitions of the productivity of capital with similar results. In line (3) of Table 3.1, both the NNP and net capital are measured in constant dollars. The pattern is similar to that obtained in the first line: the maximum slope is observed approximately in the same year (1933 instead of 1928), although the amplitude of the rise is slightly larger (cf. parameter *c*). This observation shows that the increase of capital productivity is not a result of a price effect. Quite the contrary, the variation of prices offsets to a certain extent the underlying real movement. It is also possible to consider GNP and the gross stock of fixed capital, instead of net aggregates. The results are displayed in line (4). They differ from those presented in line (1), inasmuch as $\bar{t}$ and Δ are larger. This is equivalent to saying that the rise begins at approximately the same date, but goes on longer.[7]

Labour Cost and Productivity

The historical profile of the hourly labour cost is presented in Figure 3.6. This series displays a very clear upward trend with an average growth rate of 1.95 per cent over the entire period. It increases in a stepwise fashion with two important jumps in the early 1880s and in 1921. Labour productivity is plotted in Figure 3.7. The average growth rate over the entire period is 1.92 per cent. One should notice that the historical growth pattern is very similar for the two variables (labour cost and labour productivity) depicting the same sequence, slow / fast /slow.

The results of the regressions, still using equation (3.2), are displayed in Table 3.2. For both variables the two trend values in the first and third stages are quite different (since *d* is large in comparison to *b*).[8] The slope of the asymptote for the third period, *b* + *d*, is very small for the labour cost and even negative for labour productivity. In both cases, Δ is very large. These observations imply that the curvature in the later period, corresponding to the productivity slow-down, is very strong. The actual (two) series never reach the second trend.

Figure 3.6   Labour cost (1869–1989)

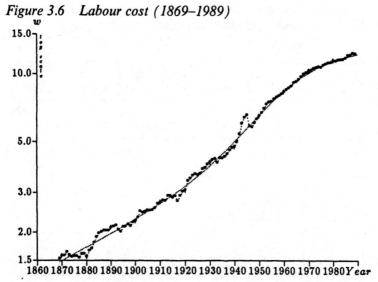

Figure 3.7   The productivity of labour (1869–1989)

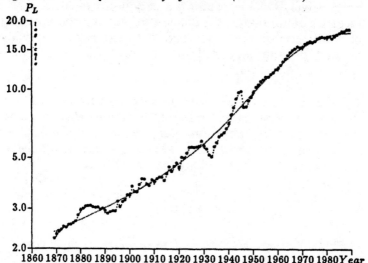

The growth rates of labour cost and labour productivity are still diminishing.

Thus, using equation (3.2) the three periods can be charac-

Table 3.2   The trend labour cost and productivity (1869–1989, with 1930–1945 omitted)

	a	b	c	d	T	Δ	R²
ln w	1.58	0.00766	0.783	0.00576	55.2	13.6	0.998
	(t=7.0)	(t=2.7)	(t=3.2)	(t=2.6)	(t=12.5)	(t=2.32)	
ln P_L*	2.56		1.39	−0.0104	61.1	16.1	0.997
	(t=64.8)		(t=59.2)	(t=11.6)	(t=34.7)	(t=13.8)	
ln P_L**	2.66		1.39	−0.00994	62.1	17.1	0.998
	(t=72.6)		(t=65.7)	(t=11.8)	(t=37.7)	(t=15.0)	

Notes:
*NNP/number of hours worked.
**GNP/number of hours worked.

terized as follows: (1) a period in which the rate of growth increases very slowly and the two series remain close to their asymptotic trend; (2) a period in which larger growth rates are progressively attained; and (3) a period in which the growth rates are diminishing. It is difficult to pinpoint the exact date of the transition from one period to the next. One viable method uses the value of the growth rate and its direction of variation. In this way:

1. We compare the growth rates along the trend lines to the average growth rate for the entire period. With this criterion, the two transitions occur in 1922 and in 1965 for labour cost, and 1922 and 1967 for labour productivity.
2. The maximum slope along the trend is reached in 1947 for labour cost and 1949 for labour productivity.[9] Prior to these dates the growth of the variables was accelerating. After these dates it is decelerating.

These findings demonstrate that, in spite of a common pattern in the three stages, the profiles of labour cost and labour productivity cannot be interpreted in the same manner as that of capital productivity. The passage from the early trend to the transition is similar to that observed for the profit rate and capital productivity, but the return to a lower growth rate does not correspond to a new stable trend.

Obviously the negative slope of the asymptotic trend of P_L for $t \to +\infty$ must not be interpreted as a pessimistic forecast concerning the future of capitalism. The large growth rates maintained in the 1960s for labour cost and labour productivity are a result of the Keynesian state policies and the high level of capacity utilization in those years. Simultaneously the economy entered a new stage of declining productivity of capital and profitability. The slowdown corresponds, at least in part, to the return to the trend after a period of evasion. Actually several plausible scenarios are compatible with these results (cf. Duménil and Lévy 1991b): prolongation of the present slowing down for a number of years, stabilization around a new trend, and others.

3   THE TREND PROFIT RATE AND OTHER VARIABLES: RECONSTRUCTIONS AND PERIODIZATIONS

In this section, we first show how the trend profit rate (as well as the capital–labour ratio and the profit share) can be reconstructed from the trends of the other variables. We then draw from this exercise some lessons concerning the choice of a periodization.

Reconstructions

As shown earlier (equation 3.1), the profit rate can be derived from the three variables considered in this study (capital productivity, labour cost and labour productivity). Figure 3.8 displays the result obtained from this derivation. The dotted line was determined on the basis of the three trends displayed in Figures 3.4, 3.6 and 3.7. A first period can be identified from the beginning of the series up to the 1900s. At this point the tendency is reversed, and the profit rate is progressively augmented from the 1910s to the 1940s. Then the new slide downward is initiated. This trend begins in 1869 at 39.3 per

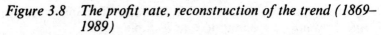

Figure 3.8   The profit rate, reconstruction of the trend (1869–1989)

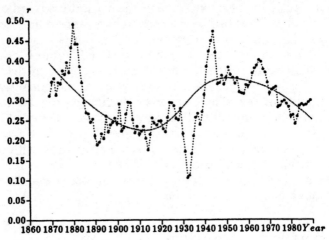

cent, falls to the minimum value of 22.5 in 1912, reaches its maximum in 1951 at 35.5 per cent and then falls back to 25.4 per cent in 1989.

Note that the sudden fall of the profit rate in the 1880s, as observed in the original series, reflects not only the variations of the general level of activity but also the fluctuation of labour cost around its trend. From 1869 to 1880, labour cost remained approximately constant, whereas labour productivity was progressing, and this explains the upward trend in the profit rate. Then labour cost increased at an annual rate of 4.8 per cent between 1880 and 1885, and the profit rate fell from 48.8 to 29.3 per cent during the same interval.

The same procedure of reconstruction can be applied to the capital–labour ratio, as shown in Figure 3.9. This ratio follows a clear upward trend, with an average rate of growth of 1.43 per cent. It stabilizes in the intermediate period, moves back to its upward trend after the Second World War, and then slows considerably. Its pattern is, in fact, a combination of the profiles observed for labour and capital productivities, the two variables from which it is reconstructed. For this reason the two temporal elements are involved, and both the

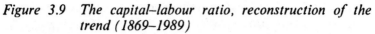

Figure 3.9   *The capital–labour ratio, reconstruction of the trend (1869–1989)*

rise of capital productivity and the productivity slowdown affect the outcome.

Lastly, Figure 3.10 applies the same methodology to the share of profits in NNP (which is equal to one minus the ratio of labour cost to labour productivity). The resulting trend line is nearly horizontal, with only a minor fluctuation. This observation is another expression of the strong correlation between labour cost and labour productivity. This correlation is too strong to be coincidental (see Duménil and Lévy, 1991b). It is clear from equation (3.1) that this invariance of the profit share is associated with the strong similarity between the profit rate and capital productivity.[10]

Periodization

The observations made in this study suggest that a distinction must be made between the two groups of variables, the 'capital' variables (the profit rate and productivity of capital) and the 'labour' variables (labour cost and labour productivity). The two variables in each group are tightly correlated. The correlation coefficient is equal to 0.897 for $ln\ r$ and $ln\ P_K$, and 0.996 for $ln\ w$ and $ln\ P_L$.

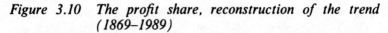

Figure 3.10   The profit share, reconstruction of the trend (1869–1989)

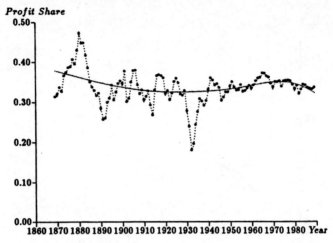

The variables in the two groups do not have exactly the same historical profile. It is, however, possible to define a single periodization, since it occurs approximately at the same time that the 'capital' variables reach their maximum and the 'labour' variables their maximum rate of growth.

The pattern observed for the productivity of capital and profit rate is the following: (1) up to the First World War, downward; (2) from the First World War to the 1950s, upward; (3) since the 1950s, downward. Applying these same divisions to labour cost and labour productivity we distinguish two sub-periods in the third stage: (1) up to the First World War, slow growth; (2) from the First World War to the 1950s, rapid growth, accelerating; (3) since the 1950s, rapid growth up to 1967 and slow growth after 1967, decelerating.

NOTES

*   Address all mail to: CEPREMAP, 142 rue du Chevaleret, 75013 Paris, France.
1.   In several earlier papers, we used the previous estimates provided by Balke and Gordon in the appendix to Gordon (1986). The main

difference in the two series is the lower figures in the new series for the period 1907–19.

2. The profit rate obtained for the corporate sector is smaller than that for the total private economy. One explanation is that the definitions of the net national product and capital stock are not identical. A second reason is that we use here an accounting definition of depreciation (instead of economic, cf. Duménil and Lévy, 1991a) and that the composition of the capital stock (the proportion as between equipment and structures) is different. Consequently the service life of fixed capital is also different and this discrepancy affects the profit rate.

3. Krzyzaniak and Musgrave (1963) contended that this increased taxation was actually the cause of the rise of the profit rate. This explanation was refuted in Gordon (1967), where it was shown that the progress of the profit rate was linked to that of capital productivity which cannot be imputed to mark-up procedures.

4. The sums implied represent a considerable fraction of public receipts. Excluding social insurances contributions, taxes from enterprises amounted to about 80 per cent of public receipts in 1929 and during the depression. After the Second World War, this percentage diminished because of the rise in personal income taxes, but these taxes still represented about 60 per cent of total receipts. Since the Second World War, and the 1970s in particular, the decline in the profit rate has been accompanied by the progressive alleviation of the tax burden imposed upon enterprises, in spite of the increasing difficulty in balancing the budget. The above percentage was reduced to about 45 per cent in the 1980s.

5. Independently of the reference to labour values or prices, and distinctions such as between productive or unproductive labour, it is easy to derive from these variables categories which are closer to Marx's. The organic composition of capital is $\gamma = P_L/wP_K$. The rate of surplus value is $\tau = P_L/w - 1$, and the profit rate is $r = \tau/\gamma$, (and not $\tau/(1 + \gamma)$, since only fixed capital is considered). Note that, because of the approximate invariance of the profit share or rate of surplus value (cf.Figure 3.10), the productivity of capital is almost proportional to the inverse of the organic composition of capital.

6. The procedure MODEL in SAS-ETS was used. As in the remainder of this chapter, we do not present the values of the Durbin-Watson test which are usually smaller than 2. The series are serially correlated since they reflect business fluctuations, and no variable can be included to overcome this problem.

7. For the last two lines, parameter d was not significative, and the regressions were rerun deleting this parameter.

8. For P_L, parameter b is not significative, and the regressions were re-estimated without this parameter.

9. Because of the difference between the two linear trends, the year in which the slope of the trend is at maximum is significantly different from that observed for the logistic (1955 and 1961 respectively).

10. It is important to keep in mind that the properties demonstrated above, and the associated reconstruction, must not be interpreted as causal relations.

REFERENCES

Balke, N. S. and R. G. Gordon (1989), 'The estimation of prewar gross national product: Methodology and new evidence', *Journal of Political Economy*, **97**, (1), 38–92.

Baran, P. and P. Sweezy (1966), *The Monopoly Capital*, New York and London: Monthly Review Press.

Bosworth, B. (1982), 'Capital formation and economic policy', *Brookings Papers on Economic Activity*, 1.

Corcoran, P. (1977), 'Inflation, taxes, and corporate investment incentives', *Federal Reserve Bank of New York Quarterly Review*, Autumn.

Denison, E. F. (1979), *Accounting for Slower Economic Growth: The United States in the 1970s*, Washington, DC: The Brookings Institution.

Duménil, G., M. Glick and J. Rangel (1987), 'The rate of profit in the United States', *Cambridge Journal of Economics*, **11**, (4), 331–60.

Duménil, G. and D. Lévy (1991a), 'Investment and technological change since the Civil War in the U.S.: A vintage model', Paris: CEPREMAP, LAREA-CEDRA.

Duménil, G. and D. Lévy (1991b), 'Technological change, distribution and stability', Chapter 10 of this volume.

Duménil, G. and D. Lévy (1991c), 'The U.S. economy since the Civil War: Sources and construction of the series', Paris: CEPREMAP, LAREA-CEDRA.

Feldstein, M. and L. Summers (1977), 'Is the rate of profit falling?', *Brookings Papers on Economic Activity*, 1.

Gillman, J. (1958), *The Falling Rate of Profit, Marx's Law and its Significance to Twentieth-Century Capitalism*, New York: Cameron Associates.

Goldsmith, R. W. (1952), 'The growth of reproducible wealth of the United States of America from 1805 to 1950', 247–309, in S. Kuznets (ed.), *Income and Wealth of the United States, Trends and Structure (Income and Wealth, series II)*, Baltimore: Johns Hopkins Press.

Gordon, R. G. (1967), 'The incidence of the corporation income tax in U.S. manufacturing', *American Economic Review*, **57**, 731–58.

Gordon, R. G. (1986), *The American Business Cycle, Continuity and Changes*, Chicago and London: University Chicago Press.

Kendrick, J. W. (1961), *Productivity Trends in the United States, NBER, General Series 71*, Princeton: Princeton University Press.

Krzyzaniak, M. and R. A. Musgrave (1963), *The Shifting of the Corporation Income Tax*, Baltimore: Johns Hopkins Press.

Lebergott, S. (1964), *Manpower in Economic Growth: The American Record since 1800*, New York: McGraw-Hill Book Co.

Lovell, M. (1978), 'The profit picture: Trends and cycles', *Brookings Papers on Economic Activity*, 3, 769–88.

Mage, S. (1963), 'The law of the falling tendency of the rate of profit', PhD dissertation, Columbia University.

Nordhaus, W. (1974), 'The falling share of profits', *Brookings Papers on Economic Activity*, 1, 169–208.

Okun, A. and G. Perry (1970), 'Notes and numbers on the profits squeeze', *Brookings Papers on Economic Activity*, 3.

Simon, H. A. (1986), 'On the behavioral and rational foundations of economic dynamics, 21–41, in R. Day and G. Eliasson (eds), *The Dynamics of Market Economies*, Amsterdam, New York, Oxford: North-Holland.

Solow, R. M. (1957), 'Technical change and the aggregate production function', *Review of Economics and Statistics*, 39, 312–20.

Solow, R. M. (1970), *Growth Theory*, Oxford: Oxford University Press.

Wolff, E. (1979), 'The rate of surplus value, the organic composition, and the general rate of profit in the U.S. economy, 1947–1967', *The American Economic Review*, 69, (3), 329–41.

APPENDIX: HISTORICAL TRENDS IN THE LITERATURE

The historical profiles of the variables considered in this study are well known (see, for example, Solow, 1970, or Simon, 1986). However, data studied in these investigations cover shorter periods of time (for example, from the First World War to the 1950s, or since the Second World War) and these studies are conducted from a different point of view.

A first example of the consequences of the limitation of the period of investigation is provided by Robert Solow's analysis of technical progress (Solow, 1957). The period covered in his study is 1919–59. It is clear from our investigation that this period is quite specific, and it is not surprising that Solow was puzzled by the size of the shift factor that he discovered. The analysis of the slide of the profit rate in the late 1960s (Okun and Perry, 1970; Nordhaus, 1974; Feldstein and Summers, 1977; Lovell, 1978; Corcoran, 1977, Bosworth, 1982) provides a second example of this difference in the duration of the period of investigation.

The perspective adopted by many studies is different from ours. A prominent example of this difference is the manner in which the productivity slowdown has been approached. It is described in the literature (see, for example, the survey in Denison, 1979) as a new phenomenon, and it is never related back to the trends observed in the nineteenth century. The slowdown is defined as the 'event' to be explained, and the intermediate stage is viewed as a natural state of affairs in modern capitalism.

The profile of the profit rate described in Marxist literature usually confirms what we have obtained. Joseph Gillman (1958) measured the profit rate for manufacturing industries for the period 1880–1952. His computation revealed a downward trend in the nineteenth century, but no restoration during the Second World War. Although Shane Mage (1963) does not consider the same unit of analysis and definition as ours, he describes a rather similar profile (for the period 1900–

60) in his pretax measure of the profit rate. The restoration of the profit rate during the Second World War is evident in his series. A difference is that he depicts a fall of the profit share after the First World War (as was also the case in Duménil, Glick and Rangel, 1987). The profile revealed by Edward Wolff (1979) for the period of 1947–67 is also quite compatible with our results.

In Paul Baran and Paul Sweezy's study (Baran, Sweezy, 1966), it is not the profit rate which is computed (in the appendix by Joseph Phillips), but the rate of surplus (surplus/ NNP). This surplus includes the profit of enterprises, interest and government expenditures (as well as 'unproductive' sectors of the economy). This ratio can be compared to our profit share, but the definition of the surplus is significantly different from our profits. In particular, because of the addition of government expenditures, personal income taxes are included in the surplus. For this reason (and possibly others), the rate of surplus is larger than our profit share and increases from 46.9 to 56.1 per cent between 1929 and 1963.

Thus, if one abstracts from the limitation of the unit of analysis and a number of biases in measurements, a general conclusion which can be drawn from the review of Marxist literature is that the case for a falling profit rate would not have been too difficult to defend, in the absence of the restoration observed during the Second World War. This is also the thesis which was presented in Duménil, Glick and Rangel (1987).

4. Unproductive Labour and the Rate of Profit in the Postwar US Economy

Fred Moseley

The rate of profit in the US economy declined significantly during the post-Second World War period. According to various estimates, the rate of profit declined approximately 30–40 per cent from the early postwar period to the mid-1970s (e.g. Bosworth, 1982).[1] This significant decline in the rate of profit is often mentioned as one of the important causes of the economic crisis of the last decade. It seems plausible that the decline of the rate of profit resulted in a slow-down of investment spending, which in turn contributed to the rise of unemployment in the 1980s. At the same time the decline in the rate of profit probably also contributed to the acceleration in the rate of inflation, as capitalist enterprises attempted to restore their rate of profit by increasing prices at a faster rate. Thus the decline in the rate of profit would seem to be at least partially responsible for both of the 'twin evils' of higher unemployment and higher inflation. It is important to understand the underlying causes of the decline in the rate of profit in order to have some idea about the likely trend in the rate of profit in the future and thus about the likelihood of a full recovery from the current economic crisis.[2]

Even though the empirical fact of the decline in the rate of profit has been rather thoroughly analysed (e.g. Lovell, 1978; Feldstein *et al.*, 1983; Holland and Meyers, 1984), there have been very few attempts by mainstream economists to explain the causes of this decline. Lovell concluded his paper with the observation that the decline in the rate of profit is 'a major puzzle for future investigations' (p. 787). Similarly Feldstein *et al.* concluded that most of the decline in the rate of profit 'remains to be explained' (p. 154) and that 'without understanding why profitability was lower in the 1970's than in the earlier period, it is not possible to say whether this has been a permanent or temporary decline' (p. 150).

Radical economists, on the other hand, have progressed further in explaining this decline in the rate of profit. The main type of explanation offered by them is the 'profit squeeze' theory, according to which the decline in the rate of profit is attributed primarily to a decline in the profit share, which is often (erroneously) claimed to be a proxy for Marx's concept of the rate of surplus-value.[3] Different profit squeeze theorists have different explanations for the decline in the profit share. Weisskopf (1979) argued that the main cause of the decline in the profit share was the lower rates of unemployment which prevailed in the postwar period, and which enabled workers to defend themselves against an increase in the relative price of wage-goods and to maintain their real wage share. Wolff (1986) presented a different explanation for the decline in the profit share: the decline in productivity growth which occurred, beginning in the mid-1960s, and which itself was due to largely accidental causes (the increase in energy prices, the faster rate of growth of the labour force and so on). Lipietz (1986) also argued that the productivity slow-down was the main cause of the decline in the profit share, but he attributed the productivity slow-down to the 'exhaustion' of the Fordist regime of accumulation, both technically (diminishing returns of a given regime of accumulation) and socially (increasing class conflict resulting in lower intensity of labour, increased absenteeism and so on).

This chapter will present an alternative explanation for the decline in the rate of profit in the postwar US economy, which is based on Marx's theory of productive labour and unproductive labour. Section 1 briefly reviews this important distinction in Marx's theory and derives a theory of the rate of profit from this distinction. Section 2 presents estimates of the variables in this Marxian theory of the rate of profit and constructs from these estimates an explanation for the decline in the rate of profit. It will be seen that, according to this alternative Marxian explanation, the main cause of the decline in the rate of profit was a very significant increase in the ratio of unproductive labour to productive labour during this period.[4] Section 3 then presents a preliminary analysis of the underlying causes of this significant increase in the relative proportion of unproductive labour in the US economy. The final section briefly states the main conclusions and implications of the chapter.

1   MARXIAN THEORY OF PRODUCTIVE AND UNPRODUCTIVE LABOUR AND THE RATE OF PROFIT

Marx's theory of the 'falling rate of profit' is well known, but it is not always recognized that this theory does not apply directly to the conventionally defined rate of profit discussed above. The main difference between the conventional rate of profit and the 'Marxian' rate of profit has to do with Marx's distinction between productive labour and unproductive labour, which will now be briefly reviewed.[5]

Marx's theory is based on the assumption that value and surplus-value are created only through *production activities*, where production is defined fairly broadly to include such activities as transportation and storage (Marx, 1977, Chapters 1 and 7).[6] The important point of this assumption for the purpose of this paper is that it implies that no value and surplus-value is created in non-production activities (Marx, 1977, Chapters 5 and 13; 1981, Chapter 6; and 1982, Chapter 17).

Non-production activities consist of two main types: (1) *circulation activities*, or activities related to the exchange of commodities, including such activities as sales, purchasing, accounting, advertising, financial relations, banking, securities exchange, insurance, real estate and legal counsel; and (2) *supervisory activities*, or activities related to the control and surveillance of the labour of production workers, including such activities as management, supervision and record-keeping.

According to Marx, no value and surplus-value are created in circulation activities, because the acts of circulation are assumed to be essentially exchanges of equivalent values. No additional value is produced as a result of these exchanges of equivalent values. Instead a given amount of value is converted from the form of commodities to the form of money, or vice versa. Similarly, according to Marx, no value and surplus-value are produced in supervisory activities because these activities are not technically required for production, but are instead necessary within the capitalist mode of production because of the class conflict inherent in capitalism between capitalists and workers over the intensity of the labour of workers.

Since by assumption value and surplus-value are created in production activities, Marx referred to the labour employed in production activities as 'productive labour' and the capital invested in production activities as 'productive capital'. Productive capital consists of two main components: *constant capital*, which is the capital invested in the material inputs to production activities (buildings, equipment and raw materials) and *variable capital*, which is the capital invested in the productive labour. Both constant and variable capital can be considered either as a stock or as a flow, but, for our purposes, constant capital will be considered solely as a stock and variable capital solely as an annual flow. Marx's theory of the 'falling rate of profit' applies only to this productive capital; that is, it assumes that all capital is productive capital.

On the other hand, since also by assumption no value and surplus-value are created in non-production activities, Marx referred to the labour employed in non-production activities as 'unproductive labour' and the capital invested in non-production activities as 'unproductive capital'.[7] According to Marx's theory, the capital invested in non-production activities is recovered, together with a profit, out of the surplus-value produced by productive labour.

These assumptions and definitions can now be used to

formulate a Marxian theory of the conventional rate of profit. Profit (P), the numerator in the conventional rate of profit, is assumed to be equal to the difference between the annual flow of surplus-value (S) and the annual flow of unproductive capital (U_f) (mostly the wages of non-production workers, but also the annual costs of non-production buildings, equipment and materials):[8]

$$P = S - U_f \tag{4.1}$$

Similarly the stock of capital (K), the denominator in the rate of profit, is assumed to be equal to the sum of constant capital (C) and the stock of capital invested in non-production structures and equipment (U_s):[9]

$$K = C + U_s \tag{4.2}$$

Combining equations (4.1) and (4.2), we obtain the following Marxian equation for the conventional rate of profit (RP):

$$RP = \frac{P}{K} = \frac{S - U_f}{C + U_s} \tag{4.3}$$

Finally, dividing all terms on the right-hand side of the above equation by the annual flow of variable capital, we obtain:

$$RP = \frac{S/V - U_f/V}{C/V + U_s/V} = \frac{RS - UF}{CC + US} \tag{4.4}$$

From equation (4.4) we can see that, according to Marxian theory, the conventional rate of profit depends not only on the composition of capital (CC)[10] and the rate of surplus-value (RS) (the determinants of the Marxian rate of profit), but also on the two ratios of unproductive capital to variable capital ($UF = U_f/V$ and $US = U_s/V$). More precisely, the conventional rate of profit varies inversely with these two ratios of unproductive capital to variable capital.

2 ESTIMATES OF THE MARXIAN VARIABLES, 1947–1977

Annual estimates of the Marxian determinants of the conventional rate of profit identified in the previous section were derived for the business sector of the US economy for the period 1947–77.[11] These estimates are presented in Table 4.1. The sources and methods used to derive these estimates are described briefly in the appendix and more fully in Moseley (1991, Appendix B).

These estimates show the following long-run trends:[12] (1) the rate of surplus-value increased 17 per cent; (2) the composition of capital increased 44 per cent; (3) the ratio *UF* increased 72 per cent; and (4) the ratio *US* increased 117 per cent.[13] Thus, according to the Marxian theory presented here, the proximate causes of the decline in the conventional rate of profit in the postwar US economy were the significant increases in the composition of capital and in the two ratios of unproductive capital to variable capital.

In order to estimate the individual contributions of each of these proximate determinants to the total decline in the rate of profit, the total decline was decomposed into four components, each one of which corresponds to the contribution of one of the four Marxian determinants to the total decline in the rate of profit. The results of this exercise are shown in Table 4.2. These estimates show that the proximate determinant which contributed the most to the decline in the rate of profit was the ratio *UF*. The increase in the ratio *UF* had a substantially greater negative effect on the rate of profit than the increase in the composition of capital, the trend which Marx emphasized in his analysis of the 'Marxian' rate of profit. These negative effects were partially offset by the increase in the rate of surplus-value, which had a significant positive effect on the rate of profit (contrary to the profit squeeze explanations of the decline in the rate of profit).

One way empirically to test the validity of this explanation for the decline in the rate of profit, compared to the two profit squeeze explanations discussed in the introduction (lower unemployment and slower productivity growth), is to deter-

Table 4.1   The rate of profit and its Marxian determinants (1947-1977)

	RS	CC	UF	US	RP
1947	1.40	3.58	0.54	0.30	0.22
1948	1.35	3.60	0.53	0.30	0.21
1949	1.50	3.81	0.59	0.32	0.22
1950	1.42	3.94	0.58	0.32	0.20
1951	1.44	3.78	0.56	0.31	0.22
1952	1.41	3.69	0.57	0.31	0.21
1953	1.35	3.56	0.58	0.30	0.20
1954	1.46	3.84	0.64	0.33	0.20
1955	1.51	3.85	0.65	0.34	0.21
1956	1.44	3.96	0.67	0.36	0.18
1957	1.50	4.08	0.70	0.38	0.18
1958	1.59	4.33	0.75	0.42	0.18
1959	1.61	4.14	0.75	0.41	0.19
1960	1.62	3.11	0.78	0.42	0.19
1961	1.68	4.18	0.81	0.45	0.19
1962	1.71	4.07	0.81	0.45	0.20
1963	1.71	3.99	0.80	0.46	0.21
1964	1.73	3.92	0.81	0.47	0.21
1965	1.73	3.92	0.80	0.48	0.21
1966	1.72	3.91	0.81	0.50	0.21
1967	1.72	4.03	0.84	0.52	0.19
1968	1.69	4.02	0.84	0.53	0.19
1969	1.62	4.07	0.85	0.54	0.17
1970	1.61	4.29	0.89	0.58	0.15
1971	1.71	4.50	0.93	0.62	0.15
1972	1.67	4.37	0.89	0.61	0.16
1973	1.59	4.39	0.87	0.61	0.14
1974	1.55	5.13	0.92	0.69	0.11
1975	1.71	5.39	0.98	0.69	0.12
1976	1.66	5.15	0.95	0.66	0.12
1977	1.63	5.03	0.94	0.66	0.12

Notes
RS: rate of surplus-value = surplus-value/variable capital.
CC: composition of capital = constant capital/variable capital.
UF = flow of unproductive capital/variable capital.
US = stock of unproductive capital/variable capital.
Sources: See Appendix.

Table 4.2   Contributions of the Marxian determinants to the decline in the rate of profit (1947–1977)

RS	0.051
CC	−0.051
UF	−0.085
US	−0.012
Total decline in *RP*	−0.099

Notes

These contributions were calculated according to the following method, which is adopted from Wolff (1986):

Let $A = RS - UF$
$\quad B = CC + US$
Then

$$\Delta RP = \frac{A_2}{B_2} - \frac{A_1}{B_1}$$

From which it can be derived that

$$\Delta RP = B^*(\Delta A) - A^*(\Delta B) \qquad (4.5)$$

where: $A^* = A' / B_1 B_2$
$\qquad\quad B^* = B' / B_1 B_2$
$\qquad\quad A' = (A_1 + A_2) / 2$
$\qquad\quad B' = (B_1 + B_2) / 2$

The contributions of each of the four Marxian variables to the overall decline in the rate of profit was calculated from equation (4.5) by allowing each variable to change one at a time and holding the other three variables constant. For example, the contributions of *RS* is given by

$B^*(\Delta RS)$.

mine the predictions implied by each explanation concerning the trend in the rate of profit after the period of study and then to compare these implied predictions with the actual trends in these variables during the post-period years (see Moseley, 1991, Chapter 4, for a more complete discussion of this empirical test of these competing explanations for the decline in the rate of profit). This exercise does not provide a conclusive empirical test of these competing explanations, primarily because none of the three implies definite and precise predictions concerning the post-period trend in the rate of profit. However these explanations do seem to imply somewhat different predictions concerning this post-period trend, so some information regarding their relative empirical validity can be gained from this exercise.

Briefly both the profit squeeze explanations (especially the lower unemployment variant) seem to imply the prediction that the rate of profit should have increased significantly over the last decade, primarily because of the higher rates of unemployment which have prevailed during this period. By contrast the 'unproductive labour' explanation presented here seems to imply that the rate of profit should *not* have increased significantly. According to this explanation, the lower rates of unemployment should have increased the rate of surplus-value, but this increase in the rate of surplus-value was probably offset by continued increase in the ratio UF.

Estimates of the rate of profit in the US economy since the mid-1970s (adjusted for different capacity utilization rates) show little or no increase in the rate of profit. Thus, although this test is not conclusive, the evidence of the past decade (specifically the absence of an increase in the rate of profit) seems to weigh in favour of the 'unproductive labour' explanation for the decline in the rate of profit presented here.

3 CAUSES OF THE INCREASE IN UNPRODUCTIVE LABOUR

The explanation for the decline in the rate of profit presented in the previous section raises the obvious further question: what were the underlying causes of the very significant increases in the two ratios of unproductive capital to variable capital, especially the ratio UF? The proximate cause of the increase in this latter ratio was a roughly proportional increase in the ratio of the number of unproductive workers to the number of productive workers in the postwar US economy.[14] Estimates of unproductive labour and productive labour in the postwar US economy are presented in Table 4.3. These estimates show that the number of unproductive workers (that is, workers employed in circulation and supervisory activities) increased 143 per cent over this period, from 10.5 million in 1947 to 25.5 million in 1977, while the number of productive workers increased only 34 per cent, from 29.6 million in 1947 to 39.6 million in 1977, thus resulting in an 83 per cent increase in the ratio of unproductive labour to productive labour, from 0.35 in 1947 to 0.64 in 1977. According to the Marxian theory presented here, this very significant increase in the ratio of unproductive labour to productive labour was the most important cause of the decline in the conventional rate of profit in the postwar US economy. The relative increase of unproductive labour required that a greater portion of surplus-value had to be used to pay the costs of unproductive labour, thus leaving a smaller portion of surplus-value as the profit of capitalists.

Thus an important task for further research along these lines is to identify the underlying causes of this very significant increase in the relative proportion of unproductive labour in the postwar US economy. This section presents a summary of a preliminary analysis of this important question (see Moseley, 1991, Chapter 5, for a more complete discussion).

To begin with, it should be recalled that unproductive labour consists of two main types: circulation labour and supervision labour. Estimates of these suggest that circulation labour accounted for approximately 80 per cent of the total unproductive labour in the US economy throughout the postwar period and supervisory labour for the remaining 20 per cent (see Moseley, 1991, Chapter 5, for a detailed presentation of these estimates). Thus, circulation labour was considerably more empirically significant than supervisory labour in the postwar US economy.

Circulation Labour

Circulation labour may in turn be divided into two subtypes: trade labour and finance labour. Trade labour is all the unproductive labour in the wholesale and retail industry, plus the

Table 4.3   *The ratio of unproductive labour to productive labour*

	PL	UL	UL/PL	Index
1947	29.6	10.5	0.35	100.0
1948	30.2	10.8	0.36	101.5
1949	28.7	10.8	0.38	106.8
1950	29.7	11.0	0.37	105.1
1951	31.2	11.7	0.37	105.8
1952	31.4	12.2	0.39	110.2
1953	32.1	12.7	0.40	112.1
1954	30.6	12.9	0.42	119.1
1955	31.4	13.4	0.43	120.3
1956	32.0	14.0	0.44	123.5
1957	31.7	14.3	0.45	127.6
1958	29.9	14.3	0.48	135.1
1959	31.0	14.8	0.48	135.1
1960	31.0	15.3	0.49	139.0
1961	30.5	15.4	0.51	143.0
1962	31.1	15.8	0.51	144.2
1963	31.4	16.2	0.52	146.3
1964	31.8	16.7	0.53	148.6
1965	32.9	17.4	0.53	149.2
1966	34.3	18.3	0.53	150.6
1967	34.5	19.0	0.55	155.6
1968	35.2	19.7	0.56	158.0
1969	36.3	20.6	0.57	160.4
1970	36.0	21.0	0.58	165.1
1971	35.7	21.1	0.59	167.5
1972	37.0	21.8	0.59	166.4
1973	38.8	22.8	0.59	166.4
1974	39.0	23.5	0.60	170.3
1975	36.9	23.5	0.64	180.1
1976	38.3	24.3	0.64	179.8
1977	39.6	25.5	0.64	181.9

Notes
PL: productive labour.
UL: unproductive labour.
Sources: See Appendix.

labour in other industries employed in the functions of buying and selling and the accounting, clerical and similar occupations related thereto. Finance labour is all the labour in the finance, insurance and real estate industry. Estimates of these two sub-types of circulation labour suggest that trade labour accounted for approximately 80 per cent of circulation labour and thus for approximately 65 per cent of the total unproductive labour. Thus the most important task in an analysis of the causes of the increase in unproductive labour is to explain the increase in trade labour, which accounted for almost two-thirds of the total increase of unproductive labour.

There are two possible causes of the relative increase in trade labour: (1) an increase in the 'sales effort'; that is, an increase in the 'services' provided with each exchange transaction, such as credit, advertising and other promotion, warranty and so on; and/or (2) slower 'productivity' growth of trade labour compared to production labour; that is, slower reduction in the labour required to provide a constant quantity of services with each exchange transaction, compared to the labour required to produce each commodity. It is very difficult to determine the relative empirical significance of these two possible causes because it is very difficult to measure the quantity of sales 'services' provided with each commodity sold. The usual estimates of productivity in the trade sector of the economy assume that the quantity of 'services' per unit of output sold remains constant and thus are of no use in determining the relative importance of these two possible causes. In order to begin to determine their relative importance, the following paragraphs present partial and indirect evidence related to changes in the 'sales effort' in the postwar US economy.

The most likely cause of a significant increase in the labour required for the 'sales effort' in the postwar US economy is an increase in the percentage of consumer sales financed by credit. Credit sales require the additional labour of investigation, record-keeping, collection and so on (all of which increase with the length of the term of the credit).

The ratio of consumer instalment credit extended to total consumer sales did in fact increase significantly (it almost doubled) during this period, from 11 per cent around 1950 (1948–52 average) to 19 per cent around 1980 (1978–82 average) (source: Federal Reserve Board). This increase in the percentage of consumer sales financed by credit was made possible by a number of innovations by lenders of consumer credit during this period, such as longer maturities, lower down payments, 'revolving' credit in department stores, 'all-purpose' bank credit cards, the extension of credit to non-durable goods and services and increased consumer loans by commercial banks. In addition, the longer maturities require more labour for a given amount of credit extended. Thus there appears to have been a significant increase in the credit-related 'sales effort' in the postwar US economy.

However most of this increase in consumer credit was held by financial institutions (commercial banks, finance companies, credit unions and so on), rather than by retail or manufacturing companies. The percentage of total consumer instalment credit held by financial institutions increased from 79 per cent in 1950 to 84 per cent in 1980. Thus almost all the additional labour required to process the increased consumer credit was employed in the finance industry, which is classified here as 'finance labour', not 'trade labour'.[15] In other words, the increase in the credit-related 'sales effort' appears to have been a significant cause of the increase in finance labour during this period, but only a minor cause of the increase in trade labour, the most important category, which is being analysed in this chapter.[16]

Another possible cause of the increase in the labour required for the 'sales effort' is an increase in advertising. However advertising cost is only a very small percentage of consumer sales, although this percentage did increase slightly, from approximately 2 per cent in 1950 to approximately 3 per cent in 1980. Furthermore employment in advertising agencies in 1980 was less than 1 per cent of the total trade labour (approximately 150 000 out of 21 million) and this percentage has even declined slightly since the 1950s (source: Bureau of Labor Statistics). Thus an increase in the advertising-related 'sales effort' does not seem to have been a significant cause of the increase in trade labour during this period.

On the other hand, the spread of 'self-service' sales (vending machines, gasoline stations, discount stores and so on) had the effect of reducing the labour required for each exchange transaction. This effect was probably minor in the aggregate, but it did at least to some extent offset any increase in the 'sales effort' from other sources.

Thus my tentative conclusions are that there was a significant increase in the 'sales effort' in the postwar US economy, especially for credit-related activities, but that this increase was not an important cause of the total increase in trade labour during this period.[17] By process of elimination it would appear that the far more important cause of the increase in trade labour was the slower 'productivity' growth of trade labour, compared to production labour. More definite conclusions would require direct estimates of the labour employed in the various aspects of the 'sales effort', which are very difficult, and perhaps impossible, to derive.[18]

If one assumes, for simplicity, that the 'sales effort' per unit of output remained constant, then the slower 'productivity' growth of trade labour follows directly from the faster increase in trade labour compared to productive labour. The quantity of output (Q) produced by productive labour (PL) must be sold by trade labour (TL). Thus the productivity of productive labour is given by Q/PL and the 'productivity' of trade labour is given by Q/TL. If TL increased at a faster rate than PL, then it follows immediately that Q/TL increased at a slower rate than Q/PL. As a result, a higher percentage of the total labour had to be employed as trade labour in order to sell the more rapidly increasing output of productive labour.

The underlying cause of the slower 'productivity' growth of trade labour would seem to be that it is inherently more difficult to mechanize buying and selling than it is to mechanize production. For example, in the automobile industry, continual mechanization has greatly increased the productivity of production workers, but the sale of each automobile requires highly personalized service, which has made it difficult to increase the number of cars sold per salesperson.

Barger (1955) attributed the relative increase in 'distribution' labour in an earlier period to this same cause: the slower

increase in output sold per labour-hour in distribution compared to the increase in output produced per labour-hour in
production. Barger's explanation for the differential is that
'technology changed far less rapidly in Retail and Wholesale
Trade than it did in Manufacturing, Mining, and Agriculture' (p. 10). Wolff (1987) also presents a similar analysis of
the causes of the relative increase in employment in wholesale and retail trade in the postwar period.

Marx argued, and the history of capitalism seems to
demonstrate, that technological change of production is an
inherent feature of capitalist economies. If, as seems to be the
case, technological change of trade is much more difficult
than technological change of production, then the slower
'productivity' growth of trade labour and the consequent
increase in the relative employment of trade labour would
also seem to be inherent tendencies of capitalist economies.
In fact the relative proportion of trade labour does seem to
have increased in all capitalist economies since the mid-
nineteenth century (for the USA, see Barger, 1955). Further,
on the basis of Marx's assumption that trade labour
produces no value, the relative increase in trade labour
causes the rate of profit to decline. Thus this analysis suggests an inherent cause of the decline of the rate of profit,
which has hitherto received very little attention, but which
seems to have been very important in the postwar US
economy.

The second sub-type of circulation labour is finance
labour. As with trade labour, analysed above, there are two
possible causes of the relative increase in finance labour: (1)
faster increase in the 'output' of finance labour (deposits,
cheques, loans, insurance policies, real estate sales and so on)
compared to the output of productive labour; and (2) slower
increase in the 'productivity' of finance labour, defined as the
output of finance labour per labour-hour. Again it is very
difficult to determine the relative significance of these two
possible causes because there are no adequate aggregate estimates of the 'output' of finance labour. Partial estimates of
the 'output' of finance labour suggests the following conclusions: (1) in the finance sub-industry (mainly banking) 'out-

put' (mainly the number of cheques processed) increased faster than the output of productive labour. 'Productivity' growth in the finance sub-industry seems to have roughly kept pace with the productivity growth of productive labour. The most likely underlying cause of the rapid increase in the number of bank cheques in the postwar period was the spread of personal cheque accounts and the increasing use of personal cheques as a means of payment in sales transactions. (2) In the insurance and real estate sub-industries, 'productivity' seems to have increased at a slower rate than the productivity of productive labour. Since labour in these sub-industries is essentially involved in sales transactions, perhaps the underlying cause of the slower 'productivity' growth in these sub-industries was similar to that of trade labour discussed above: the inherent difficulty of merchanizing sales transactions.

Supervisory Labour

We turn our attention now to the second main type of unproductive labour: supervisory labour. Following Marx (especially 1977, Part 4) and Braverman (1974), we hypothesize that the degree of capitalist control over workers depends on the following factors, in addition to the amount of supervisory labour (with the nature of the relation, whether positive or negative, in parentheses): the level of skills of workers (negative), the rate of unemployment (positive), the size of firms (negative), and the divisions among workers (positive). If these 'other factors' change in a way that reduces capitalist control, then the amount of supervisory labour will have to be increased if a given degree of capitalist control is to be maintained. In this sense, such changes in these 'other factors' may be considered as causes of the increase in supervisory labour; that is, they require an increase in supervisory labour in order to maintain a given degree of capitalist control. This response by capitalists to these various changes may not be immediate, but may instead occur after a certain time lag.

One important change which has occurred during the twentieth century, especially in manufacturing, is a significant increase in the size of firms. In 1977, 66 per cent of employees in manufacturing were in firms of more than 1 000 employees and 45 per cent were in firms of more than 10 000 employees. These percentages had increased since 1958, the earliest year for which these data are available, from 56 per cent and 33 per cent respectively (source: Bureau of the Census, *Enterprise Statistics*). Another indication of the increasing size of firms in manufacturing in the postwar period is that the percentage of production workers employed in multi-unit firms increased from 56 per cent in 1947 to 74 per cent in 1977 (source: Bureau of the Census, *Census of Manufacturing*, 'Type of Organization'). Presumably, if earlier data were available, they would show much lower percentages in large and multi-unit firms in the early twentieth century. It could be argued that some of the increase in supervisory labour in manufacturing in the postwar period was a delayed reaction to the increasing size of firms in the decades preceding this period.

Edwards (1979) argues that, as the size of firms increased in the twentieth century, the older and simpler forms of control, based on the personal and direct authority of the owners and managers, no longer sufficed to maintain an adequate intensity of labour. In response to this problem, Edwards argues, many large firms instituted a new system of 'bureaucratic control' in the postwar period. Bureaucratic control consisted primarily of elaborate and detailed systems of record-keeping, the primary purpose of which was to monitor closely the work performance of each employee. This new form of control required that more and more labour be devoted to the creation and processing of these detailed performance records. Other aspects of bureaucratic control which also required an increase in supervisory labour are detailed rules and procedures to govern all tasks which workers must perform, finely graded 'job ladders' to maintain the sense of job mobility, and an extension of incentive pay schemes. Edwards also notes that there was a significant increase in direct supervision in the postwar period to administer these new forms of bureaucratic control.

However the increased size of firms was much less significant in other industries than manufacturing. In these, other factors than increased size must have been primarily responsible for the relative increase in supervisory labour.

Another important change in the 'other' determinants of capitalist control, which may have precipitated an increase in supervisory labour, was the lower rates of unemployment which prevailed in the postwar period, compared to earlier historical periods. Marx argued in *Capital* that unemployment 'completes the despotism of capital' (1977, Chapter 25). In these terms, the lower rates of unemployment in the postwar period reduced the despotism of capital and presumably enabled workers more effectively to resist capitalist control. As a result, more supervisory labour was required in order to maintain a given degree of capitalist control.[19]

The 'other' determinants of capitalist control discussed thus far seem to have changed in ways (*ceteris paribus*) that reduced capitalist control and thus generated a need for an increase in supervisory labour. The two remaining 'other' determinants, the skills of workers and the intra-class divisions among workers, are harder to measure and to evaluate. However it does not appear likely that these factors changed in ways that reduced capitalist control and thus required an increase in supervisory labour. If anything, these two factors probably had the opposite effects.

The discussion of supervisory labour thus far has been based on the assumption that managers increased supervisory labour in the postwar period in order to maintain a given degree of control in the face of adverse changes in the 'other' determinants of capitalist control. A further possible cause of the relative increase in supervisory labour in the postwar US economy is that managers attempted not only to *maintain* a given degree of control, but also to *increase* their control. The aim of the greater control over labour would be not just to maintain a given intensity of labour, but to increase the level of intensity, and thus to increase productivity and profits. Melman (1951) suggests that such an attempt to increase managerial control was the main cause of the relative increase in 'administrative labour' in US manufacturing in an earlier period.

It is very difficult to test statistically the relative significance of these possible causes of the increase in supervisory labour. The main reasons for this difficulty are: (1) no data are available which distinguish between supervisory labour and productive labour for individual *firms* (which data are necessary to test the relations between the size of firms and the ratio of supervisory labour to productive labour) and (2) the inability to measure the degree of capitalist control and thus to distinguish empirically between attempts by managers to maintain a given degree of control and attempts to increase their control. Thus an important task for future research along these lines is to attempt to overcome these obstacles to the analysis of the causes of the increase in supervisory labour.

4   CONCLUSIONS

The above analysis has emphasized a new variable in Marxian crisis theory: the ratio of unproductive labour to productive labour. This variable has heretofore not received much attention, either by Marx himself or by later Marxist economists. But the above analysis suggests that the very significant increase in this ratio was the most important cause of the decline in the rate of profit in the postwar US economy. Thus it appears that the relative proportion of unproductive labour should be given more attention in the ongoing analysis of the causes of the decline in the rate of profit.[20]

We have also seen that the most likely cause of the significant increase in the relative proportion of unproductive labour is the slower 'productivity' growth of trade labour compared to productive labour, and that this productivity differential seems to be inherent in the nature of the two activities of production and trade. This conclusion has the important implication that the relative increase in trade labour (and of unproductive labour in general) is likely to continue in the years ahead. In addition Marx's theory of unproductive labour suggests that this further relative increase in unproductive labour will continue to exert downward pressure on the rate of profit and thus that a significant increase in the years ahead is not very likely, certainly less likely than is predicted by the profit squeeze explanations for the decline in the rate of profit mentioned in the introduction.

Finally, if the rate of profit does not increase in the coming years, as is predicted by the theory presented here, then the stagflation of the last two decades is likely to continue, and eventually perhaps to deteriorate into a deeper depression.

NOTES

I wish to express appreciation to Tom Weisskopf for his helpful comments as the discussant of this paper at the conference and to Toni Fredette for her very valuable research assistance.

1. These estimates refer to the before-tax rate of profit, with which this chapter is solely concerned.
2. This decline in the rate of profit is a world-wide phenomenon; all major OECD nations experienced a similar decline over the postwar period (see Hill, 1979).
3. For a discussion of the significant differences between the profit share and the rate of surplus-value, see Moseley (1985).
4. A similar explanation for the decline in the *share* of profit in the postwar US economy is presented in Moseley (1985) and updated in Moseley (1987).
5. For a more complete discussion of Marx's distinction between productive labour and unproductive labour, see Moseley (1991, Chapter 2). Other references on this distinction include Rubin (1972); Gough (1972); Braverman (1974, Chapter 19); and Leadbeater (1985).
6. More precisely Marx assumed that the aggregate value added produced during a given period is proportional to the aggregate amount of labour of production workers and is independent of the labour of non-production workers. From this assumption it follows that the aggregate amount of surplus-value or profit is proportional to the aggregate amount of the surplus labour of production workers.
7. Marx also used the concept of unproductive labour in the broader sense to include labour employed in non-capitalist production (for example, in government and household production). Adam Smith used the concept of unproductive labour to refer only to labour employed in non-capitalist production, not to labour employed in non-production activities within capitalist enterprises. In this chapter, the term 'unproductive labour' refers only to the latter category of labour within capitalist enterprises employed in unproductive functions.

8. The conventional rate of profit also differs from Marx's concept of surplus-value in the following minor respects, which are ignored here: indirect business taxes are not included in profit and are included in surplus-value; and various imputations for non-market transactions are included in profit and are not included in surplus-value.

9. Here we make the simplifying assumption that the stock of capital invested in the wages of both productive labour and unproductive labour is equal to zero. In reality the stock of capital invested in wages is very small, since capitalists pay workers only after they have worked for some period of time.

10. Marx's concept of the composition of capital actually refers to three distinct but related ratios: the technical, value and organic compositions of capital. Strictly speaking, Marx's theory of the falling rate of profit is presented in terms of the organic composition of capital. However, for the purpose of simplification, the composition of capital in this chapter refers to the value composition, as defined in the text. The trends in the value and organic compositions will usually be in the same direction, though with different percentage rates of change.

11. Since the mid-1970s, the rate of profit, adjusted for different capacity utilization rates, has been essentially constant. The estimates of the Marxian variables are presented for the years 1947–77 in order to focus the analysis on the period of the decline in the rate of profit.

12. These estimates have not been adjusted for cyclical fluctuations because I am interested here solely in secular trends and the capacity utilization rate at the end of my period (for example, 81.4 per cent in 1977 for manufacturing) was very close to the capacity utilization rate at the beginning of the period (82.0 per cent in 1947).

13. Since the composition of capital increased proportionally greater than the rate of surplus-value, the 'Marxian' rate of profit declined approximately 15 per cent. This decline is consistent with Marx's theory of the 'falling rate of profit'. See Moseley (1988) for a further discussion of the Marxian rate of profit in the postwar US economy.

14. The ratio *UF* also depends on the relative average wages of productive labour and unproductive labour and on the annual material costs of unproductive activities, but these other two factors were not significant causes of the increase in the ratio *UF* in the postwar US economy.

15. Data for *non-instalment* consumer credit *extended* do not exist. Data for non-instalment consumer credit *outstanding* (less appropriate for comparison to current consumer sales) do exist, but are judged to be unreliable and are no longer published by their source, the Federal Reserve Board. These data indicate that: (1) non-instalment credit has increased more slowly than instalment credit, so that non-instalment credit as a percentage of total consumer credit declined from 36 per cent in 1950 to 15 per cent in 1980; and (2) the percentage of non-instalment credit held by financial institutions increased from 43 per cent in 1950 to 75 per cent in 1980. Thus, as in the case of the more

significant instalment credit, most of the additional labour required to process non-instalment credit was 'financial labour', and not 'trade labour'.

16. For the first half of the twentieth century, Barger (1955) comes to the even stronger conclusion that there was probably a *'decline* in the relative amount of service furnished by merchants to the public in the form of credit sales' (p. 35, emphasis added). Barger attributed this decline mainly to the transfer of the financing of consumer credit from the merchant to outside financial institutions, a trend which was pioneered by the motor car industry and which, as we have seen, continued in the postwar period.

17. A further question is whether this increased 'sales effort' was due to a 'realization problem', as elaborated by Baran and Sweezy (1966) and many others, or instead was due to increased non-price competition of this type for reasons other than a 'realization problem'. An answer to this question would need to begin with an empirical determination of whether or not such a 'realization problem' in fact existed in the postwar US economy. Such an empirical determination is obviously beyond the scope of this chapter. However I do intend to return to this important question in the future.

18. Other possible forms of an increased 'sales effort' are travelling salesmen, point-of-sale promotion, warranties, returns and adjustments, free trials and so on. I have not yet been able to obtain even indirect estimates of the labour employed in these other functions. It is my hypothesis at this point that there was no significant increase in the percentage of trade labour employed in these other forms of the 'sales effort' in the postwar US economy.

19. Thanks to Tom Weisskopf for emphasizing this point to me.

20. It is often said that Marxian crisis theory consists of three main 'variants': rising composition of capital, profit squeeze and underconsumption (or realization problem). This chapter in effect suggests a fourth variant: the rising unproductive labour variant, which is compatible (or complementary) with the rising composition of capital variant. In theory the rising unproductive labour variant is also compatible with the profit squeeze variant, but not with the underconsumption variant.

REFERENCES

Baran, Paul and Paul Sweezy (1966), *Monopoly Capital*, New York: Monthly Review Press.

Barger, Harold (1955), *Distribution's Place in the American Economy since 1869*, Princeton: Princeton University Press.

Bosworth, Barry (1982), 'Capital Formation and Economic Policy', *Brookings Papers on Economic Activity*, 1.

Braverman, Harry (1974), *Labor and Monopoly Capital*, New York: Monthly Review Press.

Edwards, Richard (1979), *Contested Terrain*, New York: Basic Books.

Feldstein, Martin, Louis Dicks-Mireaux and James Poterba (1983), 'The Effective Tax Rate and the Pretax Rate of Return', *Journal of Public Economics*, **21**.

Gough, Ian (1972), 'Marx's Theory of Productive and Unproductive Labor', *New Left Review*, November–December.

Hill, T. P. (1979), *Profits and Rates of Return*, Paris: Organization for Economic Cooperation and Development.

Holland, David M. and Stewart C. Meyers (1984), 'Trends in Corporate Profitability and Capital Costs in the United States', in Holland (ed.), *Measuring Profitability and Capital Costs*, Lexington, Mass.: Lexington Books.

Leadbeater, David (1985), 'The Consistency of Marx's Categories of Productive Labor and Unproductive Labor', *History of Political Economy*, **17**, Winter.

Lipietz, Alain (1986), 'Behind the Crisis: The Exhaustion of a Regime of Accumulation', *Review of Radical Political Economics*, **18**, (1–2), Spring–Summer.

Lovell, Michael (1978), 'The Profit Picture: Trends and Cycles', *Brookings Papers on Economic Activity*, **3**.

Marx, Karl (1977), *Capital*, Volume 1, New York: Random House.

Marx, Karl (1981), *Capital*, Volume 2, New York: Random House.

Marx, Karl (1982), *Capital*, Volume 3, New York: Random House.

Melman, Seymour (1951), 'The Rise of Administrative Overhead in the Manufacturing Industries of the United States in 1899–1947', *Oxford Economic Papers*, **3**, (1), January.

Moseley, Fred (1985) 'The Rate of Surplus Value in the Postwar US Economy: A Critique of Weisskopf's Estimates', *Cambridge Journal of Economics*, **9**,(1), March.

Moseley, Fred (1987), 'The Profit Share and the Rate of Surplus-Value in the U.S. Economy, 1975–85', *Cambridge Journal of Economics*, **11**,(4), December.

Moseley, Fred (1988), 'The Rate of Surplus Value, the Organic Composition, and the General Rate of Profit in the U.S. Economy, 1947–67: A Critique and Update of Wolff's Estimates', *American Economic Review*, **78**,(1), March.

Moseley, Fred (1991), *The Falling Rate of Profit in the Postwar United States Economy*, London: Macmillan.

Rubin, I. I. (1972), *Essays on Marx's Theory of Value*, Detroit: Black

and Red Press.
Weisskopf, Thomas E. (1979), 'Marxian Crisis Theory and the Rate of Profit in the Postwar U.S. Economy', *Cambridge Journal of Economics*, **69**,(2), June.
Wolff, Edward (1986), 'The Productivity Slowdown and the Fall in the U.S. Rate of Profit, 1947–76', *Review of Radical Political Economics*, **18**(1–2), Spring-Summer.
Wolff, Edward (1987), *Growth, Accumulation, and Unproductive Activity*, New York: Cambridge University Press.

APPENDIX: DATA SOURCES AND METHODS

(For a more complete description, see Moseley, 1991, Appendix B.)

1. *Constant capital* (stock): the sum of fixed capital and circulating capital. *Fixed capital*: the current value of buildings and equipment used for production activities. Estimates are derived from BEA data for 'net private non-residential fixed capital' (current cost), excluding various types of buildings and equipment used for circulation and supervision activities (such as office, computing and accounting machines; furniture and fixtures; commercial buildings). *Circulating capital*: the current value of inventories. Estimates are derived from NIPA data for 'business inventories'.

2. *Variable Capital* (annual flow): the total compensation (including supplements and benefits) of production workers. Estimates are derived from NIPA data for 'total employee compensation' in the business sector of the economy, excluding the compensation of non-production workers. The percentage of total employee compensation within each of the eight major industry classifications that was paid to production workers is estimated using data from various sources, primarily the censuses of manufacturing, mining and construction, which provide data for the wages of 'production workers', and the BLS *Employment and Earnings* (Establishment Survey), which provides data for the numbers of 'production workers' in the manufacturing, mining and construction industries and for the number of 'non-supervisory employees' in the other industries.

3. *Surplus-value* (annual flow): the difference between new-value and variable capital. Estimates of *new-value* are derived from NIPA data for the 'net product' of the business sector, plus indirect business taxes, minus 'imputations' which do not correspond to goods and services actually sold on the market (80 per cent of which is the value of the 'housing services' of owner-occupied homes) and minus the value produced by self-employed proprietors.

PART II
SECTORAL ANALYSIS OF PROFITABILITY

5. Structural Change and the Movement of the Rate of Profit in the USA

Edward N. Wolff

The movement of the rate of profit over time has been the subject of considerable interest and debate both within and outside Marxian economics. Marx argued that the rate of profit would tend to decline over the long run. His so-called 'law of the tendency of the rate of profit to fall' states that over time the organic composition of capital would rise, thereby causing the general rate of profit to fall (Marx, 1967, Volume 3, Chapter 13). This law has been criticized on several grounds over the last 30 years or so (see, for example, Okishio, 1961; Samuelson, 1971; Roemer, 1977, 1979; Weisskopf, 1979; Wolff, 1979; Bowles, 1981; and Wolff, 1986). Despite the theoretical flaws in the argument, Marx's theory does provide a useful framework in which to analyse factors which affect movements in the rate of profit.

In this chapter, a factor is explored that has received relatively little attention in the literature – namely, the role of structural change on movements in the rate of profit. Marx (1967) himself noted the importance of structural shifts in Volume 3 of *Capital*: 'Since the general rate of profit is not only determined by the average rate of profit in each sphere, but also by the distribution of the total social capital among the different individual spheres, and since this distribution is continually changing, it becomes another constant cause of change in the general rate of profit' (p. 169). Moreover 'new lines of production are opened up, especially for the produc-

93

tion of luxuries, and it is these that take as their basis this relative over-population, often set free in other lines of production through the increase of their constant capital. These new lines start out predominantly with living labour, and by degrees pass through the same evolution as the other lines of production. In either case, the variable capital makes up a considerable portion of the total capital. . .' (p. 237). Differential growth in the various sectors will thus affect the movement of the rate of profit over time.

The particular mechanism investigated here is the effect of uneven development on the organic composition of capital. Marx defined the organic composition of capital as the ratio of constant capital, the labour value of fixed and circulating capital, to total value. He argued that it would increase over time because of the substitution of fixed and circulating capital for labour. However he noted the presence of several counteracting forces. One was the continual devaluation of constant capital owing to technical change. Another, which is focused on here, is the uneven development among the sectors of the economy. As Marx argues, the organic composition tends to increase within the various branches of the economy, particularly within manufacturing. However sectors grow at different rates over time. If employment shifts towards sectors which have a relatively low organic composition, then this will act to depress the economy-wide organic composition.

The period under investigation is primarily from 1947 to 1977 in the USA. It is found, as in previous work (Wolff, 1979 and 1986) that all in all there was very little change in the economy-wide organic composition of capital over the period. On the other hand, for the private, for-profit economy and for the productive sector, there was a moderate increase over the period. However the increase was not continuous for these two sectors and there were periods when the organic composition declined quite sharply. In addition projections to 1981, based on partial data, indicate a modest upward trend in the organic composition. It is also found that the profit rate, based on a variety of measures, fell substantially over the 1947–77 period. The decline was particularly sharp in the last decade of this period. Most of the decline was due to a fall in the profit share in national income.

Finally it is found that sectoral shifts in the distribution of employment significantly depressed the organic composition of capital. As a result, employment shifts are found to be an important counteracting infuence on the tendency of the rate of profit to fall and, without such structural change, the rate of profit would have fallen considerably more.

The paper is divided into five sections. The first presents the basic accounting framework and definitions of the variables. In Section 2, several conceptual issues concerning the measurement of the organic composition and the rate of profit are addressed. Section 3 presents the findings on movements of the organic composition of capital over time, while Section 4 focuses on movements in the rate of profit. Concluding remarks are made in the last section, and some broader implications of the results are identified.

1 ACCOUNTING FRAMEWORK AND DEFINITIONS OF VARIABLES

The basic data used for the analysis are standard Bureau of Economic Analysis (BEA) 85-sector US input–output tables and corresponding labour and capital coefficients for years 1947, 1958, 1963, 1967, 1972 and 1977.[1] All components are in constant (1972) dollars unless otherwise noted. Define:

a = inter-industry technical coefficient matrix, where depreciation is added as an endogenous row counterbalanced by an endogenous 'depreciation replacement' column and an endogenous export column is added to balance the non-competitive import row.

q = $(I - a)^{-1}$, the inverse technical coefficient matrix.

X = column vector of gross domestic output (GDO) by sector.

Y = column vector of final output (demand) by sector.

m = column vector showing the average consumption per worker by commodity.

Then the standard Leontief identity holds:

$$X = qY.$$

Also define:

L = row vector of employment by sector.

N = $\sum L$, total employment in the economy.

l = row vector of labour coefficients, where $l_i = L_i/X_i$.

s = row vector showing the distribution of employment among sectors (that is, employment shares), where $s_i = L_i/N$.

k = capital coefficient matrix of the same dimensionality as a, where k_{ij} shows the amount of net plant or equipment of type i used per (constant) dollar of output in sector j.

Then the vector of labour values λ is given by

$$\lambda = lq \tag{5.1}$$

where λ_i is interpreted as the direct plus indirect labour required per (constant) dollar of output in sector i.

The value of labour power, or the variable capital advanced per worker, is equal to λm. Total variable capital, V, is then equal to $N\lambda m$. The rate of surplus-value is defined as the ratio of total surplus-value, S, to total variable capital and is given by

$$\epsilon \equiv S/V = (N - V)/V = (1 - \lambda m)/\lambda m. \tag{5.2}$$

Total constant capital, C, is defined as the labour value of the total circulating (a) and fixed (k) capital in the economy and is given by

$$C = \lambda(k + a)X. \tag{5.3}$$

I can now define the economy-wide organic composition of capital θ as

$$\theta \equiv C/N = \lambda(k + a)X/N \qquad (5.4)$$

which shows the ratio of total constant capital to the total labour value added per year (N).[2] Here, it is implicitly assumed that the turnover rate of circulating capital (material inputs) is one year.[3] In addition, the technical composition of capital τ, defined as the ratio of the quantity of constant capital to the total labour input, is given by

$$\tau = e(k + a)X/N \qquad (5.5)$$

where e is a row vector of ones. The relation between the organic and technical composition of capital can now be derived. First, define

$$\bar{\lambda}_c = \lambda(k + a)X/e(k + a)X \qquad (5.6)$$

which indicates the average labour content of a constant dollar of fixed and circulating capital. Then

$$\theta = \bar{\lambda}_c\tau. \qquad (5.7)$$

I shall comment later about the significance of this equation.

The organic and technical composition can also be defined on the sectoral level. First, let

$d = k + a$, the matrix of fixed and circulating capital technical coefficients.

Then the organic composition in sector j, θ_j, is given by

$$\theta_j = \lambda d.jX_j/N_j \qquad (5.8)$$

where where $d.j$ is the jth column of matrix d. Likewise, the technical composition of sector j, τ_j, is given by

$$\tau_j = ed.jX_j/N_j. \qquad (5.9)$$

Let us now define $\bar{\lambda}_j$ as the average labour content per constant dollar of fixed and circulating capital in sector j:

$$\bar{\lambda}_j = \lambda d.j/ed.j. \qquad (5.10)$$

Then

$$\theta_j = \bar{\lambda}_j \tau_j. \tag{5.11}$$

Moreover the economy-wide organic composition can now be seen as a weighted sum of the organic compositions of the individual sectors, where the weights are the labour shares s:

$$\theta = \sum s_j \theta_j. \tag{5.12}$$

In like fashion, the economy-wide technical composition is also given as a weighted sum of the technical compositions of each industry, where the weights are employment shares:

$$\tau = \sum s_j \tau_j. \tag{5.13}$$

I shall comment more on these last five equations in Section 3 below.

Finally, the value rate of profit ρ is defined as:

$$\rho = S/(C + V). \tag{5.14}$$

Here it should be noted that the rate of profit is defined as the ratio of surplus value to the total value of advanced capital, including fixed capital, intermediate inputs, goods-in-process, and the wage bill. It then follows from (5.2) that

$$\rho = \epsilon/(1 + C/V) = \epsilon/[1 + \theta(1+\epsilon)]. \tag{5.15}$$

An increase in the organic composition of capital will thus lead to a fall in the (value) rate of profit. An increase in the rate of surplus-value will lead to an increase in the rate of profit, since

$$\partial \rho / \partial \epsilon = (1 + \theta)/[1 + \theta(1+\epsilon)]^2 > 0.$$

2 CONCEPTUAL ISSUES IN THE MEASUREMENT OF THE ORGANIC COMPOSITION AND THE RATE OF PROFIT

Before presenting the empirical results, there are several important conceptual issues that must be resolved about the

measurement of the organic composition and the rate of profit. As will become clear, there is no definitive answer in regard
to some of these issues, since any answer depends on the
purposes for which the measure is used. As a result alternative
measures of the organic composition and rate of profit are
developed.

The first issue is whether the government sector should be
included in the determination of the economy-wide organic
composition and rate of profit. There are several justifications
that can be made to include the government sector, First, the
government sector includes what are called 'government
enterprises', which are businesses which appear to operate in
almost all respects like capitalist enterprises. Examples are the
postal system, the Tennessee Valley Authority, many public
utilities owned and operated by local governments, publicly
owned transit systems, and state-run toll highway systems. In
each case the product or services are directly sold to customers. Moreover, even though the public enterprises are
nominally non-profit organizations, in almost all cases they
invest and expand over time. Thus, in substance, they operate
like any other capitalist enterprise and, indeed, can be considered as self-expanding value.

Second, many US governmental activities which are
financed by tax dollars provide services directly to the public.
These include public educational systems, local water and
sewerage systems, garbage collection, fire protection, the
interstate highway system and non-toll roadways, and the
like. It is important not to confuse the form of payment with
the characteristics of the exchange. In these cases services are
provided to identifiable individuals. Moreover individuals pay
for these services through taxes. The difference between this
case and the previous one is that those people who pay for the
services may not necessarily be the same as those who receive
the benefits, or at least not to the same degree for which the
payment is made. Yet such tax-financed services are activities
in which investments are made and which expand over time
and are thus not materially different from capitalist enterprises. Indeed many of these activities are often run by capitalist enterprises, as with garbage collection in many localities.

Whether a locality provides a service directly or contracts out to a capitalist enterprise to provide the service should not materially affect its classification as capital.

Third, the argument can be directly extended to the provision of so-called 'public goods', which are output that cannot be directly attributed to particular individuals. These goods are all tax-financed. The only difference between this case and the previous one is that there are not clearly identifiable substitutes among privately owned enterprises.

These three arguments all strongly suggest that the fixed and circulating capital owned by the government sector, as well as the labour employed in it, should be included in the definition of the organic composition. Moreover they also imply that the capital advanced in the government sector should be imputed an average rate of return. Though there is no profit recorded in the government sector, this is a national accounting convention. If one were to set up government accounts in analogous fashion to the corporate sector, with a separate current and capital account, then one could compute a government surplus figure in the same manner as in the corporate sector (see, for example, Ruggles and Ruggles, 1982).

The argument against the inclusion of the government sector is that there is no reason for the government to try to obtain the average (capitalist) rate of return on the capital it advances. Indeed the forces of competition, which create a tendency for the rate of profit to be equalized in the private sector, do not operate in the government sector. Moreover there is no incentive for the government to obtain a profit or even to cover its costs. Since both sets of arguments are persuasive as to whether government capital should or should not be included in the economy-wide measure of the organic composition and the rate of profit, these measures are computed both ways.

The second issue, analogous to the first, is whether non-profit institutions should be included as a sector in the measurement of the organic composition and the rate of profit. The arguments are quite similar. Many non-profit institutions, such as private universities, research institutes and hospitals, provide services to individuals on a fee-for-service basis. In this way they behave like other capitalist enterprises. Though nominally non-profit making, they invest and expand over time. Yet here, too, there are no market forces that would cause the non-profit sector to obtain the average rate of profit on its capital. Moreover, by accounting conventions, there is no profit recorded in this sector. As a result its classification is ambiguous and this sector is therefore treated both ways.

The third issue deals with the status of the so-called household sector, which consists of domestic servants directly hired by households. This sector is excluded from the social capital because, in fact, there is no capital owned by this sector. There are no forces which cause this sector to expand over time. Though there is wage labour in this sector, payment for their labour power is made out of revenue, not capital.

The fourth issue is whether unproductive labour should form part of the employment base in the computation of the organic composition. The argument for its inclusion is that, from the capitalist's point of view, payment for unproductive labour constitutes a cost just as much as wages paid to productive labour. Forces of competition necessitate that the capitalist obtain the average rate of return on the capital advanced to unproductive labour. Moreover unproductive constant capital, the inputs and capital stock employed in unproductive activity, should likewise be included in the definition of the organic composition, since the capitalist expects the normal rate of return on this capital. The argument against the inclusion of unproductive inputs in the calculation of the organic composition is that they are paid for out of surplus-value and thus do not, properly speaking, constitute capital. Since both views have some legitimacy, the organic composition and the rate of profit with and without unproductive capital will be computed.

3 MOVEMENTS IN THE ORGANIC COMPOSITION OF CAPITAL, 1947–1981

In Volume 3 of *Capital*, Marx discusses the reasons why the organic composition will tend to rise over time. The principal argument is that the technical composition will rise and this, in turn, is the result of the substitution of physical capital for labour. There are two reasons for this. First, in expanded reproduction, the demand for labour power will rise. If the demand increases faster than the growth in the labour force, the reserve army of the unemployed will become depleted. This will drive up the real wage. As a result there will be a strong inducement for capitalists to substitute physical capital for labour. This will occur through the introduction of more physical capital-intensive technology in new investment. This, in turn, will cause both the ratio of fixed plant and equipment to labour and that of materials and other intermediate inputs to labour to rise over time. Both factors will result in a rise in the technical composition (see equation (5.5)).[4] The second reason is that the forces of competition may induce the introduction of more physical capital intensive-production techniques. Even without higher real wages, more physical capital-intensive technology may be absolutely more productive than labour-intensive technology. Capitalists can thus lower costs by investing in the more capital-intensive technology. This will enable them to expand their market share and increase profits.

Table 5.1 shows movements in the technical and organic composition of capital on the aggregate level. For the whole economy, the ratio of fixed capital to labour (the 'traditional' neo-classical capital–labour ratio) increased at an annual rate of 2.3 per cent over the 1947–77 period and at 2.5 per cent over the 1947–81 period. It rose at 2.8 per cent per year from 1947 to 1958 and at about 2 per cent thereafter. The ratio of intermediate inputs to labour increased at a slightly slower pace during the 1947–77 period. As a result the technical composition of capital, a weighted average of the two, grew at 2.2 per cent per year between 1947 and 1977. From 1947 to 1958, it increased at 2.6 per cent per year; from 1958 to 1967, at 2.4 per cent; and from 1967 to 1977, at 1.5 per cent. The technical composition in the government sector was fairly stable over the 1947–77 period. As a result the technical composition of the non-government, profit-making sector grew faster than the total technical composition.[5] It increased at 3.3 per cent per year from 1947 to 1958, 2.7 per cent from 1958 to

1967, 2.0 per cent from 1967 to 1977, and 2.7 per cent per year over the whole period. Finally, for the productive economy,[6] the technical composition increased at an annual rate of 2.8 per cent per year. Thus, by all measures, there appears to be a consistent upward secular trend in the technical composition of capital.

The increase in the technical composition will cause labour productivity to increase, for two reasons. First, the increase in the physical capital–labour ratio will cause output per person hour to rise.[7] Second, insofar as the more physical capital-intensive production techniques embody more productive technology, labour productivity will increase. An increase in labour productivity will, in turn, cause total (direct plus indirect) labour requirements to fall per unit of output and thus labour values to fall. In particular, $\bar{\lambda}_c$ will tend to fall and this will act to depress the organic composition (see equation (5.7)). Marx saw this offsetting effect as relatively minor. However, historically, the fall in the labour content of physical capital has been almost as great as the rise in the technical composition.

The organic composition for the full economy showed no net change over the 1947–77 period (Table 5.1). Between 1947 and 1958, it increased at 0.5 per cent per year; between 1958 and 1967 it declined substantially; and from 1967 to 1977 it increased at 0.7 per cent per year. If we exclude the government and non-profit sector, the same pattern emerges, with the organic composition rising in the 1947–58 and 1967–77 periods and declining during the 1958–67 period. However, over the whole 1947–77 period, the organic composition rose at the rate of 0.4 per cent per year. The movement of the organic composition for the productive sector was very similar to that of the private, for-profit sector. Movements in the ratio of the labour value of fixed capital to employment behaved in similar fashion, rising in the 1947–58 and 1967–77 period and falling in the middle period. There also appeared to be a substantial increase between 1977 and 1981. Thus, from the results for this period, there appears to be no consistent secular trend in the movement of the organic composition, in contrast to that of the technical composition.

Table 5.1   Aggregate movements in technical and organic composition (1947–1981)

	Year					Average annual rate of change %				
	1947	1958	1967	1977	1981	1947–58	1958–67	1967–77	1947–77	1947–81
I. Technical composition of capital										
A. Fixed capital only (ekX/N)										
1. All sectors	12.2	16.5	20.3	24.5	28.7	2.78	2.34	1.88	2.34	2.53
2. Private-profit	9.4	13.8	17.3	22.9	24.3	3.53	2.51	2.77	2.97	2.80
3. Productive	12.5	18.8	23.9	30.2	–	3.68	2.70	2.32	2.93	–
B. Intermediate capital only (eaX/N)[a]										
1. All sectors	7.8	10.0	12.4	13.4		2.32	2.36	0.80	1.82	
C. Total capital $\tau = [e(k + a)X/N]$[a]										
1. All sectors	19.9	25.9	32.8	39.1		2.60	2.35	1.48	2.15	
2. Private-profit	18.2	26.1	33.1	40.5		3.25	2.66	2.00	2.66	
3. Productive	21.2	31.5	40.0	48.3		3.60	2.68	1.87	2.75	
2. Organic composition of capital										
A. Fixed capital only $(\lambda kX/N)$										
1. All sectors	1.41	1.63	1.43	1.67	1.91	1.34	−1.48	1.54	0.56	0.88
2. Private-profit	1.09	1.37	1.22	1.56	1.61	2.10	−1.31	2.43	1.19	1.15
3. Productive	1.45	1.86	1.68	2.05	–	2.26	−1.13	1.99	1.15	–
B. Intermediate capital only $(\lambda aX/N)$[a]										
1. All sectors	1.14	1.06	0.94	0.86		−0.66	−1.34	−0.83	−0.92	
C. Total capital $\theta = [\lambda(k + a)X/N]$[a]										
1. All sectors	2.55	2.69	2.37	2.53		0.50	−1.43	0.67	−0.02	
2. Private-profit	2.39	2.67	2.42	2.69		0.99	−1.10	1.07	0.39	
3. Productive	2.78	3.23	2.91	3.23		1.38	−1.16	1.05	0.50	

Note: Calculation includes depreciation as a separate row in matrix a.

104

Table 5.2 shows movements in the technical composition of capital by sector. There was considerable variation in the technical composition levels of the various sectors. The coefficient of variation in sectoral technical composition levels, defined as the ratio of the standard deviation to the unweighted mean, was quite high in each of the four years, ranging from 0.69 to 0.99. This indicates that changes in sectoral composition could induce major changes in the overall technical composition. Over the 1947–77 period, the technical composition increased in all sectors. Moreover, except for the government and construction sectors, it rose in every sub-period as well. Over the years from 1947 to 1977 the technical composition generally rose most rapidly in the goods-producing sectors – agriculture, mining, manufacturing, and transportation, communications and utilities – and slowest in the service sectors – trade, finance, insurance and real estate, other services, and the government. The only exception was construction, whose technical composition showed a relatively slow rate of increase. For the goods sector as a whole, the technical composition increased at an average annual rate of 3.6 per cent, whereas it increased by only 1.0 per cent per year in services as a group.

By 1977, the technical composition was highest in mining and transportation, communication and utilities; above average in agriculture, manufacturing, and finance, insurance and real estate, and the government; and below average in construction, trade and other services. The technical composition was about 2.5 times greater in the goods sector than in the services sector.

Table 5.3 shows similar statistics for the sectoral organic compositions. As with sectoral technical compositions, there is considerable variation in the organic composition levels among sectors. In 1947, it ranged from a low of 0.8 in the trade sector to a high of 7.0 in mining. In 1977, the range was from 0.8 in trade to 12.9 in mining. The coefficient of variation was quite high in each year, ranging from 0.63 in 1947 to 0.96 in 1958. Moreover there was no tendency for the variation in sectoral organic compositions to decline over time. The large variation indicates that shift effects are potentially very

Table 5.2 Movements in the technical composition of capital, by sector and year

	Year				Average annual rate of change (percentage)			
	1947	1958	1967	1977	1947–58	1958–67	1967–77	1947–77
Agriculture	10.3	19.8	32.2	96.5	5.93	5.42	10.97	7.46
Mining	61.0	140.1	162.0	194.5	7.57	1.61	1.83	3.87
Construction	13.6	15.0	22.3	22.2	0.88	4.42	−0.04	1.64
Non-durable manufacturing	18.4	34.5	43.6	52.9	5.71	2.60	1.92	3.51
Durable manufacturing	18.5	31.2	37.0	42.6	4.77	1.91	1.41	2.79
Transportation, utilities, communication	47.5	77.9	92.4	135.0	4.49	1.90	3.79	3.48
Trade	6.7	7.8	9.7	12.3	1.34	2.51	2.33	2.02
Finance, insurance, real estate	27.0	28.0	34.8	44.9	0.35	2.40	2.56	1.70
Other services	16.8	18.0	24.9	26.7	0.64	3.61	0.69	1.55
Government	31.3	29.5	32.6	33.6	−0.54	1.09	0.31	0.23
All sectors	19.9	26.5	32.7	38.0	2.60	2.35	1.48	2.15
Goods sectors[a]	20.7	35.3	46.3	60.4	4.83	3.02	2.66	3.56
Service sectors[b]	18.6	18.8	23.1	25.5	0.09	2.28	0.97	1.04
Coefficient of variation (all sectors)	0.69	0.99	0.92	0.88				

Notes:

[a] Defined as agriculture; mining; construction; non-durable manufacturing; durable manufacturing; and transportation, utilities and communication.

[b] Defined as trade; finance, insurance and real estate; government; and other services.

important in movements of the overall organic composition over time. There were also considerable differences in changes in the organic composition over time among the various sectors. In only one sector, agriculture, did the organic composition increase in each of the three sub-periods. In construction and other services, it declined in the 1947–58 and 1967–77 periods and rose in the middle one. In mining, the two manufacturing sectors and transportation, communications and utilities the organic composition increased in the 1947–58 and 1967–77 periods and declined in the middle period. In trade and finance, insurance and real estate, it fell in the first two and grew in the third. In the government sector, it declined in all three sub-periods.

Over the full 1947–47 period, the organic composition increased in six sectors and declined in four – construction; finance, insurance and real estate; other services; and the government. With the exception of construction, the organic composition increased quite substantially in the goods-producing sectors – agriculture, mining, manufacturing and transportation, communication and utilities. For the goods sector as a whole, it grew at an average annual rate of 1.2 per cent. In all four service sectors – trade, finance, insurance and real estate, other services, and the government – the organic composition showed a slight increase or an absolute decline. It declined by 0.8 per cent per year in services as a group. Thus Marx's arguments about movements in both the technical and organic composition hold most strongly for the classical Marxian sectors, the goods producers.

Next we decompose the change in the overall organic composition into three effects: an employment shift effect, a productivity effect and a technical composition effect. This decomposition follows directly from equations (5.11) and (5.12).

$$d\theta = \sum (ds_j)\bar{\lambda}_j\tau_j + \sum s_j(d\bar{\lambda}_j)\tau_j + \sum s_j\bar{\lambda}_j(d\tau_j) \qquad (5.16)$$

Because discrete time periods are used, the differential form of equation (5.15) must be modified. Various choices of weights

Table 5.3 Movements in the organic composition of capital, by sector and year

	Year				Average annual rate of change (percentage)			
	1947	1958	1967	1977	1947–58	1958–67	1967–77	1947–77
Agriculture	1.59	2.19	2.53	6.38	2.90	1.62	9.24	4.63
Mining	7.00	13.54	11.09	12.89	6.00	-2.21	1.50	2.04
Construction	1.70	1.56	1.67	1.54	-0.79	0.74	-0.77	-0.32
Non-durable manufacturing	2.99	3.83	3.41	3.51	2.27	-1.29	0.28	0.54
Durable manufacturing	2.29	3.10	2.60	2.86	2.77	-1.95	0.94	0.74
Transportation, utilities, communication	5.51	7.68	6.51	9.09	3.02	-1.84	3.34	1.67
Trade	0.75	0.74	0.68	0.79	-0.05	-1.00	1.56	0.20
Finance, insurance, real estate	3.14	2.68	2.52	2.85	-1.44	-0.70	1.23	-0.33
Other services	1.95	1.78	1.78	1.76	-0.84	0.01	-0.07	-0.33
Government	3.64	2.94	2.29	2.28	-1.96	-2.75	-0.03	-1.55
All sectors	2.55	2.69	2.37	2.53	0.50	-1.43	0.67	-0.02
Goods sectors[a]	2.80	3.65	3.40	4.05	2.40	-0.81	1.75	1.22
Service sectors[b]	2.16	1.85	1.64	1.69	-1.39	-1.36	0.28	-0.82
Coefficient of variation (all sectors)	0.63	0.96	0.88	0.88				

Notes:

[a] Defined as agriculture; mining; construction; non-durable manufacturing; durable manufacturing; and transportation, utilities and communication.

[b] Defined as trade: finance, insurance and real estate; government; and other services.

are possible. Average period weights are used here, because they give an exact decomposition.[8]

Results of the decomposition, based on 85 sectors, are shown in Table 5.4. The first panel shows the three effects in terms of the actual change in the organic composition and the second panel shows the change in the organic composition induced by each effect as a percentage of the initial organic composition. During the 1947–58 period for the full economy, employment shifts by themselves would have induced a 14 per cent decline in the economy-wide organic composition, and the growth in total labour productivity a 24 per cent decline. However the increase in the technical composition by itself would have caused a 45 per cent growth in the organic composition. This latter effect outweighed the first two and, as a result, the organic composition increased by 6 per cent. For the private, for-profit sector and the productive sector, the employment shift effects were 18 per cent and 12 per cent, respectively.

During the 1958–67 period, the employment shift effect was minimal. The productivity effect was somewhat stronger than in the previous period, causing a 33 per cent reduction in the organic composition for the whole economy, while the technical composition effect was weaker than in the preceding years, causing only a 22 per cent rise. As a result, the organic composition declined by 12 per cent during the middle period. Results are similar for the private, for-profit and productive sectors.

During the third period, the employment shift effect was again strong, causing a 17 per cent reduction in the organic composition for the whole economy, a 20 per cent reduction for the private, for-profit economy, and 17 per cent for the productive economy. The growth in labour productivity fell off considerably. As a result the productivity effect was much weaker in the third period than in the preceding two. On the other hand, the technical composition effect was greater than in the preceding period. As a result the organic composition increased during this period.

Over the entire 1947–77 period, employment shifts by themselves would have induced a 28 per cent decline in the econ-

Table 5.4 *Decomposition of the change in overall organic composition into an employment, productivity and technical composition effect*[a]

	Actual change in the organic composition				Percentage change in the organic composition[b]			
	Employ. shift effect	Prod. growth effect	Tech. comp. effect	Total change	Employ. shift effect	Prod. growth effect	Tech. comp. effect	Total change
1. 1947–58								
a. All sectors	−0.38	−0.64	1.17	0.15	−14.6	−24.3	44.5	5.7
b. Private-prof	−0.48	−0.66	1.43	0.28	−17.8	−24.3	52.4	10.3
c. Productive	−0.33	−0.78	1.52	0.41	−11.9	−28.6	55.3	14.8
2. 1958–67								
a. All sectors	−0.02	−0.87	0.57	−0.32	−0.8	−32.9	21.5	−12.1
b. Private-prof	−0.03	−0.86	0.64	−0.25	−1.0	−32.4	23.9	−9.4
c. Productive	0.03	−1.08	0.73	−0.32	1.0	−33.4	22.4	−9.9
3. 1967–77								
a. All sectors	−0.38	−0.21	0.75	0.16	−16.5	−9.2	32.5	6.9
b. Private-prof	−0.47	−0.25	0.99	0.27	−19.6	−10.4	41.2	11.2
c. Productive	−0.50	−0.27	1.09	0.32	−17.2	−9.4	37.6	11.0
4. 1947–77								
a. All sectors	−0.79	−1.72	2.49	−0.02	−27.5	−60.2	87.0	−0.7
b. Private-prof	−0.98	−1.77	3.06	0.30	−40.6	−73.3	126.3	12.4
c. Productive	−0.79	−2.14	3.38	0.45	−28.7	−77.4	122.4	16.3

Notes:

[a] The employment shift effect is defined as: $\sum d(s_i)\overline{\lambda_i}\overline{\tau_i}$. The productivity effect is defined as: $\sum s_i d(\overline{\lambda_i})\tau_i$. The technical composition effect is defined as: $\sum s\overline{\lambda_i}d(\tau_i)$. Average period weights are used in all calculations. See the text for details.

[b] Defined as the ratio of the change in the organic composition to the initial organic composition level.

110

omy-wide organic composition. In the private economy, the effect was even stronger. The growth in labour productivity caused a 60 per cent decline in the organic composition in the whole economy and a 73 per cent decline in the private economy. However, for the whole economy, the growth in the technical composition caused an 87 per cent increase in the organic composition, and the net effect was no growth in the organic composition. In the private profit-making economy, the technical composition effect induced a 126 per cent increase, and the net effect was a 12 per cent rise in the organic composition.

4 MOVEMENTS IN THE RATE OF PROFIT, 1947–1977

The definition and measurement of the rate of profit is a topic which has generated a considerable amount of discussion in recent years. In this chapter, a number of alternative measures are chosen, based on both the labour value framework and current dollar flows. Also, to avoid difficult issues concerning the division of income into a variable and surplus component, the focus is placed on the so-called capitalist profit share, defined as the ratio of total before-tax property income to value added.[9] Both gross and net profits, where the former includes the capital consumption allowance (depreciation) while the latter does not, will be used. The gross measure is closer to the familiar neo-classical rate of return or net rental rate of capital.

Table 5.5 shows the profit share in value added for four different measures: net surplus-value to total net value added, gross surplus-value (including depreciation) to gross value added, net profits to NNP, and gross profits to GNP. Though the levels differ among these four measures and among the different sectors, the pattern of movement over this period is strikingly uniform. The net profit share remained constant between 1947 and 1958 and then declined by about 20 per cent between 1958 and 1967 and by another 20 per cent or so between 1967 and 1977. Over the whole 1947–77 period, the net profit share declined by about 30 to 35 per cent. The gross profit share increased slightly between 1947 and 1958 and then declined by about 15 per cent between 1958 and 1967 and by about 10 to 15 per cent between 1967 and 1977. Over the 30-year period, the gross profit share declined by about 25 per cent.

In Table 5.6, I show movements in the rate of profit over the period. Here, again, there are various choices of measures, particularly of the denominator. I use both fixed capital (the more traditional neo-classical measure) and total Marxian capital for the base.[10] Again the results are quite invariant among measures and sectors. The rate of profit declined by about 15 to 20 per cent during the 1947–67 period, with almost all of it occurring after 1958, and then by about 25 to 30 per cent in the last 10 years. Overall the profit rate declined by about 30 to 40 per cent.

The movement of the rate of profit over time is due to two major effects: changes in the share of profits in value added and movements in the organic composition. The latter, in turn, is due to movements in sectoral organic composition levels and shifts in the employment shares among industries. It is easiest to do such an analysis for the Marxian value rate of profit, though an analogous analysis can be done for the current price version. From (5.12) and (5.15), it follows that

$$\rho = \epsilon^* / [\sum s_j \theta_j + 1 - \epsilon^*] \tag{5.17}$$

where $\epsilon^* \equiv S/N$. There is no simple decomposition of this formula (since ϵ^* appears in both numerator and denominator). However we can simulate the movement of the value rate of profit for various choices of the employment shares s_j, the sectoral organic compositions θ_j, and the surplus-value share ϵ^*.

Simulation results are shown in Table 5.7. During the 1947–58 period, the net value rate of profit in the private, for-profit sector declined from 0.142 to 0.131. The total decline was due to the increase in the sectoral organic composition. Employment shifts were an important offset. With these alone, the rate of profit would have increased by about 20 per cent (from

Table 5.5   The share of total surplus-value in total value and total profits in total income (1947–1977)

	Year				Percentage change		
	1947	1958	1967	1977	1947–67	1967–77	1947–77
1. Labour value framework							
A. Net surplus-value/total net value							
1. All sectors	0.420	0.427	0.337	0.288	−19.8	−14.5	−31.4
2. Private-profit	0.461	0.479	0.375	0.347	−18.8	−7.5	−24.9
3. Productive	0.356	0.352	0.290	0.207	−18.5	−28.8	−42.0
B. Gross surplus-value/total gross value							
1. All sectors	0.461	0.481	0.388	0.353	−15.8	−9.0	−23.4
2. Private-profit	0.499	0.528	0.425	0.408	−14.9	−3.9	−18.2
3. Productive	0.413	0.435	0.368	0.312	−11.0	−15.1	−24.5
2. Market (current) price framework							
A. Net profit/net national product (NNP)							
1. All sectors	0.406	0.406	0.322	0.251	−20.7	−22.2	−38.3
2. Private-profit	0.446	0.455	0.358	0.302	−19.7	−15.7	−32.3
3. Productive	0.344	0.335	0.277	0.180	−19.6	−35.0	−47.7
B. Gross profit/gross national product (GNP)							
1. All sectors	0.452	0.467	0.381	0.327	−15.6	−14.2	−27.5
2. Private-profit	0.489	0.513	0.417	0.378	−14.6	−9.5	−22.7
3. Productive	0.405	0.422	0.361	0.289	−10.9	−20.0	−28.7

Table 5.6 Alternative measures of the rate of profit (1947–1977)

	Year				Percentage change		
	1947	1958	1967	1977	1947–67	1967–77	1947–77
1. Labour value framework							
A. Net surplus-value/fixed capital stock $(\lambda k X)$							
1. All sectors	0.277	0.237	0.236	0.156	−14.8	−33.6	−43.5
B. Net surplus-value/total capital stock $[\lambda(k + a)X]^a$							
1. All sectors	0.123	0.117	0.111	0.080	−10.0	−28.1	−35.3
2. Private-profit	0.142	0.131	0.121	0.089	−15.0	−26.3	−37.3
3. Productive	0.102	0.090	0.089	0.058	−12.7	−35.1	−43.3
C. Gross surplus-value/fixed capital stock $(\lambda k X)$							
1. All sectors	0.327	0.295	0.271	0.211	−17.0	−22.1	−35.3
D. Gross surplus-value/total capital stock $[\lambda(k + a^g)X]^b$							
1. All sectors	0.149	0.150	0.130	0.111	−12.8	−14.6	−25.5
2. Private-profit	0.172	0.168	0.142	0.124	−17.8	−12.3	−27.9
3. Productive	0.123	0.115	0.104	0.080	−15.4	−23.3	−35.1
2. Market (current) price framework							
A. Net profit/fixed capital stock (pkX)							
1. All sectors	0.249	0.226	0.199	0.124	−19.9	−37.5	−50.0
B. Net profit/total capital stock $[p(k + a)X]^b$							
1. All sectors	0.146	0.137	0.121	0.082	−17.3	−32.5	−44.2
2. Private-profit	0.189	0.174	0.149	0.105	−20.4	−29.9	−44.2
3. Productive	0.122	0.097	0.085	0.040	−30.1	−52.6	−66.9
C. Gross profit/fixed capital stock (pkX)							
1. All sectors	0.299	0.290	0.258	0.181	−13.8	−29.9	−39.6
D. Gross profit/total capital stock $[p(k + a^g)X]^b$							
1. All sectors	0.182	0.183	0.163	0.123	−10.4	−24.3	−32.1
2. Private-profit	0.231	0.229	0.200	0.153	−13.3	−23.3	−33.6
3. Productive	0.164	0.147	0.131	0.077	−20.1	−41.1	−52.9

Notes: [a] Total capital includes depreciation as a separate row in matrix *a*.
   [b] Total capital excludes depreciation.

0.142 to 0.170, for example). Without such shifts, the rate of profit would have declined to 11.1 per cent, instead of to its actual 1958 level of 13.1 per cent.

During the second and third decades, the decline in the rate of profit was almost entirely attributable to the decline of the profit share in value added. The organic composition fell during the 1958–67 period, thus offsetting the fall in the rate of profit, but during the 1967–77 period it rose, thus exacerbating the decline. The employment effect was minimal during the 1958–67 period, but strong during the 1967–77 period. For the latter, by themselves, employment shifts would have increased the rate of profit by about 20 per cent. Without employment shifts, the rate of profit would have fallen to 7.5 per cent, instead of to its actual 1977 rate of 8.9 per cent.

Over the entire 1947–77 period, the rate of profit fell from 0.142 to 0.089, or by 37 per cent. About three-quarters of the decline was due to the decline of the profit share in value added and a quarter of the decline was attributable to the rise in the overall organic composition. However employment shifts by themselves would have increased the profit rate between one-third and one-half. Indeed, if employment shares had remained at their 1947 composition, the rate of profit would have fallen by 56 per cent instead of by its actual 38 per cent. Thus structural change acted as an important offset to the decline of the rate of profit.

CONCLUSIONS

There are four sets of findings of particular interest that emerge from this study. First, whereas the technical composition, as Marx predicted, showed a steady increase over time, the organic composition did not. It grew in the 1947–58 period and 1967–77 period but declined substantially between 1958 and 1967. Over the entire period from 1947 to 1977, the organic composition remained virtually constant in the full economy but did increase moderately in the private, for-profit sector and the productive sector.

Second, there was considerable variation in both levels and

Table 5.7　　*The effects of sectoral employment shifts, changes in sectoral organic composition and the surplus share on the value rate of profit for the private, for-profit sector (1947–1977)*

	Net value rate of profit[a]	
A. 1947–58	*1947 surplus share (ε*)*	*1958 surplus share (ε*)*
1. 1947 Sect. org. comp. (θ_j)		
1947 Employ. shares (s_j)	0.142	0.148
1958 Employ. shares (s_j)	0.170	0.177
2. 1958 Sect. org. comp. (θ_j)		
1947 Employ. shares (s_j)	0.106	0.111
1958 Employ. shares (s_j)	0.125	0.131
	1958 surplus share (ε*)	*1967 surplus share (ε*)*
B. 1958–67		
1. 1958 Sect. org. comp. (θ_j)		
1958 Employ. shares (s_j)	0.131	0.095
1967 Employ. shares (s_j)	0.132	0.096
2. 1967 Sect. org. comp. (θ_j)		
1958 Employ. shares (s_j)	0.160	0.120
1967 Employ. shares (s_j)	0.161	0.121
	1967 surplus share (ε*)	*1977 surplus share (ε*)*
C. 1967–77		
1. 1967 Sect. org. comp. (θ_j)		
1967 Employ. shares (s_j)	0.121	0.111
1977 Employ. shares (s_j)	0.144	0.132
2. 1977 Sect. org. comp. (θ_j)		
1967 Employ. shares (s_j)	0.083	0.075
1977 Employ. shares (s_j)	0.099	0.089
	1947 surplus share (ε*)	*1977 surplus share (ε*)*
D. 1947–77		
1. 1947 Sect. org. comp. (θ_j)		
1947 Employ. shares (s_j)	0.142	0.101
1977 Employ. shares (s_j)	0.213	0.149
2. 1977 Sect. org. comp. (θ_j)		
1947 Employ. shares (s_j)	0.094	0.063
1977 Employ. shares (s_j)	0.126	0.089

Note:
[a]　Defined as the ratio of net surplus-value to total capital stock in value terms $[\lambda(k + a)X]$, including depreciation.

movements of both the technical and organic composition among sectors. Though the technical composition increased in every sector between 1947 and 1977, it grew much faster in goods than in services. The organic composition increased in only six out of the ten sectors and declined in the other four. For the goods sector as a whole it increased by 45 per cent over the period, while it declined by 22 per cent for services. By 1977, the organic composition was 2.4 times greater in goods than in services.

Third, it is found that employment shares tended to shift towards sectors with lower organic composition and, as a result, tended to lower the overall organic composition. The effect was particularly strong during the 1947–58 and 1967–77 periods, where employment shifts by themselves would have induced a 14 per cent and 17 per cent decline, respectively, in the organic composition for the total economy. In the 1958–67 period the effect was minimal.

Fourth, the rate of profit showed a pronounced downward trend over the 1947–77 period. During the 1947–58 period, the total decline for the private, for-profit economy was due to the increase in sectoral organic composition. Shifts in employment would have increased the profit rate by about 20 per cent. During the 1958–67 and 1967–77 periods, the decline in the rate of profit was almost entirely attributable to the decline of the profit share in value added. The employment effect was minimal in the first of these, but in the second employment shifts would have raised the profit rate by 20 per cent again. Over the entire 1947–77 period, about three-quarters of the fall in the profit rate was due to the decline of the profit share and a quarter to the rise in the overall organic composition. However the employment shift effect was also important and, without it, the fall in the rate of profit would have been 7.9 percentage points instead of the actual 5.3 percentage points. Thus the shift of employment towards the lower organic composition services acted as an important offset to the tendency of the rate of profit to fall.

The analysis conducted in this chapter has been limited to charting the actual changes in the structural composition of employment and its effect on the organic composition and the rate of profit. No attempt has been made to explain *why* employment tended to shift towards the lower organic composition sectors. One possible explanation comes from the unbalanced growth model, originally developed by Baumol (1967) and expanded by Baumol, Blackman and Wolff (1985). The model posits two sectors, one technologically progressive and the other technologically stagnant. If real output shares remain constant over time, then relative employment will shift towards the stagnant sector. This is precisely what happened in the USA over the 1947–77 period. The service sector was technologically stagnant relative to the goods sector. As a result its technical composition rose much more slowly than in the goods sector and, consequently, so did its organic composition (which actually declined in absolute terms). Moreover, as predicted, the share of total employment in the service sector increased – in this case, from 39.6 per cent in 1947 to 64.3 per cent in 1977.

This argument, of course, still begs the question of why services are technologically stagnant. It should be noted that not all services are stagnant (exceptions include the banking and insurance sectors). However, for many of the service industries, there appear to be technological or other types of barriers, such as organizational problems, which prohibit classical Marxian forces from operating. These include difficulties of centralization and mechanization, and of the standardization and routinization of output. In legal services, as an example, output depends on individual problems and cases, for which standard operating procedures are difficult to develop. Many such barriers in the service sector appear intrinsic to the nature of the output.

Thus, in conclusion, it can be seen that, for the classic manufacturing sectors, which Marx emphasized in his works, the organic composition rose over the postwar period in the USA. What Marx did not foresee is the rapid growth in services and circulation activities, which are very different from the goods sectors and not easily amenable to the same kinds of technical change involving machine processes and the substitution of capital for labour as in manufacturing. Because of the uneven development of sectors over time, sectors with lower organic composition tended to grow faster in terms of employment than high organic composition industries. The two effects were offsetting, and, as a result, the overall organic composition tended to remain constant over time. Thus uneven development – in particular the pattern of unbalanced growth – appears as an important counteracting influence on the tendency of the rate of profit to fall.

NOTES

1. See Wolff (1986) for a complete description of the sources and methods for the input–output data for the years 1947 to 1977. See Ritz (1979) or Ritz, Roberts and Young (1979) for a listing of input–output sectors. Subsequent sector numbers refer to this sectoring scheme. Projections up to 1981 are based on Bureau of Interindustry Economics (BIE) capital stock data on computer tape prepared by Kenneth Rogers and Bureau of Labor Statistics gross output data on computer tape.

2. It is important to distinguish the organic composition of capital θ from the value composition of capital ω, defined as the ratio of total constant capital C to total variable capital V. The value composition plays a more direct role in the determination of the (value) rate of profit, as will be seen below. It is a function of both the organic composition of capital and the rate of surplus-value:

$$\omega \equiv C/V = (C/N)\cdot(N/V) = \theta(1 + \epsilon).$$

3. The turnover period can be approximated by the inverse of the ratio of the average yearly level of inventory to annual sales. On the basis of the National Income and Product Accounts of the USA, the average annual economy-wide turnover rate was estimated as follows: 1947 – 0.89; 1958 – 1.04; 1963 – 1.15; 1967 – 1.16; 1972 – 1.19; and 1977 – 1.04.

4. See Harris (1983) for a detailed discussion of this factor.

5. As discussed above, I also exclude the non-profit sector. This is a portion of the medical, educational, and non-profit sector (77). The apportionment is based on detailed industry employment data from 1977. The private, for-profit sector also includes government enterprises.

6. As Moseley (1988) and I have argued previously (see Wolff, 1987), there are two forms of unproductive activity. The first consists of sectors whose output is itself unproductive. In the classification system used here, this would include the trade sectors (sector numbers 69 and 85), finance and insurance (70), real estate rentals (71), business services (73) and a portion of government services (84). (See Wolff, 1987, for a discussion of the classification of government services into

productive and unproductive components.) The second consists of unproductive activities within sectors whose output is productive. Thus various clerical, legal, administrative and sales workers employed within productive sectors, as well as the circulating and fixed capital used in these activities, would be counted as unproductive inputs. Though it is feasible to classify employment into productive and unproductive categories (see Wolff, 1987, for details) it is quite difficult to classify fixed and circulating capital into these two components. The reason is that it is hard to assign a particular piece of equipment or plant to productive and unproductive activities within an enterprise. As a result the estimates here are based on an industry breakdown of capital and employment into productive and unproductive categories.

7. This can be seen directly in the case of an aggregate Cobb-Douglas production function of the form

$$Q = N^{\alpha}K^{(1-\alpha)}$$

where Q is aggregate output, N total employment, K total physical capital and α, the output elasticity of labour, is less than unity. Then labour productivity is given by:

$$Q/N = (K/N)^{(1-\alpha)}.$$

8. In general, if $y = a \cdot b$, then

$$y^2 - y^1 = \bar{a}(b^2 - b^1) + \bar{b}(a^2 - a^1)$$

where superscripts represent time periods and $\bar{a} = (a^2 + a^1)/2$ and $\bar{b} = (b^2 + b^1)/2$.

9. Property income is defined as the sum of corporate profits, interest, rent and proprietor income. I shall ignore here the treatment of taxes and government expenditures.

10. In the case of gross profits, the denominator must exclude depreciation as an element of cost. For this I use a matrix a^0, defined as equal to matrix a except for the depreciation row and corresponding column, which are set equal to zero.

REFERENCES

Baumol, William J. (1967), 'Macroeconomics of Unbalanced Growth: The Anatomy of Urban Crisis', *American Economic Review*, **57**,(3), June, 415–26.

Baumol, William J., Sue Anne Batey Blackman and Edward N. Wolff (1985), 'Unbalanced Growth Revisited: Asymptotic Stagnancy and New Evidence', *American Economic Review*, **75**,(4), September, 806–17.

Bowles, Samuel (1981), 'Technical Change and the Profit Rate: A

Simple Proof of the Okishio Theorem', *Cambridge Journal of Economics*, **5**, (2), June, 183–6.

Harris, Donald J. (1983), 'Accumulation of Capital and the Rate of Profit in Marxian Theory', *Cambridge Journal of Economics*, **7**,(3/4), September/December, 311–30.

Marx, Karl (1967), *Capital*, 3 Volumes, Moscow: International Publishers.

Moseley, Fred (1988), 'The Marxian Macroeconomic Variables and the Postwar U.S. Economy: A Critique of Wolff's Estimates', *American Economic Review*, **78**, (1), March, 298–303.

Okishio, N. (1961), 'Technical Change and the Rate of Profit', *Kobe Economic Review*, **7**, 86–99.

Ritz, Philip M. (1979), 'The Input–Output Structure of the U.S. Economy, 1972', *Survey of Current Business*, **59**,(2), February, 34–72.

Ritz, Philip M., Eugene P. Roberts and Paula C. Young (1979), 'Dollar Value Tables of the 1972 Input–Output Study', *Survey of Current Business*, **59**,(4), April, 51–72.

Roemer, John (1977), 'Technical Change and the "Tendency of the Rate of Profit to Fall" ', *Journal of Economic Theory*, **16**, (2), December.

Roemer, John (1979), 'Continuing Controversy on the Falling Rate of Profit: Fixed Capital and Other Issues', *Cambridge Journal of Economics*, **3**,(4), December, 379–98.

Ruggles, Richard and Nancy Ruggles (1982), 'Integrated Economic Accounts of the United States, 1947–1980', *Survey of Current Business*, **62**,(5), May, 1–53.

Samuelson, Paul (1971), 'Understanding the Marxian Notion of Exploitation', *Journal of Economic Literature*, **9**,(2), June, 399–431.

Weisskopf, Thomas E. (1979), 'Marxian Crisis Theory and the Rate of Profit in the Postwar U.S. Economy', *Cambridge Journal of Economics*, **3**,(4), December, 341–78.

Wolff, Edward N. (1979), 'The Rate of Surplus Value, the Organic Composition, and the General Rate of Profit in the U.S. Economy, 1947–67', *American Economic Review*, **69**,(3), June, 329–41.

Wolff, Edward N. (1986), 'The Productivity Slowdown and the Fall in the U.S. Rate of Profit, 1947–76', *Review of Radical Political Economy*, **18**,(1&2), 87–109.

Wolff, Edward N. (1987), *Growth, Accumulation, and Unproductive Activity: An Analysis of the Postwar U.S. Economy*, Cambridge: Cambridge University Press.

6. Using US Input–Output Data for Marxian Empirical Research: Values, Production Prices and Wage–Profit Curves

Eduardo M. Ochoa

INTRODUCTION

This chapter presents actual labour values and production prices inherent in the structure of the US economy during the years 1947, 1958, 1961, 1963, 1967–70 and 1972, using a 71-industry fixed-capital model of the economy. This will be done in order to measure the deviations of production prices from labour values and actual market prices, as well as their relationship over time. In addition. US wage–profit curves for five of these years will be presented.

The above project acquires its significance when viewed in the context of the emergence of neo-Ricardian economic theory. Sraffa's analysis of the relationship between prices and distribution was aimed at a critique of the reigning marginalist orthodoxy (Sraffa, 1960). In this purpose it was eminently successful. In a well-known debate carried out in a series of articles originating primarily from both Cambridges, the aggregate neo-classical theory of production and distribution was dealt a severe – some would say fatal – blow.[1]

This was owing to two results of the Sraffian model. First, it showed that the neo-classical concept of capital as a 'real' factor of production whose quantity is measurable prior to exchange and distribution was unsustainable, since the prices used to measure the value of capital goods depend on distribution. Second, by raising the possibility of reswitching of techniques as the rate of profit (and distribution) varies, it showed that the results of marginal productivity theory – inverse relation between capital intensity and the rate of profit, the rate of profit as the scarcity price or efficient allocator of capital – were theoretically untenable.

The same analysis, however, contained an implicit criticism of the Marxian labour theory of value. The criticism soon turned explicit (Steedman, 1977). The Sraffa system was said to make Marx's value analysis (and the subsequent transformation to prices of production) redundant. Moreover the economic structure which emerged from a labour value analysis, it was argued, did not necessarily match the observed structure in terms of prices. Specifically the rate of profit in value terms did not equal the rate of profit in terms of production prices, the sum of prices did not equal the sum of values, and the sum of profits did not equal the sum of surplus-value. Moreover their deviations were not systematic, but depended on the vagaries of distribution. In fact the adoption of new techniques did not follow a clear pattern in terms of value quantities (such as a rising organic composition of capital) but again depended on distribution and the ensuing price changes, since the decisions of individual capitalists are based on the observable prices alone.

The possibility of reswitching was once again invoked as an illustration of adjustments in the system in response to price changes which are independent of any changes in value magnitudes. This argument relies on the logical or algebraic possibility of magnitudes of the technical coefficients such that price–value deviations will be very large, and wage–profit rate curves will have the shapes required for reswitching of techniques, or distributional effects so large that value and price analyses will lead to different conclusions.

There is no question that these are mathematical possibilities of the model. Whether they are real possibilities of any actual economy, however, is another, more questionable matter. This chapter will attempt to shed some light on this last question.

1 THE SRAFFIAN CRITIQUE OF MARXIAN VALUE THEORY

The reswitching phenomenon in a Sraffian system can be briefly characterized as follows. Given a capitalist economy which produces *n* commodities using *n* single-product processes, the production-determined equilibrium prices which are formed depend on the distribution of the net product between wages and profits. Moreover it is possible to construct two viable matrices of technical coefficients differing only in one column (set of sectoral inputs) such that one of the matrices (technologies) is more profitable than the other at high average rates of profit, less profitable at intermediate rates of profit, and once again more profitable at very low rates of profit. This is described as a switch out of, and a reswitch back to, the original technology as π assumes its range of values.

The criticism of Marxian value theory implicit here is that, since changes in distribution can reverse the ranking of techniques in price terms, their ranking according to which produces the given use value at the lowest value (that is, embodied labour-time) is irrelevant to economic decision making by individual capitals, and hence to the aggregate of those decisions. It follows that aggregate value analysis ('capital in general') cannot predict any dynamic tendencies operating at the price level (that is, the laws of motion of capitalist production as a whole).

If the examples constructed to illustrate reswitching are representative of the techniques of production present in real economies, then this criticism has powerful practical force. However, if a careful study of all the available data on actual technology matrices which have existed over time yields no such cases, then the likelihood increases that reswitching is a mathematical curiosum of no real significance, rather like negative prices (on the caveats to this statement, see Section 8 below). By examining the technologies of the US economy for the period for which data is available (1947–72) and the associated production prices and wage–profit rate curves, this chapter seeks to make a contribution to this necessary empirical determination of the character of the reswitching phenomenon.

On a more general level, the neo-Ricardian criticism of Marxian value analysis rests on an emphasis on the quantitative divergence of prices from values. In this criticism prices of production are identified with market prices; in other words, the economy is assumed to be in equilibrium. No real economy, however, is ever in equilibrium. The distinction between actual prices (market prices) and equilibrium prices (prices of production for all but the marginalists) is therefore crucial. The argument usually made against value analysis is that, since individual capitalists base their decisions on observed prices, value quantities which differ markedly from prices yield incorrect predictions of capitalists' behaviour.

A number of methodological objections which are independent of the magnitude of price–value deviations have elsewhere been made to this argument (Steedman, 1981). In this chapter, however, we will focus on two narrower points on which empirical evidence can be brought to bear. First, the divergence of theoretical predictions and actual behaviour of capitalists is equally likely to occur when comparing prices of production and market prices. It would seem in fact quite likely that values and prices of production are quantitatively closer to each other than either is to market prices, which would imply that value analysis is as good a practical tool of analysis of real economies as equilibrium–price analysis. Empirical confirmation of this hypothesis would be highly significant.

Second, one of the purposes of the value category in Marx's analysis is to show that the amount of socially necessary labour time required to produce commodities is the essential reality behind the formation of prices, and that therefore changes in the former will be the main long-run determinants of changes in the latter. This is likewise an empirically testable hypothesis.

2 PRICE SYSTEMS

We now present labour values and three different types of price systems for the US economy for the years 1947, 1958, 1961, 1963, 1967, 1968, 1969, 1970 and 1972.

Labour Values

Labour values are here assumed to be identical to total (direct and indirect) labour requirements for unit of output. The approach followed in dealing with the problem of heterogeneous labour is discussed in the appendix. In addition we are ignoring dynamic effects such as rapidly changing technology and changing patterns of demand. The former effect would make the socially necessary labour time – as determined in the sphere of production by the state-of-the-art technology – different from the (average) total labour requirements for the industry as a whole. The latter effect would imply a disjunction between the two senses of socially necessary labour time (the second sense being the amount of social labour time which 'society' is willing to allocate to the production of a given good, as evidenced by the level of demand). Assuming these effects away is an abstraction comparable to assuming that the rate of profit is uniform across industries. Moreover it should be possible to infer the real importance of these effects from the empirical results.

The system of 71 linear equations which define the labour values is:

$$v = a_0 + v(A + D) \qquad (6.1)$$

where a_0 is the homogeneous-labour-coefficients row vector, A is the matrix of input coefficients whose elements a_{ij} represent the amount of good i used by industry j, and D is the physical capital depreciation matrix (see the appendix for a discussion of data sources and methods). The solution to (6.1) is given by

$$v = a_0(I - A - D)^{-1} \qquad (6.2)$$

Equation (6.2) defines the row vector v as the amount of

labour required directly and indirectly to produce one unit of sectoral output. That physical unit is a 'market-dollar's worth', given the way a_0, A and D are defined. When we use their deflated versions, the unit is a constant (1972) market-dollar's worth, which is then a constant measure of physical output. The vector v thus has the units of labour time per physical unit of output.

Direct Prices

We define the row vector of direct prices d, following Shaikh (1977), as the set of prices directly proportional to labour values, where the constant of proportionality relates the money unit to a unit of labour time (that is, worker-hours/dollar). We define the money unit by requiring that the sum of sectoral outputs at direct prices equal the sum of sectoral output at market prices. In vector notation,

$$dq = mq \qquad (6.3)$$

where the vector of market prices m is the unit vector, since q is measured in market prices. The proportionality constant μ (the value of money) is therefore given by:

$$d = (1/\mu)v = \frac{mq}{vq} v \qquad (6.4)$$

Marxian Prices of Production

Marx defines prices of production as the sum of costs plus an inter-sectorally uniform rate of profit on capital advanced. These magnitudes are seen to be the centres of gravity of the continually fluctuating market prices. By capital advanced, we mean the capital invested in plant and equipment (fixed capital), plus the accumulated investment in inventories of materials, plus the stock of money necessary to pay out wages. The level of material inventories and wages fund is related to their flows by the turnover time of circulating capital t_j in each industry. If we have the flows per year, and the turnover time in (fractions of) years, then the necessary stocks are simply (annual flows × turnover time). This would give us the stock levels necessary to produce one year's output. Dividing through by the output level we obtain the stocks required per unit of output.

In order to specify the wage we must include the real counterpart of the value of labour power. This is given by the column vector b', which is the real wage basket per unit of homogeneous labour time. The expression for p, the Marxian prices of production vector, is then as given below:

$$p = p(b'a_0 + A + D + <g>) + \pi p [K + (A + b'a_0)<t>]$$
(6.5)

where $b'a_0$ is the matrix of wage–good inputs, $<g>$ is the diagonal matrix of indirect tax coefficients (see the appendix), and π is the uniform rate of profit. Let $A^+ = (b'a_0 + A + D + <g>)$ (that is, total costs) and $K^+ = [K + (A + b'a_0)<t>]$ (total capital advanced). Then (6.5) reads

$$p = pA^+ + \pi p K^+$$

or

$$(1/\pi)p = pK^+(I - A^+)^{-1}$$
(6.6)

Equation 6.6 is the eigenvalue problem for the matrix $K^+(I - A^+)^{-1}$.

The economically meaningful solution requires p to be a strictly positive, real vector. If we assume that $K^+(I - A^{+1})^{-1}$ is an indecomposable matrix – and we know it is non-negative – then the Perron-Frobenius theorem ensures that the only such eigenvector is the one associated with the largest eigenvalue $(1/\pi)_{max}$ (to which corresponds the lowest π).

Since p is an eigenvector, it is defined up to a constant. In other words, (6.6) only defines a set of relative prices. To set the price level, we need a normalization condition similar to (6.3):

$$pq = mq$$
(6.7)

Let p^* and p be the unnormalized and normalized eigenvectors, respectively. Then we define the normalization constant β such that $p = \beta p^*$. We can then rewrite (6.7) as

$$\beta p^* q = mq \tag{6.8}$$

which implies

$$\beta = \frac{mq}{p^* q} \tag{6.9}$$

Therefore

$$p = \frac{mq}{p^* q} p^* \tag{6.10}$$

Summing up, Marxian prices of production are given by solving for the eigenvector associated with the maximum eigenvalue of the system of equations (6.6) and then normalizing this eigenvector according to (6.10).

Sraffian Prices of Production

The generalized price system developed by Sraffa in Part II of his book (Sraffa, 1960) treats fixed capital as a joint product. Consider the following price system with joint products:

$$(1 + \pi)sK + sA + a_0\omega = sB \tag{6.11}$$

K is the capital stock (which becomes a flow in a joint-product model) and A is the flow of circulating capital (materials), B is the matrix of joint products, ω is the scalar wage, and s is the price vector.

We shall present the conditions under which the Sraffian joint-product model of fixed capital reduces to a standard depreciation model. Define $\hat{B} = B - I$. Then $B = \hat{B} + I$, so that the joint-product matrix B is the sum of the identity matrix (that is, the unit output of each industry) and the matrix $\hat{B}$, now interpreted to be the used-machinery coefficients (that is, capital as a joint product). Then the above equation can be rewritten as follows:

$$s(K - \hat{B}) + \pi sK + sA + a_0\omega = s \qquad (6.12)$$

The matrix $(K - \hat{B})$ represents the difference between the stock of capital going into the production process and the stock of capital which emerges out of it; in other words, the scrappage matrix. This is precisely the series which we use to construct the matrix D in our price systems, so the above equation is none other than

$$s = s(A + D) + \pi sK + a_0\omega \qquad (6.13)$$

This approach to fixed-capital models is discussed and criticized by Varri (1980) because the scrappage matrix $(K - \hat{B})$ cannot be defined independently of prices. Nevertheless, in any discussion of *actual* economies and calculations using empirically-obtained coefficients, this is all that is available. What the above discussion shows is that a joint-production treatment of fixed capital is equivalent to the standard treatment, provided we assume that the price of old machines (and hence the decision to scrap) is not sensitive to changes in the distribution of income.

Even if this is the case, however, Sraffa's model is still different from Marx's, since he computes the profit rate on fixed capital advanced only. Also he does not have a concept of the value of labour power, so the distribution of the surplus product between wages and profits if left open as a degree of freedom of the system. We can solve for the resultant system as follows:

$$s = \omega a_0(I - A - D - \pi K)^{-1} \qquad (6.14)$$

This is a system of n linear equations and $n + 2$ unknowns: s, ω and π. We also have our usual normalization condition

$$sq = mq \qquad (6.15)$$

Combining (6.14) and (6.15) and specifying the level of π, we get:

$$\omega a_0 (I - A - D - \pi K)^{-1} q = mq$$

or

$$\omega = \frac{mq}{a_0 (I - A - D - \pi K)^{-1} q} \tag{6.16}$$

Solving (6.16), we obtain the money wage, which we can use in (6.14) to obtain the price vector s. This can be done for a number of values of π in the range (O, R), where R is the inverse of the maximal eigenvalue of the system given below, which is (6.16) with $\omega = 0$:

$$s_R = s_R (A + D) + R s_R K \tag{6.17}$$

3 SECTORAL PRICE–VALUE DEVIATIONS

Following the definitions presented above, labour values v, direct prices d, and Marxian production prices p for the nine years studied were calculated. This section will present results based on those basic computations.

In order to measure the extent of the pairwise cross-sectional deviation between direct prices, Marxian prices of production and market prices in a real economy, we developed the following statistics (here illustrated for the production price–direct price case of Table 6.1):

Mean Absolute Deviation (%): (6.18)

$$MAD(p,d) = (1/n) \sum_i \frac{|p_i - d_i|}{d_i} (100)$$

Mean Absolute Weighted Deviation (%): (6.19)

$$MAWD(p,d) = \sum_i \frac{|p_i - d_i|}{d_i} \cdot \frac{q_i}{\sum_j q_j} (100)$$

Normalized Vector Distance (%): (6.20)

$$NVD(p,d) = \frac{[\sum_i (p_i q_i - d_i q_i)^2]^{1/2}}{[\sum_i (d_i q_i)^2]^{1/2}} (100)$$

Both MAD and $MAWD$ are the mean of the absolute value of the deviations of one set of prices from another as a fraction of the latter. The NVD measures the vector distance between the priced output vectors using two sets of prices as a fraction of the vector length of one of the former.

We also computed the cross-sectional correlation coefficient, which we report squared as R^2. In order to minimize spurious correlation – since prices and values must be correlated as $p_i q_i$ and $v_i q_i$ to have any variation in the market-price data – we computed R^2 on the logged data points. Nevertheless, as has been shown elsewhere (Ochoa, 1984; Petrovic, 1987), measures of covariance such as R^2 are not the proper statistics to assess the cross-sectional relation between alternative price systems. Rather measures of deviation such as those presented above should be used.

The choice of numeraire should be the money unit, since that is how the exchange value of goods is actually measured. But the money unit's exchange value is in effect given by the equation of purchase price of total output to the quantity of total output. In effect the unit of value is represented by a quantity vector with the proportions of the gross output vector, whose price is one dollar. Let

Q = gross output vector
p = computed-price vector
T = scalar market price of output vector $= mQ$
q = composite numeraire (vector)
m = market-price vector

Then

$$q = Q / mQ = Q / T$$

and the normalization condition is

$$pq = 1 \text{ or } pQ/mQ = 1 \text{ or } pQ = mQ$$

which is in fact the condition adopted in this study.

To measure the extent to which individual values determine the behaviour of production prices over time, we also performed 71 time series linear regressions of values on Marxian production prices, using constant-dollar market prices as a pseudo-quantity measure. The associated correlation coefficients were averaged and squared to obtain a general measure of explained variation which is dimensionally comparable to the cross-sectional R^2. (The reason we squared after averaging was that we did not want to take credit for negative correlations over time. Using this procedure, the latter actually reduce the magnitude of the R^2-like time series statistic.) Unlike the case of cross-sectional deviations, here it is legitimate to use R^2 as a measure of correlation, because all three sets of prices (market, direct, and production prices) are varying over time independently of output levels.[2]

Calculated values for all these measures are presented below.[3] The results show clearly that labour values have a very high degree of cross-sectional correlation with prices of production. This admittedly inconclusive result is similar to results reported elsewhere (Wolff, 1979; Petrovic 1987). More significantly the average correlation over time is also quite high: approximately 93 per cent of the variation in individual prices of production over time are due to changes in the underlying labour values, suggesting of all things a Ricardian 93 per cent labour theory of value. In addition average price–value deviations – whether weighted or unweighted – are quite small: around 17 per cent. The 'transformation problem', therefore, appears to be of limited empirical significance.

It might be objected that our deviation measures are 'small' because we are using market prices (one dollar's worth) as the quantity unit of each sector, so that all computed prices cluster around unity. However, just as the mean value of a distri-

Table 6.1   Marxian production price–direct price relations

Year	1947	1958	1961	1963	1967	1968	1969	1970	1972	Average
MAD (p,d) (%)	18.2	13.8	14.9	16.3	17.7	18.1	17.8	16.9	17.9	16.9
MAWD (p,d) (%)	14.5	15.1	16.4	17.5	18.7	18.6	18.6	17.8	19.8	17.4
NVD (p,d) (%)	13.4	14.3	15.4	16.5	18.3	18.3	18.6	18.3	18.4	16.8
X-sect. R^2	0.972	0.979	0.976	0.972	0.967	0.965	0.966	0.971	0.970	0.971
T-sers. R^2	–	–	–	–	–	–	–	–	–	0.926

bution is irrelevant when we measure its coefficient of variation (standard deviation/mean), so are the absolute values of the percentage deviation of one set of prices from another (see equations (6.18) and (6.20) above) independent of the scaling factor used. Whether we have actual p_i or p_i/m_i as we do, the terms being summed in equations (6/19) and (6.20) would be the same:

$$\frac{|d_i/m_i - p_i/m_i|}{p_i/m_i} = \frac{|d_i - p_i|}{p_i}$$

Moreover, in the case of our *NVD* measure, market prices are eliminated from the expression of computed prices because we use the value of the full sectoral output: (p_j/m_j) $(m_j q_j) = p_j q_j$.

The results presented above become even stronger when we consider the actual extent of the deviation between production prices and market prices, shown in Table 6.2 below. A comparison of the results of Tables 6.1 and 6.2 shows that prices of production are nearly as far away from market prices as they are from direct prices. Since there is no reason to expect that these deviations are correlated, and from theoretical considerations, we would expect that the deviation between direct and market prices would be more than that of production prices from market prices, but substantially less than the sum of the two deviations. It was surprising to find that, in fact, the observed direct price–market price deviations are smaller than the production price–market price deviations (with the exception of the *MAD* in one year) as shown in Table 6.3 below.

While both *MAD* and *MAWD* measures are smaller between direct and market prices than between production

Table 6.2   Marxian production price–market price relations

Year	1947	1958	1961	1963	1967	1968	1969	1970	1972	Average
MAD (p,m) (%)	18.5	13.1	12.7	12.6	13.7	13.2	12.8	12.5	13.0	13.6
MAWD (p,m) (%)	16.8	13.4	14.1	14.3	15.0	14.5	14.1	13.1	14.5	14.6
NVD (p,m) (%)	19.6	15.5	16.4	16.7	17.4	16.8	16.1	15.3	17.6	16.8
X-sect. R^2	0.963	0.987	0.986	0.987	0.983	0.983	0.984	0.986	0.982	0.982
T-sers. R^2	–	–	–	–	–	–	–	–	–	0.760

and market prices, their R^2s are smaller as well. This suggests the possibility of systematic bias on the computation of production prices, leaving them farther away from market prices, even though more covariant with the latter than direct prices (we see here the usefulness of calculating R^2s as a means of estimating relative degree of correlation, even though the absolute values are biased upward by the spurious correlation of output levels). The likely source of bias in the production–price computation is the capital stock series. The capital stock series issued by the Bureau of Industrial Economics of the US Department of Commerce (1983) is based on the 'perpetual inventory' method. The latter is essentially integration of past investment flows coupled with a probabilistic scrappage function. This function uses a distribution centred around estimated asset lives. The results of the integration are very sensitive to the asset lives used, and the values used are known to be unreliable estimates.

Over time, prices of production account for somewhat more of the variation in market prices than do direct prices (R^2s equal 0.760 and 0.754, respectively), but the improvement is quite small compared to the amount of variation left unaccounted for. This suggests that labour values are the dominant deterministic influence over market prices, with the distribution effects of production prices playing a far less important role. Moreover the distribution effects – the improvement obtained by the 'transformation' from values to prices of production – are themselves a fraction of the 'noise' component of market prices (the stochastic disequilibrium effects).

These results suggest that the labour theory of value is not only a powerful methodology for a critical understanding of

Table 6.3. Direct price–market price relations

Year	1947	1958	1961	1963	1967	1968	1969	1970	1972	Average
MAD (d,m) (%)	19.9	11.8	12.1	11.8	10.8	10.7	10.2	10.3	12.0	12.2
MAWD (d,m) (%)	16.0	11.8	12.7	12.5	11.8	11.1	11.5	11.1	13.8	12.5
NVD (d,m) (%)	17.3	12.0	13.6	13.4	13.2	12.2	13.2	12.7	15.8	13.7
X-sect. R^2	0.957	0.978	0.975	0.974	0.975	0.974	0.977	0.978	0.974	0.974
T-sers. R^2	–	–	–	–	–	–	–	–	–	0.754

the social relations of production in capitalism. It also appears that labour values are quantitatively dominant influences in the formation of market prices. The conceptual equalization of the rate of profit which defines prices of production as the centre of gravity of market prices thus provides only a marginally better approximation to the latter than labour values themselves.

4 PRICE–VALUE DEVIATIONS AND WAGE SHARES

The results presented above relative to price–value deviations are so startling that there has been and will be a tendency to minimize their importance by attributing them to the high wage shares in the US economy. In the limit, when profits go to zero and wages take all the net product, prices of production would become identical to values. Hence, if the distribution of the net product between profits and wages were close to this limit, prices of production would be close to values regardless of the manner in which the structure of the economy would transform values.

In order to investigate this possibility, we should vary the distribution of the net product between wages and profits, derive the corresponding prices of production, and observe the price–value deviations which ensue. To do this, we begin by replacing the real wage vector b' with a variable scalar wage ω. From (6.5) we have:

$$p = pb'a_0 + p(A + D + <g>) + \pi pb'a_0<t> + \pi p(K + A<t>)$$

But pb' is a scalar (the production price of the real wage vector); so we designate it ω. Solving the above equation for p we thus obtain:

$$p = \omega a_0(I + \pi<t>)[I - A - D - <g> - \pi(K + A<t>)]^{-1}$$

This is no longer an eigenvalue problem, but a linear system with two degrees of freedom. Combining the above expression with our usual normalization condition leaves one degree of freedom. By setting π equal to values from 0 to π_{max}, we can obtain the desired prices of production. The resultant price–value deviations for 1967 (a typical year) are shown in Table 6.4 below. It should be noted that it is the presence of indirect taxes as a component of costs in the price equation (6.5) that prevents the measures of deviation between production prices and direct prices from vanishing when $\pi = 0$.

These results show several things. First, the wage share of income in the USA was by no means as high as is usually implied: the year 1967 shows an average wage share of income (after depreciation and indirect business taxes) of 52.2 per cent. Second, the measures of deviation predictably become larger as the wage share is reduced, but they increase only moderately: even when the wage share drops to zero, the *MAD* is only 34.4 per cent. The cross-sectional R^2s average 0.939 even for this extreme case. Similar results were obtained for the remaining eight years in this study. We conclude that

Table 6.4   *US price–value deviations as a function of wage share (1967)*

Wage share	π/R	MAD (%)	MAWD (%)	R^2
1.000	0.000	4.3	4.7	0.997
0.858	0.100	7.9	8.4	0.990
0.729	0.200	11.6	12.3	0.988
0.610	0.300	15.0	15.9	0.985
0.501	0.400	18.3	19.3	0.981
0.401	0.500	21.3	22.4	0.975
0.308	0.600	24.2	25.8	0.969
0.222	0.700	27.0	28.9	0.961
0.142	0.800	29.6	31.9	0.953
0.069	0.900	32.0	34.7	0.945
0.000	1.000	34.4	37.4	0.935
	Actual wage–profit point			
0.522	0.382	17.7	18.7	0.982

the remarkably close correspondence between direct prices and prices of production is a feature of the actual US economy which is not sensitive to the level of the wage share.

5   RESWITCHING AND MARXIAN THEORY

Implicit in Marxian theory is the belief that an analysis of technical change carried out in value terms is not qualitatively modified in actual capitalist economies owing to the deviations of prices from values. It is the essence of the reswitching argument, however, that such 'distributional' sources of variation can generate phenomena all of their own and thus not only destroy the neo-classical parable, but also cause an analysis of choice of technique in terms of labour values to be inconsistent with the results in terms of prices (of production).[4]

We must first of all point out that, in a fundamental sense, the Cambridge attack on the neo-classical concept of capital as a homogeneous factor of production only needs to rely on an economy of fixed-proportions techniques and heterogeneous goods, not on reswitching or capital reversing. That is, the Hicks case of uniform capital–labour ratios but dissimilar (incommensurable, really) capital- and labour-intensities is sufficient to deprive the neo-classical construction of meaning.[5] And yet this 'Hicks case' poses no problem for Marxian value analysis, since it in fact eliminates the deviation of prices from values by definition.

The fact remains, however, that the cases of capital reversing and especially reswitching pose a serious challenge to Marxian value analysis. In the latter case, consider Figure 6.1. In this case, technique A has higher unit values than technique B (lower output per worker); it also has a higher capital-output ratio (lower π). In terms of value analysis, such a technique is clearly inferior and should not be expected to be adopted in the presence of B. And yet, because of the curvature of one or both of these techniques, double switching occurs, with the consequence that for a large and important range of values of the wage rate, technique A would be

Figure 6.1　Wage–profit frontiers with alternative techniques

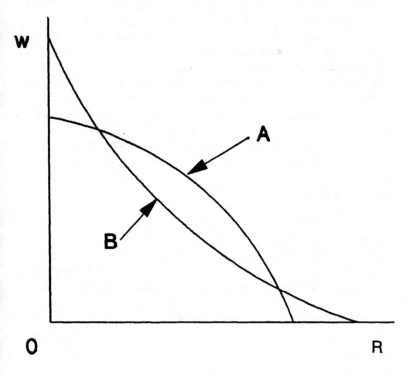

adopted, since it yields a higher rate of profit. This is clearly a blow to those who would claim that value relations underlie and impose clear limits to the surface phenomena of capitalist production.

6　EMPIRICAL WAGE-PROFIT CURVES

There is no question that it is possible to construct numerical examples of two or more sector economies which will exhibit reswitching properties. The question emerges, however, as to whether such cases are merely logical curiosities or real possibilities for actual economic systems.

Unfortunately we do not possess the information about all available techniques in each sector of production which would be necessary to calculate wage-profit frontiers (see Section 8 below). Using our 'Sraffian' prices of production,[6] we can generate wage–profit *curves* for each year's economy. While these are not the wage–profit frontiers which are invoked in the reswitching argument (see below), they are the only computable wage curves, and provide suggestive evidence on the empirical relevance of reswitching. To obtain them we simply solve equations (6.14) and (6.16) above for values of π from 0 to *R*. By using coefficients and output levels measured in constant dollars, we obtain values of the money wage which are directly comparable from year to year. The wages are, in effect, deflated.[7]

The results of this procedure for the years 1947, 1958, 1963, 1967 and 1972 are plotted in Figure 6.2 below, which shows the wage–profit curves of the US economy for the five years in question, spanning a period of 25 years. The most striking feature of all of them is how nearly linear they are: they exhibit very slight convexity, with extremely small 'wiggles' close to

Figure 6.2   US wage–profit frontiers

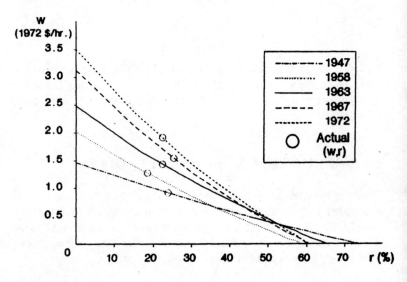

the π-intercept. (The significance of near-linear wage–profit curves is discussed below.) This results from the remarkable closeness of labour values to prices of production for the US economy.

There is also a strong trend towards higher net product per worker, as evidenced by the rising ω-intercept. The output–capital ratio (or maximum rate of profit R) fell dramatically from 1947 to 1958; after which it rose steadily until 1967. Between then and 1972 it fell once again.[8] In other words, the character of technical change from 1947 to 1958 and from 1967 to 1972 follows Marx's characterization (falling unit values and falling R); from 1958 to 1967, however, the wage–profit curve moved strictly outward, so that the new techniques were unambiguously more profitable regardless of the wage rate. This implies that the new techniques were both capital- and labour-saving in this period.

Another noteworthy feature is the actual position of the economy during these years, as shown by the small circles on the curves. Notice that, in every single instance, the new curve would have yielded a higher rate of profit if the wage rate had remained unchanged from one time period to the next. The higher wage rates alone were responsible for the fall in the profit rate in the two periods when this happened; in the other two periods, the rise in the wage rate was more than compensated for by the outward expansion of the wage–profit curve (specifically, by the rise in R).

In fact the only periods where the actual π fell are precisely those for which the associated R fell; also the rise in the wage rate closely mirrors the rise in output per worker. Both of these characteristics are consequences of the fact that the rate of surplus-value remained relatively steady throughout this entire period, as shown in Table 6.5 below.

Table 6.5   US rate of surplus-value

Year	1947	1958	1963	1967	1972
s/v (%)	95.1	86.9	101.4	116.7	111.7

Note: std. dev. = 12.1; mean = 102.4; std. dev./mean = 0.12.

7 NEAR-LINEARITY AND STANDARD PRODUCT

We have interpreted the near-linearity of the wage–profit curves of the postwar US economy as being due to the characteristic structure of industrial economies; namely, that the vertically-integrated compositions of capital for each sector show only moderate variance.[9,10] In a word, prices of production and direct prices do not deviate very much. However it is theoretically possible to have linear wage-profit curves even when price–value deviations are large and value compositions of capitals show high variance. This happens when the numeraire used is the standard product, in the sense given to it by Sraffa. It follows – given that we used the actual output vector in our normalization condition – that if the actual composition of output for the US economy is fairly close to the standard-product proportions, this alone might be responsible for the near-linearity of the observed wage-profit curves.

To investigate this possibility, we simply derived the standard product q^* for the years in our study and compared it to the actual product. The results for 1967 – a typical year – yielded a *MAD* of 386.4 per cent between the standard and actual products, and a correlation coefficient of -0.192 ($R^2 = 0.037$). These values effectively rule out any similarity of the actual to the standard product as the source of the near-linearity of the US wage–profit curves. The latter must therefore be due entirely to the relatively uniform value compositions of capitals and the consequent closeness of prices of production to direct prices.[11]

8 WAGE-PROFIT CURVES AND WAGE-PROFIT FRONTIERS

Any attempt to draw conclusions on the empirical relevance of reswitching based on Figure 6.2 must contend with the fact that the curves we have calculated differ significantly from the wage–profit frontiers referred to in the reswitching debate. In the latter, the curves refer to the envelope of all alternative techniques at a given point in time, whereas we have only presented the (average) technique which was chosen. Moreover, in order to make the switchpoints invariant with respect to numeraires, the assumption is made that, in the neighbourhood of a switchpoint, two techniques differ only in one industry (if they differed by more, an additional non-interior technique could be fashioned by taking the best of both). For our actual wage curves, all industries show different coefficients from year to year, so that, even if all we wanted to show was the envelope of all techniques actually used during the period 1947–72, we would have to construct $5^{71} = 4 \times 10^{49}$ curves.

The above raises the interesting question of what empirical significance the choice-of-technique argument has if it invariably involves the change of only one method at each switchpoint. The real-world situation of n industries and many firms means that the choices of technique are made at existing prices (which depend on distribution) simultaneously by many firms and industries. The cost minimization assumption assures us that the emerging wage–profit frontier (with multiple changes in sectoral methods) will be further out (yield a higher rate of profit) at the current wage rate. But it does allow for the possibility of switchpoints at different wage rates (other than the current one) for different numeraires. In fact, when we used each of the 71 different commodities in our study as numeraires to generate 71 sets of wage–profit curves, we found that switchpoints did vary from numeraire to numeraire (Ochoa, 1984).

It follows that the choice of numeraire becomes important in establishing the real-world switchpoints of the real-world historical technologies (also the observed point in the frontier of the economy should always lie on the envelope of historical curves up to that time, which it does). As we have already argued above, the actual purchasing power of the money unit (and hence the total output of the economy) is the most meaningful choice, and was used for this study.

There remains the problem of inflation and changing gross output composition. This means that in the real world the composite numeraire q shrinks from year to year, as well as changing its proportions. Hence the decision to adopt a given technique, which was originally made on the basis of one purchasing power level of the dollar, will, instead, be implemented on the basis of a different purchasing power level (Marzi and Varri (1977) discuss this problem as well). We can correct for the effect of this by using a base year's prices and current output or a base year's constant prices and output. The latter represents the intended aggregate effect of the individual firms' decisions on the technology of the economy. The former represents the actual impact of changes in techniques and output proportions on the wage–profit frontier of the economy.

Strictly speaking, then, the historical wage–profit frontiers do not address the reswitching scenario, since not all options available are shown, but only those five which were historically chosen. In fact, even with all possible combinations of the historical column vectors, we would not have the true wage–profit envelope, because (1) the empirical input–output coefficients are actually averages of the spectrum of coexisting techniques in each industry, (2) the techniques which were available but not used in each year do not show up in our input–output tables, and (3) the calculated wage–profit curves span a period of 25 years, so that technical change has occurred throughout, violating the assumptions of the choice of technique. This latter argument is not so serious if we view the resultant envelope of the five curves calculated as that available to the economy in 1972, but the absence of techniques which were not used is a more serious problem.

It is therefore conceivable that, for any one of these years, the unobserved wage–profit frontiers which would obtain from considering alternative but unused techniques then available might be switching out of and into the frontier envelope, for unobserved levels of distribution. This would be so provided that these alternative technologies were odd enough (different enough in their coefficients spectrum) to significantly distort the shapes of the unobserved curves. The observed curves' linearity suggests that this would be unlikely; that an economy which is highly integrated would exhibit qualitatively similar curves even when using some of the alternate techniques. (We are not even making the additional argument here that the way much technical progress occurs involves the clear superiority of a new technique under a broad range of income distributions, owing to the incorporation of new scientific principles.) All we can say is that the observed frontiers suggest – though by no means show – that reswitching may not be a real possibility for advanced capitalist economies.

9 CONCLUSION

This chapter has shown that labour values and prices of production for the US economy in the postwar period were remarkably close to each other as well as to market prices. The scale of the errors to be expected in the available data suggests that little if any accuracy is to be gained by calculating prices of production, so that either value or market-price series should be adequate in studying the behaviour of the economy in the aggregate and over time. This is a startling empirical postscript to the long-standing debate on the 'transformation problem' which now appears to involve relatively insignificant magnitudes in real economies.

Equally remarkably, the wage–profit curves implicit in the input–output coefficients for the period were all very nearly linear. This latter result was shown not to depend on the composition of output or the weighting scheme used to homogenize labour inputs. While the wage–profit curves calculated cannot be brought directly to bear on the reswitching debate, the fact remains that over a period of 25 years the economy has exhibited wage–profit curves (that is, techniques) which are a far cry from the – it would appear – unlikely shapes required for reswitching and capital reversing to occur. While the presence of heterogeneous capital goods and fixed proportions dealt fatal blows to the neo-classical concept of aggregate physical capital, the near-linearity of actual wage–profit curves appears to support the labour theory of value as a powerful practical tool to analyse and understand the global character of production and growth in capitalist economies.

NOTES

1. See Ferguson (1969) for a comprehensive statement of the neo-classical aggregate production and distribution theory. As was argued by Samuelson and others during the debate between the two Cambridges, reswitching did not affect the internal consistency of neo-classical theory in its full generality, in the Walrasian manner developed by Arrow and Hahn (1971), among others. But for a 'Classical' critique of even this general form, see Duménil and Lévy (1985).

2. The following set of relations were estimated:

$$d_i(t) = \alpha_i + \beta_i m_i(t) + u_i(t); \qquad i = 1, \ldots, 71; \ E(u_i) = 0. \tag{1}$$

The relation above refers to unit prices, where the physical unit remains constant throughout the time series. Our actual results use a current market dollar's worth as the physical unit; we needed to convert it to a constant (1972) market dollar's worth to obtain prices for an unchanging physical unit. Our actual results were

$$D_i(t) = d_i(t)q_i(t); \quad M_i(t) = m_i(t)q_i(t) \tag{2}$$

We could not regress $D_i(t)$ on $M_i(t)$ without spurious correlation, owing to the appearance of $q_i(t)$ on both sides. So we can divide through by $M_i(t)$:

$$\frac{D_i(t)}{M_i(t)} = \frac{d_i(t)q_i(t)}{m_i(t)q_i(t)} = \frac{d_i(t)}{m_i(t)}; \qquad \frac{M_i(t)}{M_i(t)} = 1 \tag{3}$$

This is the form in which we have presented direct prices: d_i/m_i. While this eliminates $q_i(t)$ from both expressions, it turns market prices into a constant (one), which means there is no variation left to correlate. Equation (1) is equally valid when divided through by a constant $(m_i(1972))$.

$$\frac{d_i(t)}{m_i(1972)} = \alpha_i + \beta_i \frac{m_i(t)}{m_i(1972)} + u_i(t) \tag{4}$$

which gives prices per 1972 market dollar's worth of sectoral output. But

$$\frac{d_i(t)}{m_i(1972)} = \frac{d_i(t)}{m_i(t)} \cdot \frac{m_i(t)}{m_i(1972)}$$

Since $m_i(t)/m_i(1972)$ is nothing but the price-index $e_i(t)$, we may write (4) as

$$\frac{d_i(t)}{m_i(t)} e_i(t) = \alpha_i + \beta_i e_i(t) + u_i(t) \tag{5}$$

Equation (5) is equivalent to (1). The price-index $e_i(t)$ is clearly a time series of market prices; but the left-hand side appears to contain the same variable. A glance at (4), however, quickly dispels that impression: the $e_i(t)$ is there precisely to eliminate the influence of $m_i(t)$ in the denominator of the left-hand side of (5).

3. Empirical results not presented in this chapter are available to readers from the author upon request.
4. In this regard, see Parys (1982).
5. See Ferguson (1969), 255–66.
6. We chose to use what we call Sraffian prices because these most closely approximate the terms of the reswitching debate. Marxian prices of production, however, yielded nearly identical curves.
7. They are not, however, deflated by the equivalent of the GNP deflator. Rather by what we might call 'gross output deflator' in the input–output sense of the term.
8. Correcting for capacity utilization does not alter these results (Ochoa, 1984).
9. This point is developed in Ochoa (1984) and Petrovic (1987).
10. Our description of the wage–profit curves as nearly linear can be justified by a simple quantitative measure: a stepwise linear regression of w on powers of π using our calculated points. For 1967 – a typical year – we observed levels of explained sum of squares of deviations shown below:

SS explained by each variable when entered in the order given

Due to	SS
π	9.682445
π^2	0.108906
π^3	0.000975
π^4	0.000009
Residual	0.000001
TOTAL	9.792335

Alternatively when we regress w on π alone (that is, approximate the wage–profit curve with a straight line) we obtain for 1967 an R^2 of 0.989. Similar results hold for the other years.
11. An anonymous reviewer raised the question of whether the use of relative wages as weights to homogenize labour inputs might not unduly bias the results on price–value deviations, if they influence the sectoral variations in organic compositions of capital. This possibility was considered in Ochoa (1984), where it is reported that the cross-

sectional R^2 between wages and organic compositions of capital was never higher than 0.026. Moreover the calculations are generally robust to the effect of variations in the weighting of labour inputs: values were calculated using unweighted labour inputs, without significantly altering the results.

REFERENCES

Arrow, K. J. and F. H. Hahn (1971), *General Competitive Analysis*, San Francisco: Holden-Day.

Carter, A. (1970), *Structural Change in the U.S. Economy*, Cambridge, Mass.: Cambridge University Press.

Duménil, G. and D. Lévy (1985), 'The classicals and the neoclassicals: a rejoinder to Hahn', *Cambridge Journal of Economics*, **9**,(4), December.

Ferguson, C. E. (1969), *The Neoclassical Theory of Production and Distribution*, Cambridge, Cambridge University Press.

Marzi, G. and P. Varri (1977), *Variazioni di Produttivita nell'Economia Italiana: 1959–1967*, Bologna: Società Editrice Il Mulino.

Ochoa, E. (1984), *'Labour Values and Prices of Production: An Interindustry Study of the U.S. Economy, 1947–1972'*, unpublished PhD dissertation, New York: New School for Social Research.

Parys, W. (1982), 'The deviation of prices from labour values', *American Economic Review*, December.

Petrovic, P. (1987), 'The deviation of production prices from labour values: some methodology and empirical evidence', *Cambridge Journal of Economics*, **11**,(3), September.

Research Data Associates (1982), *Draft Documentation for Interindustry Data Tape*, Worcester, Mass.

Shaikh, A. (1977), 'Marx's Theory of Value and the Transformation Problem', in J. Schwartz, (ed.), *The Subtle Anatomy of Capitalism*, Santa Monica, Cal.: Goodyear.

Sraffa, P. (1960), *Production of Commodities by Means of Commodities*, Cambridge: Cambridge University Press.

Steedman, I. (1977), *Marx after Sraffa*, London: New Left Books.

Steedman, I. (ed.) (1981), *The Value Controversy*, London: New Left Books.

US Department of Commerce (1975), 'Summary Input–Output Tables of the U.S. Economy: 1968, 1969, 1970', BEA Staff Paper No. 27, Washington, DC.

US Department of Commerce (1964–79), *Survey of Current Business*, Nov. 1964, Nov. 1969, Feb. 1974, Feb. 1979, March 1979 issues, Washington, DC.

US Department of Commerce (1981), *GNP and components (14) by industry, 1948–79; 1980 benchmark*, Magnetic tape, Washington, DC.

US Department of Commerce (1983), *Bureau of Industrial Economics Capital Stock Data Tape*, Washington, DC.

US Department of Labor (1979), *Capital Stock Estimates for Input–Output Industries: Methods and Data*, Washington, DC.

US Department of Labor (published yearly), *Supplement to Producer Prices and Price Indexes*, Washington, DC.

Varri, P. (1980), 'Prices, Rate of Profit and Life of Machines in Sraffa's Fixed-Capital Model', in Luigi Pasinetti (ed.), *Essays on the Theory of Joint Production*, New York: Columbia University Press.

Wolff, E. (1979), 'The rate of surplus value, the organic composition, and general rate of profit in the U.S. economy, 1947–1967', *American Economic Review*, March.

APPENDIX: DATA SOURCES

This is an account of the sources and methods used to perform the calculations reported in this chapter. For further details see Ochoa (1984). We have, from the US Department of Commerce, A, the matrix of input–output coefficients for the US economy for the years mentioned above, at various levels of disaggregation. We worked at the 82-industry level, aggregated to 71 industries, in order to match the capital-stocks data available. Unlike the technical coefficients matrix used in Sraffian models, these matrices show the input requirements in dollars per dollar of output (the Sraffian technical-coefficients matrix shows the inter-industry requirements in real terms). From the same source we have q, the dollar value of output-by-industry vector, at 82-order.

We have, from the US Department of Labor, the direct-labour requirements, in worker-hours, per dollar of output, at 82-order, for the years listed above. Since these labour times are heterogeneous (different skills and intensities), we used the relative wage structure in these industries, obtained from the same source, to reduce skilled or more intense labour to unskilled labour of minimum intensity, as exemplified by the lowest-wage sector. We thereby assume that the labour markets have no significant barriers to entry, so that the relative wage structure is a good measure of the relative values of heterogeneous labour powers and the rate of surplus-value is uniform across industries. We call the resultant reduced-labour requirements vector a_o.

From the US Department of Commerce (1983), we have the vector k, the dollar value of gross capital stock in current dollars for each industry. Since this capital stock is heterogeneous, we used asset weights w to disaggregate k in G, the gross capital-stock matrix, whose elements G_{ij} show the dollar value of the stock of the ith capital good in the jth industry. Dividing each column j of G_{ij} by q_j, we obtain the matrix of capital-stock coefficients K_{ij}. The set of asset weights were derived by assuming that the stock of every capital good has a uniform age distribution, so that the fraction scrapped each year is the inverse of the asset lifetime (given in the US Department of Commerce, 1979). We then assumed further that the composition of the capital stock for each industry, in terms of the 71-commodity structure we are using, changes slowly over time. It follows that there is a straightforward relation between the composition of gross investment – which is given for 1963, 1967 and 1972 – and the composition of the capital stocks. The composition of net investment will be the same as that of replacement investment, and clearly the same as their sum (gross investment). By assumption, the following relation holds between replacement investment (depreciation) and stock of the ith good in the jth industry:

$$D_{ij} = \frac{K_{ij}}{l_i} \text{ or } K_{ij} = l_i D_{ij} \tag{6A.1}$$

where l_i is the lifetime of the ith asset. The relative composition of the capital stock w_{ij} is therefore given by

$$w_{ij} = \frac{K_{ij}}{\sum_i K_{ij}} = \frac{l_i D_{ij}}{\sum_i l_i D_{ij}} \tag{6A.2}$$

and we obtain K from k using the expression below:

$$K_{ij} = w_{ij} k_j \tag{6A.3}$$

We also have 71-order depreciation vectors d_j (gross discards) of capital stock for the relevant years (US Department of Labor, 1980). These depreciation levels are straightforwardly disaggregated – given our assumption of constant composition – as follows:

$$D_{ij} = \frac{H_{ij}}{\sum_i H_{ij}} d_j \tag{6A.4}$$

where H_{ij} is the known gross investment matrix. This also allows us to compute w_{ij} as outlined above.

We go on to discuss the conditions under which it is appropriate to use gross discards as a measure of the physical wear-
and-tear of capital goods. Assume a uniform distribution of
ages for each kind of asset held by each industry. If this
assumption is reasonable, then each year's gross discards of
equipment by each industry will equal total physical wear-
and-tear for all assets held by that industry. The latter quantity (which is defined prior to distribution) need not be
obtained by assuming linear depreciation: in fact, in the statistics which we used, it is not. This proposition can be shown to
be true as follows. Let d_i, $i = 1, \ldots, n$ be the fractional physical
wear-and-tear which occurs for a given kind of asset in a given
kind of industry in year i of this asset's life (which is n years).
The d_i may all be different, but we require that $\sum d_i = 1$ (that
is, the machine transfers its value to the product exactly over
its life). Given our assumption that we have a uniform distribution of ages, the fraction of the total assets of this kind in
this industry of age i years if $f_i = 1/n$, for all i. Now we show
that the physical amount of gross discards equals the total
amount of physical wear-and-tear on all the assets (of this
kind in this industry).

1. Every year, $1/n$ of all the assets are discarded (as given by
    our gross-discards series).
2. Also every year, the total amount of physical wear-and-
    tear is given by

$$\sum_i f_i d_i = \sum_i (1/n) d_i = (1/n) \sum_i d_i = (1/n)$$

Hence the physical amount of gross discards equals the
physical amount of wear-and-tear, assuming a uniform distribution of vintages for this kind of asset, but without having to
assume linear wear-and-tear.

It might be questioned how we could define wear-and-tear
in purely physical terms, or rather gross discards. This was
done the same way we measured all other physical quantities
in this project: by making one current-market dollar's worth
the physical unit of measurement. Hence the gross discards

were measured at replacement cost in current dollars. Then depreciation is given as sD (that is, not before distribution).

To obtain the real unit wage vector b, we use the sectoral proportions in the personal consumption expenditures component of final demand, which is part of the input–output data developed by the Department of Commerce. By multiplying it by the wage rate in current dollars of the lowest-wage sector, we obtain the dollar amount of each consumer good required per unit of reduced labour.

The treatment of indirect business taxes in this study assumes that they represent a cost like any other in the formation of a uniform rate of profit. We therefore compiled a vector of indirect-tax coefficients, g, from US Department of Commerce (1981).

We required a 71-order price-index vector, e, to factor out changes in input–output coefficients which are due to market price changes. This is necessary if we are to compare technologies over time, since we are using a 'dollar's worth' as a measure of physical quantity of a product (see Carter, 1970, page 21). The US Department of Labor (1979) provides price indices for most input–output industries. Except for 1947, all the required indices are included in the data tape of Research Data Associates (1982). We used the price index vector implicit in US Department of Commerce (1970), which gives 1947 input–output data in 1947 and 1958 dollars, to obtain the 1947 values.

Summarizing, we have

A Input–output coefficients matrix
k Fixed-capital coefficients row vector
a_0 Direct reduced-labour coefficients row vector
w Capital-assets weights matrix
G Gross-capital-stocks matrix
b' Real-wage column vector per unit of reduced labour
l Asset-lifetime column vector (per asset type)
e Price-index row vector
q Dollar value of output-by-industry row vector
K Capital-stocks coefficients matrix
D Depreciation coefficients matrix

H Gross-investment coefficients matrix
g Indirect-tax coefficients row vector

Given this data base, we could perform all the computations outlined in the chapter. In all cases, we can compute prices and values using the data in current dollars or in constant dollars. The former is more accurate when investigating relations in a single year; the latter is necessary for intertemporal comparisons.

To deflate the *A* matrix we compute:

$$A^* = \ <e^{-1}> \ A \ <e> \tag{6A.5}$$

where $<e>$ is the diagonal matrix obtained from the vector *e*.

To deflate the output row vector *q*:

$$q^* = q \ <e^{-1}> \tag{6A.6}$$

To handle the capital valuation problem, we could take the capital coefficients matrix *K* at current dollars and deflate it like *A*. This is valid since current dollar gross-stocks measure current replacement value of assets still in place.

The real unit-wage vector *b*, also measured in 'dollar's worth', can be deflated as *q* above.

7. Prices, Wages and Profits in Brazil: an Input–Output Analysis, 1975

Ednaldo Araquém da Silva and Jean-Luc Rosinger

INTRODUCTION

In the history of economics we can observe a persistent interest in the trade-off relationship between pairs of variables, such as between price or wage inflation and unemployment. The objective of this chapter is to analyse the trade-off relationship between the wage share and the profit margin in the Brazilian economy, and the effect of this trade-off on production prices.[1] Although still undeveloped here, we examine also the *empirical* relationship between the wage share and the value of the gross output. Thus we intend to give empirical content to some important concepts of Marxian political economy, which until recently have been given primarily theoretical attention (Pasinetti, 1977; Lipietz, 1982; Garegnani, 1984).[2] The empirical results are based on the 1975 Brazilian input–output accounts, aggregated into 20 sectors.

The chapter is organized as follows: first, we develop the equation system necessary to calculate production prices and the distribution of income between wages and profits; second, we calculate the trade-off relationship between the wage share and the profit margin and the associated system of production prices. Third, we examine the effect of hypothetical changes in the wage share on the production prices and on the value of the gross output. The chapter concludes with a brief discussion of some of the policy implications of the empirical results. The principal hypothesis being examined is that a policy increase in the wage share can cause some key sectoral production prices to fall as well as the value of economic activity to increase.

1 ANALYTICAL FRAMEWORK

The basic model of an n-sector capitalist economy where each sector produces a single output, can be specified as follows:[3]

$$p = (1 + r) [p A + w L] \tag{7.1}$$

$$p z = v z = 1 \tag{7.2}$$

where p $(1,n)$ is a vector of sectoral production prices; A (n,n) is the input–output matrix in which each non-negative element a_{ij} $(i_{jd} = 1, 2, \ldots, n)$ denotes the input i used per unit of gross output j; L $(1,n)$ is the vector of direct labour used per unit of gross output; v $(1,n)$ is the vector of sectoral labour values; z $(n,1)$ is the vector of net output per unit of total employment of production workers; and r, w are scalars denoting the profit margin and the wage share.

Equation (7.1) is a standard expression of production prices (Marx, 1971, volume 3, p. 157). Likewise the numeraire equation (7.2) is a recent interpretation of Marx's 'invariance postulate' that total value equals total price.[4] Equation (7.2) has the advantage that it does not assign a special role to any one of the n-sectors in the economy, such as was done in earlier stages of capitalism with agricultural or gold production. Another advantage of equation (7.2) is that it gives expression to Marx's theorem (1971, Volume 3, p. 164; see also Lipietz, 1982) that relative production prices generally deviate from their corresponding labour values.

This is an open system with $(n + 1)$ equations and $(n + 2)$ unknown variables to be determined, counting the n-sector production prices, the profit margin and the wage share. As in the classical tradition, we make some basic assumptions which constitute part of the 'core' of the surplus approach (see Garegnani, 1984, pp. 293–4):

1. The technology (A, L) of the economy and the level and composition (consumption, investment) of the net output (z) per unit of total employment are fixed magnitudes.
2. The input–output matrix A is assumed to be productive and indecomposable (see Bródy, 1970; Pasinetti, 1977) and each of its elements $a_{ij} \geq 0$ $(i, j = 1, 2, \ldots,n)$ is constant over scale.
3. The net output is distributed between workers and capitalists, and both the money wage rate and the profit margin are uniform in the economy.

From these assumptions we can show the following analytical results:

(a) $p = (1 + r) w L [I - (1 + r) A]^{-1} > 0$
   if $0 \leq r < R$ = maximum profit margin, where $I(n,n)$ is an identity matrix;
(b) $R = (1/\mu_1) - 1 > 0$
   if μ_1 (the Frobenius root of A) < 1 by the assumption that A is productive;
(c) $p = (1 + R) p A > 0$
   if $r = R$;
(d) $p = L [I - A]^{-1} > 0$
   if $r = 0$;
(e) $w = 1 / (1 + r) L [I - (1 + r) A]^{-1} z$
(f) $w = 0$ if $r = R$.

We solve this sytem of sectoral production prices as a function of the profit margin by expanding (7.1) and then transposing the vector $[(1 + r) p A]$ to the left-hand side of the equation:

$$p = (1 + r) p A + (1 + r) w L$$
$$p [I - (1 + r) A] = (1 + r) w L$$
$$p = (1 + r) w L [I - (1 + r) A]^{-1} \qquad (7.3)$$

where, from some familiar theorems of Frobenius and Perron

(see Bródy, 1970; Pasinetti, 1977), we know that the matrix in brackets has an inverse in the interval $\mu_1 \leq 1/(1 + r) < 1$. The profit margin is treated as an independent variable. It follows from (7.3) that the n-sector production prices can be calculated for any ordered pair (r, w), where r lies in the closed interval $(0, R)$. We now proceed to find the upper and lower bounds of the profit margin.

2 THE MAXIMUM PROFIT MARGIN

The hypothetical maximum profit margin can be computed by setting $w = 0$ in equation (7.1), which now becomes:

$$p = (1 + R) \, p \, A$$
$$\mu \, p = p \, A, \text{ where } \mu = 1/(1 + R) \text{ is a scalar;} \qquad (7.4)$$
$$p \, [\mu \, I - A] = 0.$$

The solution of equation (7.4) is an n-th order polynomial in μ such that each root μ_i $(i = 1, 2, \ldots, n)$ can be obtained by setting the determinant of (7.4) equal to zero:

$$det \, [\mu \, I - A] = 0 \qquad (7.4')$$

For each root μ_i $(i = 1, 2, \ldots, n)$ there is a vector satisfying (7.4), as follows:

$$\mu_i \, p_i = p_i \, A, \text{ for } i = 1, 2, \ldots, n.$$

From the maximum Frobenius root (μ_1), we can obtain the maximum profit margin as its reciprocal minus one, that is, $R = (1/\mu_1) - 1$. This is our result (b) above. It means that there exists a positive profit margin in at least one of the n-sectors, making possible the expansion of the capitalist economy (see Bródy, 1970, pp. 23–4).

Labour Values

As a special case of (7.1), in which $r = 0$, and thus $w = 1$, we can calculate the n-sector labour values according to the following system of equations:

$$v = L [I - A]^{-1} \qquad (7.5)$$

where v_i denotes the labour value of the i-th sector.

For Marx (1971), labour values represent the total (direct and indirect) amount of homogeneous labour required to produce a unit of gross output.[5] Labour values can facilitate economic analysis because they are independent of income distribution between wages and profits; they only depend on the technology of the economy. Thus the value of gross output aggregated with labour values as weights would remain the same even after variations in the distributive variables r and w.

The Wage Share

Like the sectoral production prices, the wage share can be computed as function of the profit margin. In view of the numeraire equation (7.2), we can postmultiply equation (7.3) by z $(n, 1)$, and then solve for w as a function of r. This gives the wage share in national income:

$$p z = 1 = (1 + r) w L [I - (1 + r) A]^{-1} z$$
$$w = 1 / (1 + r) L [I - (1 + r) A]^{-1} z \qquad (7.6)$$

where r is regarded as an independent variable.

In equation (7.6), w represents both the real wage rate and the wage share in national income; thus, for any given set $(A, L; z)$, the wage share varies inversely with the profit margin. This formulation of the wage equation expresses Marx's suggestion (1969, Part II, p. 419; emphases added) that 'wages have to reckoned according to the *relative share* of the value of the total product . . . The position of the classes to one another depends more on *relative wages* than on the absolute amount of wages.'

3 EMPIRICAL RESULTS

The empirical measurement of this Marxian model of production prices and income distribution has been made with the Brazilian input–output accounts of 1975, aggregated into 20 sectors. Table 7.1 contains the relevant 20 sectors classification along with their respective code numbers. All the relevant data come from IBGE (1987). Following the procedure outlined in equation (7.4), the dominant Frobenius root for Brazil in 1975 was estimated as being equal to $\mu_1 = 0.423$; therefore the corresponding maximum profit margin became equal to $R = (1/\mu_1) - 1 = 1.41$. Using equation (7.6), different values for the wage share were interpolated as the profit margin was allowed to increase from zero to its estimated maximum level. The results are shown in Table 7.2.

Table 7.1   Brazil, 1975: 20-sector input–output classification

Sector	IBGE activity code
1. Agriculture, fishing and forestry	101 to 499
2. Mining and fuels	501 to 504
3. Non-metallic minerals	1001 to 1091
4. Metal industries	1101 to 1191
5. Machinery	1201 to 1208
6. Electrical equipment	1301 to 1308
7. Transport equipment	1401 to 1491
8. Wood and furniture	1501 to 1602
9. Paper and cardboard	1701 to 1703
10. Rubber, leather and plastics	1801, 1802, 1999, 2301, 2302
11. Chemicals	2001 to 2009
12. Cosmetics and pharmaceutics	2199 to 2299
13. Textile and clothing	2401 to 2502
14. Food, beverages and tobacco	2601 to 2899
15. Printing and miscellaneous	2901, 2902, 3001, 3099, 5601
16. Electricity	4001
17. Construction	4201
18. Public utilities and other services	4101, 5401 to 5504
19. Transport and communications	5201 to 5301
20. Retail and distribution	5101, 5102

Source: IBGE (1987) pp. 49–51.

Figure 7.1 shows that the wage–profit curve in Brazil is convex to the origin (for comparisons, see Marzi and Varri, 1977; Özol, 1984; Cekota, 1988). The presumably uniform profit margin and the average (weighted by value added) wage share are equal to 71.9 and 29.9 per cent, respectively. This relatively low wage share shows the historical weakness of Brazilian workers compared to capitalists.

Table 7.2 also contains the value of the gross output measured by sectoral production prices for selective pairs of (r, w); that is, $p\,x$, where x (20,1) is the given vector of gross output per sector. Figure 7.2 shows that the value of the gross output increases when the wage share increases beyond a certain level; coincidently, this level corresponds to the actual wage share. For an unrealistic interval of the wage share up to about 20 per cent, an increase in the wage share is also compatible with a decrease in the value of the gross output. As can be seen from equation (7.2), the value of the gross output has the same dimension as total employment. The positive rela-

Figure 7.1   Brazil, 1975: wage–profit curve

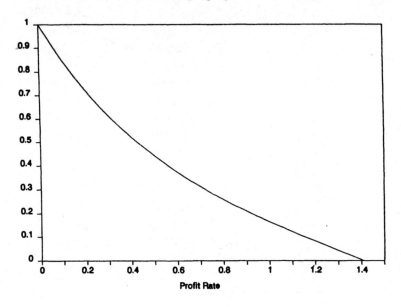

Profit Rate

Table 7.2   Brazil, 1975: wage–profit curve and the value of gross output

r	w	p X
0	1.0	23660962
0.05	0.9198	23633364
0.1	0.847	23606815
0.15	0.7807	23581383
0.2	0.7201	23557145
0.25	0.6644	23534185
0.3	0.6131	23512597
0.35	0.5657	23492486
0.4	0.5218	23473970
0.45	0.4809	23457183
0.5	0.4429	23442274
0.55	0.4072	23429415
0.6	0.3738	23418801
0.65	0.3424	23410655
0.7	0.3129	23405237
0.75	0.2849	23402846
0.8	0.2584	23403832
0.85	0.2331	23408606
0.9	0.2091	23417655
0.95	0.1861	23431561
1	0.164	23451022
1.05	0.1426	23476888
1.1	0.122	23510203
1.15	0.1018	23552263
1.2	0.082	23604701
1.25	0.0624	23669609
1.3	0.0429	23749712
1.35	0.0232	23848648
1.4	0.003	23971413
1.4073	0.0	23991609

tionship between the wage share and total employment corroborates a basic postulate of classical economics that decreases in the profit margin are compatible with increases in the value of gross output or the level of total employment. The reason is that, as Sylos-Labini (1984, pp. 214–17) has argued, wages are not only costs of production but also an important source of effective demand. Substituting equation (7.6) into (7.3), we can obtain a vector of sectoral production prices for each pair of the profit margin and the wage share (r, w). The resulting equation system is as follows:

$$p(r) = \frac{L\ [I - (1 + r)\ A]^{-1}}{L\ [I - (1 + r)\ A]^{-1}\ z}$$

In Table 7.3 we reproduce the computed production prices, for each of the 20 sectors of the Brazilian economy in 1975, associated with selected pairs of the profit margin and the wage share. As the wage share increases, the production prices of sectors 1, 2, 3, 16, 18, 19, and 20 increase, while those of

Figure 7.2   Brazil, 1975: gross output as f(w)

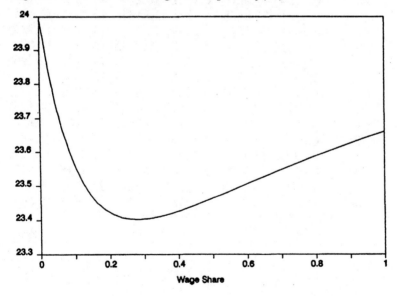

Table 7.3 *Brazil, 1975: relative prices as function of the wage share*

r	w	p_1	p_2	p_3	p_4	p_5
0	1	44.3632	7.4197	11.5105	8.6841	9.372
0.05	0.9198	43.3517	7.3497	11.422	8.8452	9.4005
0.1	0.847	42.3372	7.2812	11.3342	9.014	9.4355
0.15	0.7807	41.3187	7.2141	11.247	9.1912	9.4775
0.2	0.7201	40.2955	7.1484	11.1607	9.3777	9.5272
0.25	0.6644	39.2665	7.0842	11.0753	9.5742	9.5854
0.3	0.6131	38.2305	7.0214	10.9907	9.7818	9.6529
0.35	0.5657	37.1863	6.9601	10.9072	10.0013	9.7307
0.4	0.5218	36.1323	6.9002	10.8247	10.2341	9.8199
0.45	0.4809	35.067	6.8418	10.7434	10.4815	9.9216
0.5	0.4429	33.9885	6.7849	10.6633	10.745	10.0374
0.55	0.4072	32.8947	6.7294	10.5847	11.0263	10.1689
0.6	0.3738	31.7832	6.6754	10.5075	11.3274	10.3178
0.65	0.3424	30.6512	6.623	10.4318	11.6508	10.4864
0.7	0.3129	29.4955	6.5721	10.358	11.9989	10.6772
0.75	0.2849	28.3124	6.5228	10.286	12.375	10.8931
0.8	0.2584	27.0976	6.4751	10.216	12.7827	11.1376
0.85	0.2331	25.8458	6.4291	10.1483	13.2263	11.4147
0.9	0.2091	24.5512	6.3849	10.083	13.7109	11.7295
0.95	0.1861	23.2064	6.3426	10.0205	14.2428	12.0877
1	0.164	21.8027	6.3023	9.9609	14.8295	12.4967
1.05	0.1426	20.3296	6.2642	9.9047	15.4801	12.9653
1.1	0.122	18.7742	6.2287	9.8523	16.2061	13.5045
1.15	0.1018	17.1203	6.1961	9.8041	17.022	14.1284
1.2	0.082	15.3477	6.1671	9.761	17.9463	14.8549
1.25	0.0624	13.4308	6.1426	9.7239	19.0036	15.7074
1.3	0.0429	11.3361	6.124	9.6943	20.2266	16.7177
1.35	0.0232	9.0195	6.1138	9.6746	21.6615	17.9295
1.4	0.003	6.4212	6.116	9.6686	23.3757	19.4064
1.4073	0	6.016	6.1178	9.6693	23.6534	19.648

r	w	p_6	p_7	p_8	p_9	p_{10}
0	1	7.6458	8.7889	18.8767	9.1623	8.8825
0.05	0.9198	7.713	9.0945	18.9577	9.332	9.0084

r	w	p_6	p_7	p_8	p_9	p_{10}
0.1	0.847	7.7859	9.4203	19.0302	9.5096	9.1425
0.15	0.7807	7.8649	9.7683	19.0938	9.6956	9.2849
0.2	0.7201	7.9507	10.1409	19.1482	9.8905	9.436
0.25	0.6644	8.0439	10.5406	19.1932	10.095	9.5959
0.3	0.6131	8.1451	10.9703	19.2283	10.3096	9.7649
0.35	0.5657	8.2552	11.4334	19.2531	10.5349	9.9434
0.4	0.5218	8.375	11.9336	19.267	10.7718	10.1315
0.45	0.4809	8.5055	12.4753	19.2695	11.0211	10.3297
0.5	0.4429	8.6479	13.0636	19.2599	11.2835	10.5383
0.55	0.4072	8.8034	13.7041	19.2375	11.56	10.7576
0.6	0.3738	8.9735	14.4038	19.2013	11.8517	10.9881
0.65	0.3424	9.16	15.1703	19.1504	12.1596	11.2302
0.7	0.3129	9.3648	16.013	19.0835	12.485	11.4843
0.75	0.2849	9.5902	16.9427	18.9991	12.8292	11.751
0.8	0.2584	9.8389	17.9725	18.8957	13.1935	12.0308
0.85	0.2331	10.1141	19.1178	18.7712	13.5796	12.3242
0.9	0.2091	10.4196	20.3973	18.6232	13.989	12.6319
0.95	0.1861	10.7598	21.8337	18.4489	14.4235	12.9545
1	0.164	11.1403	23.4549	18.2448	14.885	13.2926
1.05	0.1426	11.5678	25.2953	18.0065	15.3755	13.6468
1.1	0.122	12.0506	27.3982	17.7288	15.8969	14.0179
1.15	0.1018	12.5993	29.8184	17.4049	16.4513	14.4064
1.2	0.082	13.2271	32.6265	17.0263	17.0405	14.8124
1.25	0.0624	13.9516	35.915	16.5819	17.6662	15.236
1.3	0.0429	14.7962	39.8078	16.057	18.3296	15.676
1.35	0.0232	15.7933	44.4753	15.4315	19.0313	16.1295
1.4	0.003	16.9895	50.1599	14.6772	19.771	16.5899
1.4073	0	17.1836	51.0894	14.5547	19.8815	16.6565

r	w	p_{11}	p_{12}	p_{13}	p_{14}	p_{15}
0	1	6.6816	5.1665	17.4711	25.0766	7.5635
0.05	0.9198	6.8988	5.297	17.8416	25.8253	7.585
0.1	0.847	7.1115	5.4315	18.231	26.543	7.612
0.15	0.7807	7.3196	5.5699	18.6409	27.2284	7.6447
0.2	0.7201	7.523	5.712	19.073	27.8798	7.6836
0.25	0.6644	7.7214	5.8577	19.5293	28.4954	7.729
0.3	0.6131	7.9145	6.0068	20.0121	29.0729	7.7814

r	w	p_{11}	p_{12}	p_{13}	p_{14}	p_{15}
0.35	0.5657	8.1022	6.159	20.5237	29.6102	7.8413
0.4	0.5218	8.284	6.3141	21.067	30.1043	7.9091
0.45	0.4809	8.4596	6.4717	21.645	30.5524	7.9856
0.5	0.4429	8.6286	6.6316	22.2614	30.9509	8.0712
0.55	0.4072	8.7905	6.7934	22.9199	31.2957	8.1668
0.6	0.3738	8.9447	6.9565	23.6253	31.5823	8.2731
0.65	0.3424	9.0905	7.1205	24.3824	31.8054	8.3909
0.7	0.3129	9.2271	7.2847	25.1974	31.9586	8.5214
0.75	0.2849	9.3537	7.4483	26.0768	32.0348	8.6654
0.8	0.2584	9.469	7.6105	27.0284	32.0255	8.8243
0.85	0.2331	9.5719	7.7701	28.0613	31.9205	8.9994
0.9	0.2091	9.6606	7.9259	29.1857	31.708	9.1923
0.95	0.1861	9.7335	8.0761	30.4137	31.3735	9.4047
1	0.164	9.7883	8.2189	31.7595	30.8996	9.6386
1.05	0.1426	9.8221	8.3517	33.2394	30.2654	9.8962
1.1	0.122	9.8318	8.4714	34.8725	29.4446	10.1801
1.15	0.1018	9.8132	8.5742	36.681	28.4051	10.4931
1.2	0.082	9.7613	8.6551	38.6899	27.1058	10.8387
1.25	0.0624	9.6697	8.7077	40.9273	25.4947	11.2205
1.3	0.0429	9.5303	8.7236	43.4217	23.5041	11.643
1.35	0.0232	9.3332	8.6916	46.1975	21.0444	12.1111
1.4	0.003	9.0652	8.5968	49.26	17.9943	12.6303
1.4073	0	9.0195	8.5767	49.7268	17.4931	12.7103

r	w	p_{16}	p_{17}	p_{18}	p_{19}	p_{20}
0	1	4.4634	15.5557	10.5118	12.7796	6.9064
0.05	0.9198	4.3972	15.5129	10.3053	12.6192	6.7172
0.1	0.847	4.3318	15.4735	10.1011	12.4656	6.5295
0.15	0.7807	4.2672	15.4379	9.8988	12.3191	6.3433
0.2	0.7201	4.2033	15.4062	9.6983	12.1798	6.1584
0.25	0.6644	4.1403	15.3789	9.4992	12.0482	5.975
0.3	0.6131	4.0782	15.3561	9.3014	11.9245	5.7929
0.35	0.5657	4.0169	15.3383	9.1045	11.8091	5.6122
0.4	0.5218	3.9566	15.3259	8.9082	11.7025	5.4327
0.45	0.4809	3.8972	15.3194	8.712	11.6051	5.2544
0.5	0.4429	3.8388	15.3194	8.5156	11.5175	5.0772
0.55	0.4072	3.7815	15.3263	8.3184	11.4405	4.9012

r	w	p_{16}	p_{17}	p_{18}	p_{19}	p_{20}
0.6	0.3738	3.7254	15.3411	8.1199	11.3748	4.7261
0.65	0.3424	3.6704	15.3644	7.9194	11.3213	4.5519
0.7	0.3129	3.6168	15.3972	7.7162	11.2811	4.3786
0.75	0.2849	3.5647	15.4407	7.5094	11.2556	4.2059
0.8	0.2584	3.5141	15.4961	7.2981	11.2463	4.0337
0.85	0.2331	3.4652	15.5649	7.081	11.2551	3.8619
0.9	0.2091	3.4183	15.6491	6.8568	11.2843	3.6902
0.95	0.1861	3.3735	15.7508	6.6238	11.3367	3.5184
1	0.164	3.3313	15.8726	6.38	11.4156	3.3463
1.05	0.1426	3.2919	16.0179	6.1231	11.5256	3.1733
1.1	0.122	3.256	16.1907	5.8501	11.6718	2.9991
1.15	0.1018	3.224	16.3964	5.5574	11.8614	2.8232
1.2	0.082	3.197	16.6416	5.2402	12.1032	2.6447
1.25	0.0624	3.1761	16.9353	4.8929	12.4092	2.4628
1.3	0.0429	3.163	17.2897	4.5076	12.7956	2.2763
1.35	0.0232	3.1603	17.7223	4.0745	13.2845	2.0835
1.4	0.003	3.1718	18.2588	3.5799	13.9083	1.8822
1.4073	0	3.175	18.3476	3.5019	14.0127	1.8521

sectors 4, 5, 7, and 9 to 15 decrease. In the other sectors (6, 8, and 17), the production prices are apparently insensitive to increases in the wage share above the 30 per cent level measured in 1975. These results are shown in graph form in Figure 7.3 (a–f).

A close inspection of Figure 7.3 reveals certain common characteristics to the grouping of industries with increases or decreases in production prices when the wage share increases. It appears that, in the primary sectors such as agriculture and mining, along with public utilities, transport and trade, there is a positive relationship between production prices and the wage share; modern industrial sectors show a negative relationship; and in traditional industrial sectors, such as wood and furniture and construction, there is no apparent relationship between changes in the wage share and production prices.

Also Figure 7.3 shows that virtually all the production prices are non-linear functions of the wage share of the profit margin. These curves represent the sectoral production prices

Figure 7.3a   Brazil, 1975: relative prices as f(w)

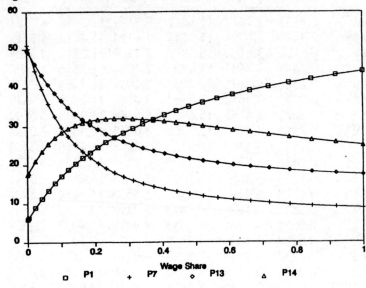

Figure 7.3b   Brazil, 1975: relative prices as f(w)

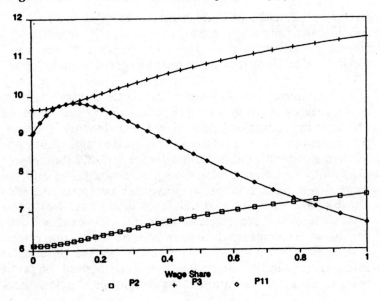

Figure 7.3c   Brazil, 1975: relative prices as f(w)

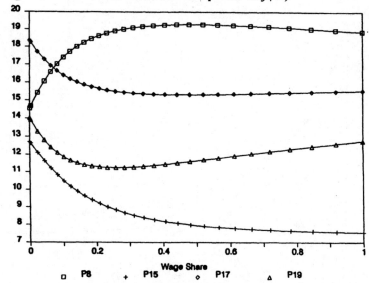

Figure 7.3d   Brazil, 1975: relative prices as f(w)

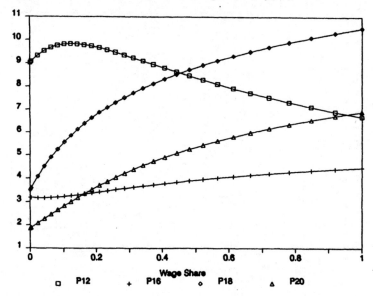

Figure 7.3e   Brazil, 1975: relative prices as f(w)

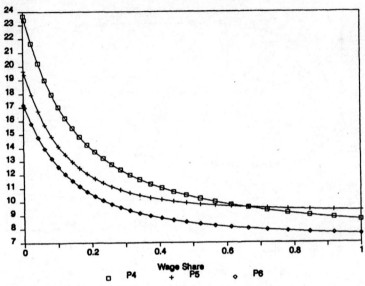

Figure 7.3f   Brazil, 1975: relative prices as f(w)

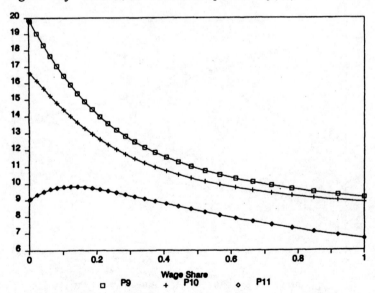

relative to the production price of the net output per unit of labour.[6] The vertical intercept of each curve, where the profit margin is null, is thus the labour value relative to the labour value of the net output. Since the production prices have the same dimension as labour values, they can be interpreted as absolute prices measured in terms of labour employment per unit of gross output.

4 CONCLUDING REMARKS

The absence of capital stocks poses an important restriction on the empirical results, which must then be interpreted with caution. Nevertheless we think it interesting to find substantial variations in some sectoral production prices resulting from hypothetical changes in the income distribution between wages and profits. In fact we observe that an increase in the wage share can cause some sectoral production prices to fall, others to increase, while others are insensitive to changes in income distribution. The empirical results also show that an increase in the wage share can *stimulate* the Brazilian economy, because the gain in the value of the gross output or the level of total employment more than compensates the hypothetical fall in the profit margin. Although we do not explore them here, the shape of the wage–profit relationship and the variations of the sectoral production prices provide interesting insights into modern capital controversies (see Pasinetti, 1977; Garegnani, 1984; and Özol, 1984).

NOTES

This research was financed by a grant from PNPE-IPEA (Rio do Janeiro). We are grateful for the assistance of Troy L. Haines and the comments of Thijs ten Raa and an anonymous referee.
1. Marx established an inverse relationship between the wage share and the *profit rate*. But, in the absence of a capital stock matrix for the Brazilian economy, we work with a circulating capital model; thus we estimate the profit margin instead of the profit rate.
2. However, Bródy (1970) and Wolff (1987) have a strong empirical con-

tent. Also the empirical application of Sraffa's system has been pioneered by Marzi and Varri (1977), Özol (1984) and Cekota (1988).

3. See Bródy (1970, 43–4) for a specification of the production price equation with fixed capital stocks.

4. The numeraire equation (7.2) can also be expressed in terms of the net output:

$$p \, y = v \, y = L \, x = N \qquad (7.2')$$

where y $(n,1)$ is a vector of net output, v $(1,n)$ is a vector of sectoral labour values, $x(n,1)$ is a vector of gross output and $N(1,1)$ is a scalar denoting total employment of workers directly engaged in production. Multiplying (2') through by $(1/N)$, we obtain our numeraire equation:

$$p \, z = v \, z = 1, \qquad (7.2)$$

where $z = (1/N) \, y$. This implies that the sum of production prices is equal to the sum of labour values. Again it may be useful to expand the numeraire equation so we can see explicitly that the value of the net output is equivalent to total employment in the economy:

$$v \, y = v \, (I - A) \, x = L \, (I - A)^{-1} \, (I - A) \, x = L \, x \qquad (7.2'')$$

Alternatively we can choose $p \, (I - A)^{-1} \, z = 1$ as the numeraire equation; however this is unsuitable for examining the trade-off relationship between labour and capital.

5. This analysis is restricted to the quantitative, that is, the determination of the magnitude of labour values. Marx (1971, Volume 1, 46–7 and 84–5) analysed labour values in terms of its three aspects; that is, 'form', 'substance' (abstract labour) and 'magnitude'.

6. In this analysis the sectoral production prices are measured by the number of workers directly engaged in production per million of 1975 Brazilian cruzeiros.

REFERENCES

Bródy, A. (1970), *Proportions, Prices and Planning*, Amsterdam: North-Holland.

Cekota, J. (1988), 'Technological change in Canada (1961–80): an application of the surrogate wage function', *Canadian Journal of Economics*, **21**,(2), May.

Garegnani, P. (1984), 'Value and distribution in the classical economists and Marx', *Oxford Economic Papers*, **36**,(2), June.

IBGE. (1987), *Matriz de Relaçoẽs Intersetoriais: Brasil – 1975*, Rio de Janeiro: Instituto Brasileiro de Geografia e Estatistica.

Lipietz, A. (1982), 'The so-called "transformation problem" revisited', *Journal of Economic Theory*, **26**,(1), February.

Marx, K. (1969), *Theories of Surplus Value*, Part II, Moscow: Progress Publishers.

Marx, K. (1971), *Capital*, Volumes 1 and 3, Moscow: Progress Publishers.

Marzi, G. and P. Varri (1977), *Variazioni di Produttività nell'Economia Italiana: 1959–1967*, Bologna: Il Mulino.

Özol, C. (1984), 'Parable and realism in production theory: the surrogate wage function', *Canadian Journal of Economics*, **17**(2), May.

Pasinetti, L. (1977), *Lectures on the Theory of Production*, New York: Columbia University Press.

Sylos-Labini, P. (1984), *The Forces of Economic Growth and Decline*, Cambridge, Mass.: MIT Press.

Wolff, E. (1987), *Growth, Accumulation and Unproductive Activity*, London: Cambridge University Press.

8. The Regimes of Accumulation of the USA: 1950–1987

Michel Juillard[1]

For a long time, technical change has been recognized as being at the core of theories of economic growth. The relationship is already present in the writings of Adam Smith. It is a central aspect of the dynamic of the mode of production for Marx. It is present in a different, but no less essential, manner in Schumpeter. In examining the neo-classical framework, all studies of aggregate production functions have pointed towards the importance of an unexplained residual, naming it total factor productivity. Others, like Denison (1974, 1985), have tried to decompose productivity growth into many factors.

In modern literature, the model of cumulative causation developed by Kaldor (1966) has tried to integrate technical change and macroeconomic dynamics in a manner in which the feedbacks of economic growth on technical change are taken into account. The originality of this model resides in its use of the Verdoorn law which links productivity gains with the growth of demand. More recently French authors regrouped around the 'Regulation School' have generalized this approach by introducing the concept of regime of accumulation. This notion describes the articulation between technical change, income distribution and transformation of the norm of consumption (see Aglietta, 1976, 1986; Bertrand, 1983; Boyer, 1986, 1987; Lipietz, 1979, 1982).

This articulation can be schematically illustrated through the relation between technical change and income distribu-

174

tion. When productivity gains are only absorbed by profits and hence the real wage remains constant, two circumstances may threaten the pursuit of accumulation in the long run: first, if productivity gains are obtained primarily in the development of mass production for consumer goods, the economy may run into problems of profit realization owing to the insufficiency of effective demand from wage earners. On the other hand, if the relative lack of demand from wage earners is balanced by an increase in investment, the economy may enter a crisis of over-accumulation along the lines of the Marxian falling rate of profit argument. Allowing for changes in the wage to examine the other extreme, the modalities of adaptation of the nominal wage to productivity gains and to inflation may be such that real wage increases threaten the profit margin and result in a slow-down of accumulation.

The foundations of the concept of the regime of accumulation derive from this very moment: the coherency between technical change, the evolution of income distribution and the transformation of the norm of consumption.

The macroeconomic structure crystallized in the regime of accumulation could not exist without the institutional arrangements, formal or implicit, which serve to codify and organize the coercive laws of the mode of production in a given period. Without entering into details which are beyond the scope of this chapter, it is worth mentioning the wage relationship, the form of competition, the formation of prices, the system of credit and money supply, the role of the state and the type of integration in the international order. This set of institutional arrangements is often referred to as the mode of regulation.

Intensive accumulation is based on a transformation of the productive forces through the application of more and more capitalist intensive methods of production. The stability of this mode of growth requires a distribution of income such that in order to expand the market for consumption goods a regular increase in the real wage is ensured, without damaging the profitability of capital. This seemingly contradictory condition is met by an adequate sharing of productivity gains and through an increase in the productivity of Department I which is composed of sectors that produce capital goods, such that the increase in the technical composition of capital is balanced.

As will shortly be seen, these conditions were by and large met during the 1950s and early 1960s, what is known as the 'Golden Age' of the regime of intensive accumulation. Its crisis began when the gains in efficiency derived from the methods of production slowed down markedly in the late 1960s. This fall in efficiency manifests itself in the slow-down of the growth of labour productivity and the increase in the capital–output ratio. These changes in the conditions of production will induce a transformation of the regime of accumulation towards a regime that is more extensive than intensive. Extensive accumulation is characterized by continuing growth in employment, but with low gains in labour productivity and real wages.

The changes in the distribution of income which were imposed on workers from the mid-1970s – but which are more characteristic of the 1980s – as well as some recovery of the growth of labour productivity in the 1980s, were generally favourable to profits. But this advantage in terms of the profit margin did not translate into a recovery of capital accumulation. This difficulty arose because the problems induced by a relatively high composition of capital were not solved and a large part of the surplus made available during the Reagan years was allocated to the military build-up. Furthermore the cumulative effects of poor productivity performance for many years also express themselves in a tremendous loss of market share inside the USA and reinforced competition abroad. The following sections successively analyse the changes in intensive accumulation, the modifications of wage relations, the evolution of profitability and its feedback on the dynamic of accumulation. The chapter concludes with an examination of the new tendencies of the 1980s.

1   FROM INTENSIVE TO EXTENSIVE ACCUMULATION

The primary characteristic of intensive accumulation is the mechanization of the labour process. This phenomenon can be approximated through the evolution of the ratio between the stock of fixed capital, measured in constant prices, and employment (capital–labour ratio). Figure 8.1 shows the evolution of this ratio for the main departments of the economy. Department I supplies fixed investment goods and Department II produces consumer goods.

Since the beginning of the period under examination, Department II is more capital intensive and the difference between the two departments has a tendency to increase through time. As with all the series between stock and flows, the short-term fluctuations of the ratio indicate changes in the level of productive capacity utilization. However the late 1970s seem to display a net slow-down in the rate of mechanization. This indication can be seen more clearly if we examine the evolution of the quantity of investment per worker, in constant dollars, in Figure 8.2.

Figure 8.3 shows this ratio for the private sector until 1987. In this case the turning-point in the formation of fixed capital

Figure 8.1   Capital–labour ratio, by department

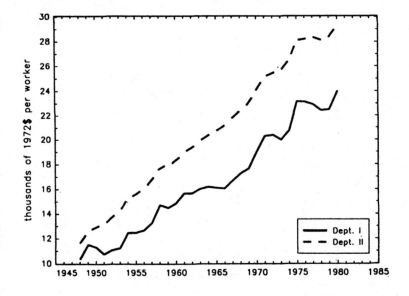

Figure 8.2 Gross investment per worker, by department

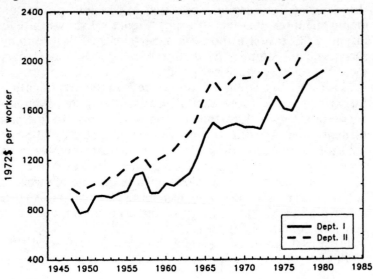

Figure 8.3 Investment per worker in the private economy

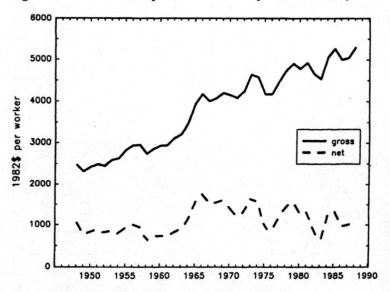

per worker seems to take place as early as the mid-1960s. In the 1980s, the increases in gross investment per worker come to a halt. The surge in investment which occurred in the mid-1980s is barely able to compensate this diminution during the recession of 1981–2. The net investment per worker has a somewhat different evolution. Although nearly constant in the 1950s, it experiences a surge in the early 1960s. From that point on it has exhibited a declining trend. As a consequence, since 1966, capital depreciation accounts for a growing part of gross investment.

The primary reason for capitalists to invest in the mechanization of the labour process is to increase the relative surplus-value obtained through an increase in labour productivity. Remarkable results were indeed achieved during the two first decades of the postwar period. The average rate of productivity growth was larger than in any previous period in the history of capitalism. However these favourable conditions came to an end as early as the mid-1960s. Figure 8.4 plots the labour productivity series for the sphere of production.[2]

The turning-point experienced in the mid-1960s is clearly visible, as is the vigorous recovery after the 1981–2 recession. Figures 8.5 and 8.6 show labour productivity by department (I and II) and sub-department ('i' for intermediary and 'd' for direct). The turning-point of 1966 can be seen to be the same for all the departments, with the exception of the sub-department which produces intermediary goods for the production of consumer goods. The growth of labour productivity is more rapid in Department II as a result of transformations in the sub-department of intermediary goods which has a quite distinct evolution.

In a previous study (Juillard, 1988a and 1988b), an attempt was made to explain statistically the growth in labour productivity of the two departments, using the growth of output and the increase in the capital–labour ratio, based upon a theoretical framework of a generalized Kaldor relationship. A study of the stability of the coefficients shows the disappearance, around 1966, of the constant term, which in this framework corresponds to the effect of

Figure 8.4   Labour productivity in the sphere of production

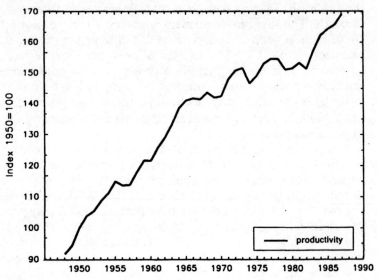

Figure 8.5   Labour productivity index, by department

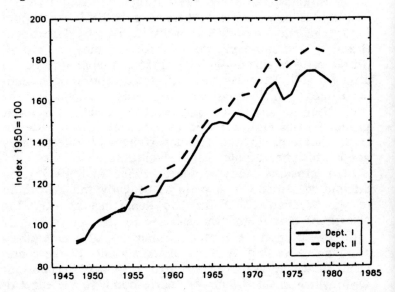

innovation and disembodied technical change.[3] The slow-
down in productivity remains difficult to explain in a satisfactory manner. In an attempt to explain this situation, the
authors of the regulation school refer to an exhaustion of
Fordism, both in its technical and social dimensions
(Aglietta, 1986; Boyer, 1987; Lipietz, 1986). Utilizing a
somewhat different theoretical framework, others, like
Bowles, Gordon and Weisskopf (1984), concentrate their
analysis on the social and subjective factors surrounding
workers' motivations. To the contrary, Shaikh (1987)
stresses the relative slow-down in the accumulation of capital. From yet another perspective, Mandel (1980) concentrates on the exhaustion of the third industrial revolution.
Using any of these theoretical frameworks, it is difficult to
avoid making the slow-down in labour productivity dependent on some factor that is exogenous to the model. At best,
the slow-down in productivity can only be thought of as

Figure 8.6   Labour productivity index, by sub-department

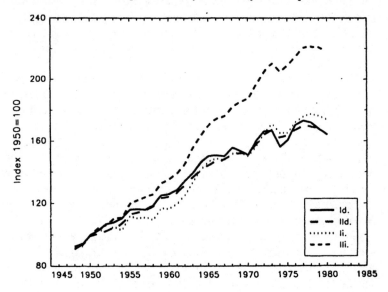

endogenous if it is the result of cumulative and diffuse effects of a large number of the variables. However, on the other hand, the productivity slow-down is sudden and dramatic enough to appear to be triggering the transformation of the regime of accumulation.

2　REAL WAGES AND RELATIVE SURPLUS-VALUE

In Fordism, intensive accumulation must be accompanied by a regular increase in the purchasing power of wage earners and an expansion of the market for consumer goods. This expansion is made possible only through a transformation of the norm of consumption. It implies not only a larger volume of consumption per capita but also the introduction of new types of commodities at a price which makes them affordable to wage earners. Historically this can first be represented by the diminution of the proportion of necessary goods and an increasing importance of durable goods and, later, personal services. In the USA, more than anywhere else, the commodities symbolizing this transformation have been individual homes and motor cars (Aglietta, 1976).

Figure 8.7 shows the evolution of real compensation and real wages per worker on a yearly basis. Compensation includes payments for social security and other benefits. It reflects the total labour cost for enterprises. Wages and salaries are closer to workers' direct earnings before taxes. Both series show a relatively regular growth path. The widening gap between them reflects the growing importance of the components of the indirect wage, mainly composed of employers' contributions to social security, to other social insurances and to pension funds.

The evolution of real compensation shows a net slow-down at the end of the 1960s. In an experiment similar to the one described above for productivity, an attempt was made to regress the rate of growth of real compensation on

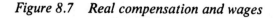

Figure 8.7   Real compensation and wages

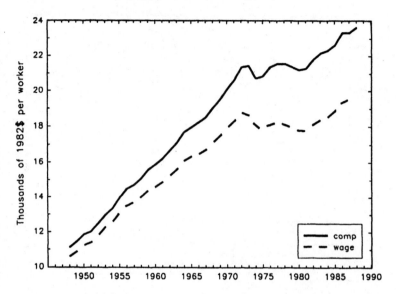

labour productivity growth rate and the change in unemployment. The study of structural stability of the coefficients again shows the disappearance of the autonomous trend, but this time only in 1972 (Juillard, 1988a, 1988b).[4] If confirmed, this result would indicate an inertia in the modalities of wage determination that is not altogether surprising. In conjunction with the productivity slow-down, this inertia had nefarious effects on profitability between 1966 and 1972.

A rough indicator of the evolution of relative surplus-value is given by the real social labour unit cost (Aglietta, 1976). This measure is derived from the wage share corrected for the ratio of the price index of value added to the implicit price index of consumer goods. Figure 8.8 gives the evolution of this ratio for the sphere of the production, both on a compensation basis and on the basis of wages and salaries. Wages and compensation figures have been corrected by taking into account the diminishing weight of self-

Figure 8.8   Real unit labour cost in sphere of production

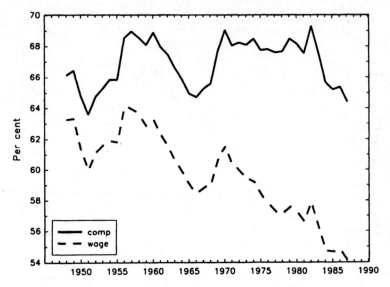

employed people in the labour force.[5] The implicit price deflator for consumer goods is the one corresponding to corrected
consumption as described below.

Labour costs in terms of compensation rise on average from
the early 1950s to the beginning of the 1970s, where they reach
a plateau. The exceptional period of the early 1960s should be
noted as very favourable to the accumulation of surplus-
value. In addition there is a sharp inversion after 1966, which
reflects the lag between the evolution of productivity and of
wage formation. The plateau established during the 1970s is
only briefly broken during the recession in 1982. Following
that, there is a falling tendency of the labour cost indicator.
On the contrary, the picture offered by labour cost in term of
wages is of continual decline since the mid-1950s. The exceptions are, of course, the period between 1966 and 1970 and the
recession of 1981–2. The difference between the two curves is
obviously explained by the rising importance of the indirect
wage.

3   PROFITS AND INVESTMENT

The dynamic of income distribution has a tendency to increase labour costs through an increase in the contributions to social insurances. Figure 8.9 shows the evolution of the share of capital income (depreciation and net interest included) in gross value added by department. The ranking of the two main departments remains the same throughout the period, corresponding to the hierarchy of the intensity of capital usage. Again we find the exceptional character of the early 1960s and the sudden drop in profitability following the turning-point of 1966. The decomposition of value added for the private sector as a whole is presented in Figure 8.10.

Wages are declining, but supplements to wages in the form of contributions to social insurances are increasing, as are capital consumption allowances (depreciations). As a result profits have been declining since 1966. Indirect taxes remain constant.

Figure 8.9   Profit margin, by department (%)

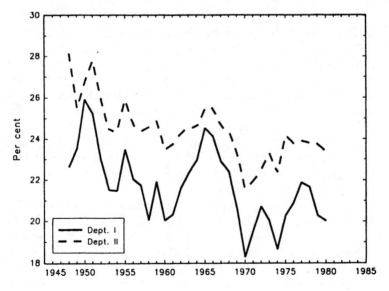

Figure 8.10   Components of value added

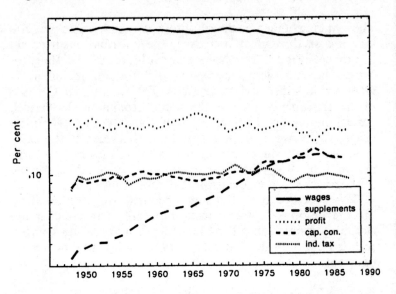

The fall in the rate of profit seen in Figure 8.11 is the result of both the evolution of profit margins and of the capital-output ratio. As shown in Figure 8.12, the capital–output ratio displays increases in the value composition of capital in both departments. In relative terms the phenomenon is more important for Department I. The primary reason for the increase in the capital–output ratio lies in the fact that the gains in labour productivity are not able to be completely offset by the effects of the rise in the technical composition (capital–labour ratio) induced by mechanization. The fact that the productivity of Department I grows more slowly than the average only reinforces this effect.

The trend towards a rising composition of capital is also shown by the evolution of the ratio between gross investment and gross value added. Figure 8.13 shows the evolution of this ratio for the private sector until 1987. The tendency towards a growing importance of investment is only reversed in the 1980s. However, as can be seen, net investment has been

Figure 8.11   Profit rate, by department

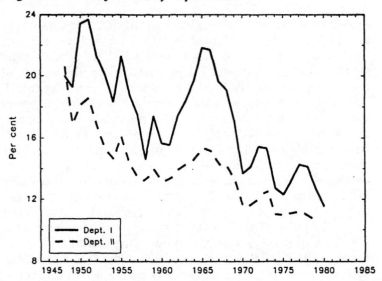

Figure 8.12   Capital–output ratio, by department

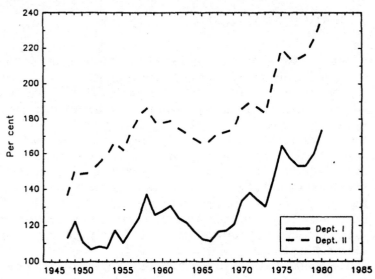

declining since 1966. Figure 8.14 shows the same ratio by department.

The movements of the rate of profit define cycles in the rate of accumulation of fixed capital. They are here approximated by the ratio of gross investment to gross capital stock shown in Figure 8.15. Department I exhibits a rate of accumulation slightly higher than that of Department II. This feature seems consistent with a classical adjustment mechanism from which one would postulate that accumulation would be relatively more important in the sectors with the higher rate of profit. In the same manner, the increasing value composition of capital in these sectors creates a differential in accumulation that induces a faster fall in the rate of profit. The rate of accumulation does not display a downward trend which is comparable to the trend of profitability. This is a reflection of both the increase in the share of profit accumulated and the possibility of using funds made available as a result of the development of the system of indirect wages, primarily by the pension funds.

4   NEW TENDENCIES OF THE 1980s

In many respects the adaptation of the US economy to the crisis of Fordism may appear successful, insofar as the new regime of accumulation seems capable of reproduction without generating insurmountable contradictions. The growth patterns previously based on the growth of productivity and real wages have been replaced by growth of employment, slow gains in productivity and a constant, or even declining, real wage. The very noticeable loss of membership and of power of the trade union movement did not allow a defence of the real wage. In this light, the US experience could provide an example of an adaptation to the crisis where the adjustment cost is mainly shouldered by the working class.

The switch to extensive accumulation was also favoured by the demographic evolution. The 1960s were the time

Figure 8.13 Investment–value added ratio in the private economy

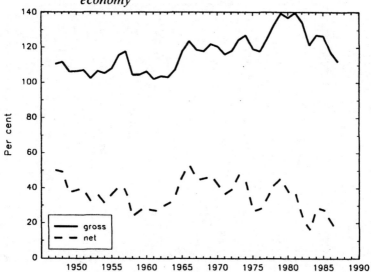

Figure 8.14 Investment–value added ratio, by department

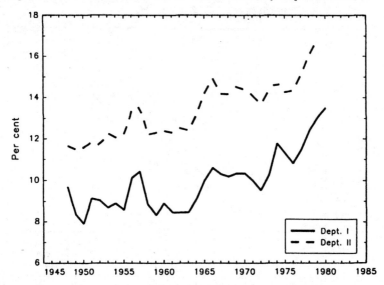

Figure 8.15   Rate of accumulation (I/K), by department

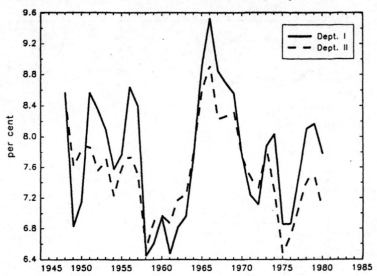

Figure 8.16   Real family income distribution for the lowest and highest fifth of population

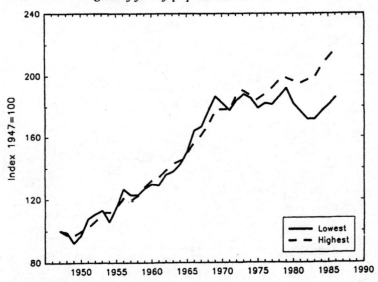

when the first generations of the postwar baby-boom reached the labour market. This increase in the population of working age and the constant increase in the participation rate of women provided the economy with a labour supply ample enough to accommodate this mode of growth without putting upward pressure on wages. On the other hand, even though real wages were not growing, the increase in the average number of household members employed resulted in an increase in average household income, making the freeze of real wages socially more acceptable.

The slow-down in the progression of real income is, however, accompanied by a sharp increase in the inequality of income distribution (see Figure 8.16). Because it could be the source of growing social tensions, the increase in social inequality may be one of the main internal contradictions of a regime of extensive accumulation.

Figure 8.17   Import shares

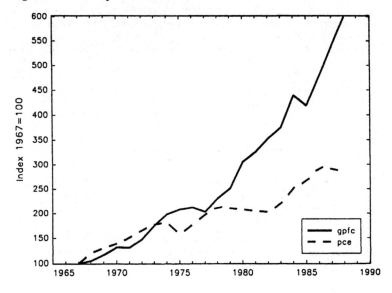

Difficulties appear on the international front. The primary drawback of extensive accumulation is the loss of competitiveness to foreign competition. This occurs not only in relation to Europe and Japan, but also with the newly industrialized countries. The loss of domestic market shares, endemic throughout the 1970s, reaches qualitatively new levels in the 1980s, particularly where production goods are concerned, as shown in Figure 8.17 (where gpfc stands for gross private capital formation and pce for personal consumption expenditures). Obviously the strongest indicator of this is the change in the role of the USA from that of the primary creditor power of the postwar period to that of net debtor.

NOTES

1. I am grateful to Susan Pashkof for her editorial comments in the preparation of this chapter.
2. The sphere of production is defined in this chapter as the private sector less finances, insurance, real estate, business and professional services, and radio/tv.
3. The results of the econometric estimation between 1950 and 1980 are the following. For Department I:

$$P_t = 0.015 + 0.101 \ Q_t + 0.395 \ (K_{t-1} - N_{t-1}) - 0.017 \ D66_t$$
$$(0.005) \quad (0.057) \quad\quad (0.063) \quad\quad\quad\quad (0.006)$$
$$R^2 = 0.66 \ D.W. = 1.58$$

For Department II:

$$P_t = 0.010 + 0.340 \ Q_t + 0.306 \ (K_{t-1} - N_{t-1}) - 0.014 \ D66_t$$
$$(0.003) \quad (0.071) \quad\quad (0.088) \quad\quad\quad\quad (0.003)$$
$$R^2 - 0.84 \ D.W. = 2.54$$

D66 is a dummy variable taking value of 0 before 1966 and 1 later.
4. The results of the econometric estimation between 1950 and 1980 are as follows. For Department I:

$$RW_t = 0.015 + 0.602 \ P_t - 0.228 \ U_{t-1} - 0.208 \ DP_t - 0.018 \ D72_t$$
$$(0.008) \quad (0.226) \quad\quad (0.130) \quad\quad (0.612) \quad\quad (0.009)$$
$$R^2 = 0.71 \ D.W. = 1.74$$

For Department II:

$$RW_t = 0.011 + 0.624\ P_t - 0.049\ U_{t-1} - 0.011\ D72_t$$
$$(0.005)\quad (0.147)\qquad (0.109)\qquad\quad (0.006)$$
$$R^2 = 0.71\ D.W. = 2.05$$

$D72$ is a dummy variable taking value of 0 before 1972 and 1 later. DP is an indicator of the difference in productivity between the two departments.

5. Self-employed people are imputed a wage figure corresponding to the average for employees. The part of noncorporate profit-type income in excess of this imputed wage is then treated as profit.

REFERENCES

Aglietta, Michel (1976), *Régulation et crises du capitalisme*, Paris: Calmann-Lévy.

Aglietta, Michel (1986), 'Etats-Unis: persévérance dans l'être ou renouveau de la croissance' in R. Boyer (ed.), *Capitalismes fin de siècle*, Paris: Presses Universitaires de France.

Bertrand, Hugues (1983), 'Accumulation. régulation, crise: un modèle sectionnel théorique et appliqué', *Revue Economique*, **34**, 305–43.

Bowles, S., D. Gordon and T. Weisskopf (1984), *Beyond the Waste Land*, New York: Anchor Press.

Boyer, Robert (1986), *La théorie de la régulation. Une analyse critique*, Paris: La Découverte.

Boyer, Robert (1987), 'Formalizing growth regimes within a regulation approach: A method for assessing the economic consequences of technological change', Cahier No 8715, Paris CEPREMAP.

Denison, Edward (1974), *Accounting for United States economic growth, 1929–1969*, Washington, DC: The Brookings Institution.

Denison, Edward (1985), *Trends in American economic growth, 1929–1982*, Washington DC: The Brookings Institution.

Juillard, Michel (1988a), *'Un schéma de reproduction pour l'économie des Etats-Unis: 1948–1980. Tentative de modélisation et de quantification'*, PhD dissertation, University of Geneva.

Juillard, Michel (1988b), 'A reproduction scheme for the U.S.: 1950–1980', Working Paper No. 7, Political Economy, New York: New School for Social Research.

Kaldor, Nicholas (1966), *Causes of the Slow Rate of Growth of the United Kingdom*, Cambridge: Cambridge University Press.

Lipietz, Alain (1979), *Crise et inflation, pourquoi?* Paris: Maspéro.

Lipietz, Alain (1982), *Le monde enchanté. De la valeur à l'envol inflationniste*, Paris: La Découverte.

Lipietz, Alain (1986), 'Behind the crisis: The exhaustion of a regime of accumulation. A "regulation school" perspective on some French empirical works', *Review of Radical Political Economy*, **18**, 13–32.

Mandel, Ernest (1980), *Long Waves of Capitalism Development*, London: Cambridge University Press.

Shaikh, Anwar (1987), 'The current economic crisis: Causes and consequences', *Review of Radical Political Economy*, **19**.

PART III
PROFITABILITY, ACCUMULATION AND THE SOCIAL WAGE

9. A Marxian–Keynesian Theory of Investment Demand: Empirical Evidence

James R. Crotty and Jonathan P. Goldstein

In Marxian economic theory, the fundamental laws of motion of capitalism are based, on the microeconomic level, on the individual capitalist's imperative to accumulate capital and, on the macroeconomic level, on the contradictory tendencies of the accumulation process that lead either to periods of disaccumulation (crisis), to strategic microeconomic transitions in the predominant form of the accumulation of capital, or both. Yet the Marxian theory of accumulation has not advanced beyond or fully exploited the simple, although powerful, analysis in Volume I of *Capital*. In particular, the Marxian theory of accumulation must be redirected and extended in order to (1) explain how finance capital both enhances and impinges on the accumulation process; (2) re-emphasize and clarify the mechanisms through which competition acting as a coercive force influences investment decisions; and (3) explain strategic transitions in the mode of accumulation, particularly between the widening and deepening of capital. In addition the theory must be micro-founded in order to avoid the criticisms advanced in Elster (1982, 1983), Goldstein (1985, 1986b) and Roemer (1981, 1982). Finally the resulting theory must be tested empirically. The theory should provide both quantitative and qualitative explanations of postwar economic history.

The purpose of this paper is to: (1) summarize briefly the extensions to the Marxian theory – or more appropriately, the Marxian–Keynesian theory[1] – of investment developed in

Crotty and Goldstein (1990a, 1990b); and, more importantly, (2) specify and conduct econometric tests of the theory. A micro-founded Marxian theory of investment demand and an associated rate of accumulation are developed in which the optimal investment decision depends on expected profitability, the degree of competition, the degree of financial fragility, and managerial attitudes towards a growth–financial safety trade-off. Empirical support for our theory is obtained from regression analysis of the determinants of the rate of accumulation in the US manufacturing sector between 1954 and 1986. Our econometric results establish a strong positive Marxian competition effect and a growth–financial safety or growth–autonomy trade-off in the determination of the level of investment. We find that perceived increases in the degree of 'unsafe' leverage lead to reductions in the rate of accumulation and thus an increased emphasis on financial safety relative to growth. In addition our results support the standard positive effect of expected profitability in Marxian theories of accumulation.

This chapter is divided into three sections. Section 1 summarizes our theory of investment demand. Section 2 specifies and conducts econometric tests of our investment theory. Section 3 contains our concluding remarks.

1   A MARXIAN–KEYNESIAN THEORY OF INVESTMENT DEMAND

The main characteristics of the Marxian theory of accumulation in Volume I of *Capital* can be summarized as follows: (1) competition, acting as a coercive force, compels individual capitalists to maximize surplus-value through the progressive accumulation of capital; (2) given that reinvested surplus-value is the primary defence of the value of the firm's existing capital, the expected profitability of investment is a major determinant of investment demand – the firm, in order to survive, must undertake all projects that are expected to be profitable; (3) under the implicit assumption in Volume I that investment is financed internally, the level of profits also influences investment by acting as a financial constraint on investment demand; (4) the accumulation of capital proceeds either through the widening of capital, the deepening of capital, or combinations of widening and deepening; (5) transitions from one predominant mode to the other (and thus from one microeconomic investment strategy to another) are determined by the nature of the capital–labour relationship and/or the intensity of the competition among capitals and may have important feedback effects on these class relations; (6) under the implicit assumption that capital is illiquid (the firm cannot avoid adverse financial conditions by selling its capital), accumulation is irreversible and increases in the intensity of competition result in either defensive increases in capital-deepening, labour-saving investment, or in a gradual shrinking of the firm that results in its ultimate demise.

Thus the intensity of competition is also a major determinant of the level of investment. Competition as a coercive force can generate 'invest or die' situations for the firm. This effect of competition on investment, which we refer to as the Marxian competition effect, clearly distinguishes the Marxian theory of investment from alternative theories, yet this effect has been neglected and/or sublimated in Marxian analyses of accumulation that focus on profitability as the main determinant of investment activity.

In Crotty and Goldstein (1990a, 1990b), the Marxian theory of the accumulation of capital and thus investment demand is: (1) extended to consider external financing and thus the management–finance capitalist class relationship; (2) extended to include the separation between ownership and control of the firm and thus the manager–stockholder class relationship (or the principal–agent problem); (3) extended to incorporate the influence of Keynesian uncertainty and of financial fragility on accumulation; (4) revised to bring to the forefront the importance of the intensity of competition and thus the capital–capital class relationship and the strategic shifts in investment policy set off by competitive pressures; and (5) restructured as a formal optimization problem (microfoundation) for the capitalist–managerial firm. At the same time the intent of the original theory is preserved: (1) while profits no longer act as a binding financial constraint, expected profitability is still a major determinant of the firm's investment policy because, *ceteris paribus*, the level of investment must maximize profits; (2) the capital–labour relationship affects the investment decision through its effect on expected profits;[2] (3) both forms of accumulation – widening and deepening – are incorporated; (4) the uncertainty of profit flows is modelled; and (5) industrial capital is assumed to be illiquid.

The core assumptions that underlie the models in Crotty and Goldstein (1990a, 1990b) can be summarized as: (1) managers and owners are qualitatively different economic agents and management is in control of the firm; (2) the firm operates in a Marxian competitive environment;[3] (3) the manager, who exerts control over the firm, maximizes a preference function $O(G(I^W,I^D), S(I^W,I^D))$ (subject to the constraints that competition, as a coercive force, places on this decision) where G reflects the growth objectives of the enterprise including expected profitability, S embodies management's concern both for the financial security of the enterprise and for its own decision-making autonomy from finance capitalists (creditors and stockholders) – its financial safety–autonomy objectives – and I^W and I^D are respectively investment by capital widening and investment by capital deepening; (4) industrial capital is illiquid – accumulation of capital by widening or deepening is irreversible; and (5) the firm operates in an environment of 'true' or Keynesian uncertainty.[4]

Thus the I^W, I^D combination that maximizes O is determined by the nexus of class relations impinging on the managerial firm. In particular the managerial–labour, capital–capital and managerial–finance capital relationships interact to determine I^W and I^D.

The managerial firm's optimal investment strategy and the resulting comparative static results are best understood by considering the core of management's decision-making problem: the *growth–safety trade-off* that exists when a marginal increase in investment is considered. But, before we consider this trade-off, some additional discussion of the behaviour of G, S, the competitive constraint, the firm's cash flows, stock of debt, and the firm's relative preference for growth versus financial security are in order.

In our model G is a function of two sub-goals: (1) R, the profits of enterprise in the current period – gross profits flows (total revenue minus total costs) minus the costs of decision-making autonomy (dividends and interest payments); and (2) K, the firm's capital stock in the current period – a measure of the size-status of the firm.[5] R and K represent the profit and size dimensions of management's desire for healthy growth.

Given the existence of external debt, the financing of investment – external or internal – generates, respectively, explicit or implicit cash flow commitments to finance capitalists. Under the assumptions of illiquid capital (irreversible accumulation and debt commitments) and true uncertainty (unknowable future gross profits and cash flows), the manager can never be sure that the finance capital the firm needs for growth purposes will generate enough gross profits to cover its cash flow commitments to finance capitalists – its costs of autonomy. Failure to meet these commitments results in an autonomy crisis. Thus the management's growth strategy is constrained by its need to preserve the financial security of the enterprise and its own decision-making autonomy.

The S function has two arguments: F and D'. F is a short-term index of the likelihood of an autonomy crisis in the current period. In particular, it is the perceived likelihood, based on management's subjective pseudo-probability distribution, that this period's expected gross profit flows (from a given capital stock) will not exceed the firm's costs of autonomy – interest and dividend payments. D' on the other hand, is a measure of the firm's longer-term vulnerability to bankruptcy. It is defined as $(D - D^*)$, the difference between the current level of firm debt and that level of debt that management considers reasonably safe. D^* varies with the size of the firm and with shifts in managerial attitudes towards, and assessments of risk. In particular, $D^* = L^*K$ where L^* is the critical debt–equity ratio that management considers safe. To borrow Minsky's terms (1975, 1986), F and D' are measures of management's perception of the extent to which the firm is either financially fragile or robust in the short and long run, respectively.

The coercive aspects of competition are modelled as follows. Given an uncertain future, the firm makes projections of the determinants of profitability over the course of an investment planning horizon and attempts to maximize the function O. However, if this strategy fails to keep the firm in a position to survive the potential competitive struggles that may take place beyond the planning horizon, it has to be replaced. Suppose that the firm feels it must keep its market share above some critical level below which it will not have the financial, technical or marketing power to withstand future competitive attacks. This critical market share becomes a constraint on O maximization.

Should competitive pressure increase sufficiently to violate the market share constraint, the O maximization strategy *must* be replaced. The firm is coerced into considering strategies it previously considered to be too disruptive and too risky. The firm may undertake major new investment programmes designed to lower unit variable costs through labour substitution, labour reorganization and technological improvement. In addition major bureaucratic restructuring, firing masses of blue- and white-collar workers, closing plants, attacking unions and so on are complementary, but disruptive, parts of the same strategy.

While this new investment programme results in a lower value of O, particularly since the new strategy is likely to have large start-up costs or costs of adjustment, if it is successful it *will* lower variable costs, make the firm 'leaner and meaner', and put the firm in a better position to survive the next round of competitive attack.

Specifically in our model we concentrate on foreign competition and specify the competitive constraint as $P^F - U(I^W, I^D; LS) > C^*$, where P^F is the average foreign price, U is the firm's unit variable cost, LS reflects the firm's labour relations strategy, and C^* is the minimal cushion the firm needs to be able to protect its market share and to survive in a competitive environment. Violation of the constraint must trigger either a change in LS, or less I^W, or more I^D, or more likely some combination of the three.

Our main intention here is to help resolve two problems in the Marxian treatment of the effect of competition on accumulation. First, our approach clearly specifies the way in which competition can 'coerce' firms into investing in the face of deteriorating profitability. Second, we want to insulate our argument against the typical attacks which argue that Marxian firms that do not implement profit-augmenting, cost-cutting investments prior to competitive attacks are operating irrationally and inefficiently.

In our model, the new I^D-dominated strategy was not optimal prior to the violation of the constraint. O maximization over the investment planning horizon may well have entailed an I^W-dominant strategy, and since the constraint was satisfied the firm considered itself to be adequately positioned for any competitive wars that might develop beyond the planning horizon. An I^D-dominant strategy, on the other hand, is dangerous and costly. It might entail a disastrous confrontation with labour, and tension between management and short-sighted shareholders or between upper and lower strata of management. To put the matter more neo-classically, an I^D-dominated strategy might have enormous 'costs of adjustment', such that it will never appear to be optimal over an intermediate-length investment planning horizon.[6] However, when competitive pressure causes a constraint violation that threatens long-term survival, the firm has no choice but to adopt the I^D-dominant strategy and absorb the costs in the short run. *A competition-induced, cost-cutting investment programme undertaken in the face of battered profits and rising financial fragility is a rational development in our model. Moreover the model helps explain transitions in investment strategy, such as the one that took place in manufacturing in the late 1970s and 1980s.*

Finally we consider the firm's relative preferences for growth and safety. Recognizing that $O_G > 0$ and $O_S > 0$ (where subscripts denote partial derivatives), the relative growth–safety preference $\frac{O_G}{O_S}$ depends on the behaviour of O_{GG} and O_{SS}. In the case where the competitive constraint is not binding, we assume that $O_{GS} = O_{GG} = 0$ and $O_{SS} < 0$: the firm's imperative to grow in response to general competitive pressures is a constant unyielding commitment that is independent of the growth level of the firm, while the firm's response to financial security and uncertainty is variable. In particular, at lower levels of financial security, management responds to weakened decision-making autonomy by placing more weight on the financial security objective relative to the growth objective. In the case where the competitive constraint is binding, which is the only case under demand growth conditions where the size of the firm could be reduced by meeting the constraint through I^W reductions, it is assumed that $O_{GG} < 0$ and $O_{SS} < 0$. Furthermore it is assumed in this intensely competitive period that movements in O_G dominate movements in O_S: the investment strategy that satisfies the constraint by shrinking the firm is not the preferred strategy.

Thus the firm's optimization problem can be roughly sketched as to maximize

$$O(G[R(I^W,I^D,C), K(I^W,I^D)], S[F(I^W,I^D,C), D'(I^W,I^D)])$$

subject to

$$C(I^W,I^D) \geq C^*$$

where $C = P^F - U$, $R_C > 0$ and $F_C < 0$: decreases in competition (an increase in C) increase the firm's mark-up, gross profit flows, R, and cash flows and thereby reduces the probability that cash flows cannot meet financial commitments.

We now consider the optimal solution and comparative static results through the G–S trade-off facing the firm. For simplicity we begin with the case where the competitive constraint is not binding and where $I^D = 0$, that is, the costs of adjustment render I^D unprofitable. In this case total investment, $I = I^W$. In Crotty and Goldstein (1990a), it is shown for this case that in the neighbourhood of equilibrium the marginal growth gains from an additional unit of I are positive ($G_I > 0$) and the marginal security gains are negative

(S_I < 0): a *G–S* trade-off exists. Increases in *I* increase *K* and either increase or decrease *R* in such a way that *G* rises,[7] while increases in *I* raise *D'* (as *D* rises faster than the admissible level of debt, *D**) in such a way that its negative impact on *S* is either reinforced by increases in *F* or outweighs the effect of a reduction in *F* on *S*.[8] In addition it is shown that, under standard assumptions about the firm's demand curve and production function, $S_{II} < 0$ and $G_{II} < 0$.[9]

The *G–S* trade-off and optimal level of *I*, *I** are depicted in Figure 9.1. The manager maximizes *O* by choosing *I* at the point where $G_I = -(O_S/O_G)S_I$: increments in *I* are optimal until the point where the marginal growth gains equal the absolute value of the marginal security losses.

While the optimal *I* solution in this case is not determined by the Marxian competition effect, it is consistent with the fundamental principles of a Marxian theory of accumulation, including the more general effect of competition, which work through the imperative to maximize growth, particularly profits. *I** is determined by the full nexus of class relations, discussed above, impinging upon the managerial firm. The extension of the theory to include finance capital under conditions of true uncertainty and illiquid capital establishes the *G–S* trade-off and thus extends the Marxian theory of accumulation and crisis to include one important interaction between the sphere of production and the sphere of circulation. In contrast to the unidirectional financial sector–real sector integration found in the Post-Keynesian literature (Crotty, 1990), where accumulation crises are rooted solely in the financial sector, the integration in our theory is bidirectional. Accumulation-induced or exogenous changes in real sector profitability affect investment both directly through *G* and indirectly through their effect on financial security/autonomy, while independent changes in the firm's relationship with finance capitalists affect *S* and thus *I*.

Comparative static results are best understood by considering changes in the intensity of the *G–S* trade-off set off by a parameter change. Increases in the firm's profit per unit which are generated as the result of demand growth or manager–labour struggle that results in increases in productivity or reductions in wages result in increases in investment demand. In particular, increases in the profit per unit: (1) increase the marginal increment to growth from higher marginal gross profits (shifting G_I to the right); (2) reduce the marginal decline in safety because F_I is reduced by the increase in marginal gross profits (shifting $-(O_S/O_G)S_I$ to the right); and (3) increase the level of S, through higher gross profits that reduce F, such that the relative preference weight on S_I is reduced (O_S/O_G declines, shifting $-(O_S/O_G)S_I$ to the right). Thus I unambiguously rises as the G–S trade-off is weakened – less security must be sacrificed to obtain additional growth.

This result, on both the micro and macro levels, establishes the important Marxian linkage between expected profitability and I. On the micro level, it serves as the basis for understanding profit-induced changes in I demand. On the macro level, it provides a feedback mechanism via which macroeconomic variables, particularly the pace of accumulation, determine

Figure 9.1   The optimal I solution and the G–S trade-off

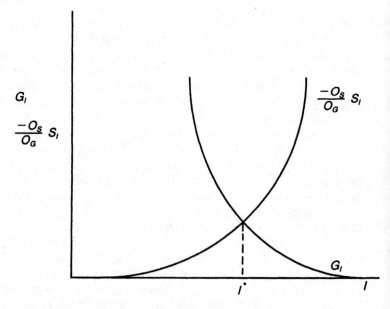

microeconomic profitability and security and thus I. In addition it serves as the basis for an endogenous theory of accumulation crisis that has its roots in both the spheres of production and of circulation.

We now consider the financial determinants of the managerial firm's investment demand. Both increases in the firm's initial stock of debt or in its debt–equity ratio and decreases in L^*, the critical debt–equity ratio that determines the amount of admissible debt, lead to a reduction in I. Both of these parameter changes intensify the $G–S$ trade-off by decreasing the level of S through an increase in D' and thus increasing the relative preference for S (O_S/O_G rises). In addition a decrease in L^* causes the marginal security loss to increase – marginal increments to debt remain unchanged while the marginal increase in admissible debt declines, thus $|D_I'|$ increases and I is further reduced. These effects respectively emphasize that the degree of leverage, along with the mode of financing and the firm's historically and institutionally specific attitude towards long-term debt dependency/vulnerability, affect I behaviour. They infuse the model with important Keynesian insights concerning uncertainty and the importance of financial structures.

In addition it is shown in Crotty and Goldstein (1990a) that, under a reasonable set of conditions, increases in uncertainty, as reflected in the variance of the distribution of the firm's expected profits,[10] increase the intensity of the $G–S$ trade-off by reducing S (F increases) and by increasing marginal security losses (F_I increases). As a result, I declines.

Finally, under realistic assumptions, changes in other parameters produce standard results. Increases in the interest rate, rate of depreciation and price of capital, all of which increase the costs of autonomy,[11] reduce the level of I by increasing the intensity of the $G–S$ trade-off.

In summary, the basic model establishes expected profitability, financial fragility/robustness, and the costs of autonomy as the main determinants of investment demand.[12] The extension of the model to include two forms of investment, I^D and I^W, and the Marxian competition constraint (Crotty and Goldstein, 1990b) does not alter the qualitative nature of the

G–S trade-off or the comparative static results for total $I = I^W + I^D$, discussed above. This extension integrates the special Marxian competitive effect on investment demand and allows competition-coerced transitions in the dominant mode of accumulation to be explained.

In the case where $I^D = 0$ and $I^W > 0$, a decrease in C that causes the competition constraint to bind will force a transition in I policy as I^D becomes the dominant form of I.[13] Depending on the historical conjuncture the transition to I^D may result in a protracted managerial labour struggle over the implementation of new technology. After the transition, either I^W is driven to zero or both I^D and I^W are simultaneously employed.

It is in the post-transition case that all previous comparative static results hold.[14] In this case, it is also shown that the Marxian competition effect is positive. Abstracting from the effect of C on gross profits and under the assumption that movements in O_G dominate movements in O_S when competition intensifies, an increase in C^* or a decline in C increases total I and achieves the necessary cost reduction by stimulating I^D more than I^W is depressed. This is the Marxian competition effect. It is a partial effect which is to be distinguished from the total effect of C on I. In contrast, the total affect of C on I includes the Marxian effect and the negative effect of C on gross profits and thus I. On a priori grounds, this total effect is sign-indeterminate. In situations in which the total effect is positive an interesting profitability–fragility–competition nexus results.[15] *Increases in competition compel the firm to invest more at the same time that profits are declining. As a result the firm's financial position is eroded* on two planes, the higher levels of I increase financial commitments at the same time as cash flows (gross profit flows) are reduced. The likelihood of a short-run autonomy crisis is increased, but I policy is not altered to avert it. Thus an interesting and historically relevant dimension is added to the Marxian theory of accumulation and economic crisis, one rooted in the interaction between the spheres of production and circulation. *In the midst of both profitability and financial crises, competition may compel the firm to continue to accumulate and thus postpone an* *accumulation crisis, while at the same time it creates the conditions for an economic crisis of greater proportions.*[16]

In conclusion, the Marxian theory of investment demand developed in Crotty and Goldstein (1990a, 1990b): (1) preserves the original intent of the Marxian theory of accumulation; (2) extends the theory in several relevant directions; (3) reinterprets the mechanism underlying the Marxian competition effect and re-establishes its importance; (4) provides a microfoundation for Marxian theories of economic crisis rooted in both the spheres of production and of circulation; and (5) formalizes the theory in a manner suitable for econometric testing.

With respect to econometric testing, the above theory establishes: (1) expected profitability; (2) financial fragility/robustness; (3) the intensity of competition; and (4) the costs of autonomy as the main determinants of investment demand. In the next section we specify and conduct econometric tests of our theory of investment demand.

2 ECONOMETRIC SPECIFICATION AND TESTS

In this section we: (1) discuss the theoretical specification of an investment equation; (2) consider an appropriate statistical specification for a test of our I theory using time series data for the US manufacturing sector; (3) discuss the data employed; and (4) report the results of our statistical estimation.

Theoretical Specification

In the last section we concluded that our theory of total investment demand can be summarized as:

$$I = f(R,A,C,B) \tag{9.1}$$

where R is expected net revenues (profits of enterprise), A are the costs of autonomy, $C = P^F - U$ is an index of international competitive pressure, and B is the level of financial robustness/fragility. Recognizing that A affects both B and R, equation (9.1) can be rewritten as

$I = f(R,C,B)$.

In Crotty and Goldstein (1990a, 1990b) it is shown that our theory of I demand is derived from a theory of the desired (optimal) capital stock, K^*.[17] Thus our theory of the desired capital stock is summarized as

$K^* = g(R,C,B)$

Considering the formal specification of our model, (1) $R = \Pi - rD$ where r is the nominal interest rate and D is the stock of debt; and (2) B combines the short- and long-term indices of financial security: F and D'. Since F is based on the dynamically unstable functional form and parameters of the firm's subjective probability density function for expected gross profits and thus cannot readily be made operational in an econometric sense, we restrict B to equal $D' = D - D^*$. D^*, an attitudinal variable, can be thought of as also incorporating the influence of the variance of expected gross profits, a component of F. Finally the level of competition is adequately captured by $C = P^F - U$ at this stage of the specification.

We now consider non-linearities in the formal model. Recognizing that $O_{ss} < 0$ in all cases covered by the model, a non-linearity exists in the effect of financial fragility on investment demand and K^*. The effect of a change in D' on I and K^* depends on the existing level of financial security or D'. Thus the I and K^* functions are non-linear in D'. Considering the simplest non-linear form, I and K^* are specified as quadratic in D'. This specification allows us to test the important interaction between financial conditions and I demand based on a G–S trade-off that intensifies at lower values of S and thus results in deeper declines in I and K^* for a *ceteris paribus* increase in D'. While we recognize that other non-linearities may exist in the model, particularly in the cases where $O_{GG} < 0$, we confine our analysis of non-linear effects to those associated with D'.[18]

In summary, the theoretical specification of our desired capital stock equation can be restated as

$$K^* = g((\Pi - rD), C, D', (D')^2) \qquad (9.2)$$

An equation for net investment, I^N, can be derived from equation (9.2) and the definition for net investment:

$$I^N \equiv K^* - K_{-1} \tag{9.3}$$

where K_{-1} is the actual capital stock in the previous period.

Substituting equation (9.2) in equation (9.3) results in a general equation for I^N:[19]

$$I^N = g((\Pi - rD), C, D', (D')^2) - K_{-1} \tag{9.4}$$

If it is assumed that replacement investment is approximately proportional to the capital stock in the previous period, gross investment, I^g, can be expressed as

$$I^g = g((\Pi - rD), C, D', (D')^2) - (1 - \delta)K_{-1} \tag{9.5}$$

where δ is the rate of depreciation.

We now consider the functional form of g in equations (9.4) and (9.5). In order to separate out the Marxian competition effect from the effect of C on Π and thus I, it is necessary for g to be linear in C and $\Pi - rD$. Expressing the non-linear relationship between D' and I as a quadratic requires that g is linear in D' and $(D')^2$. The most general specification of equation (9.5) requires that the coefficients on Π and rD not be restricted to equal each other. Thus g is also linear in Π and rD. The practical restriction that the impact of financial fragility on I is limited to the effect of D', where D' is not a function of Π, implies that g must also be linear in Π, D' and $(D')^2$. Finally the impact of D' on I is independent of the level of C; thus g is linear in D', $(D')^2$, and C.

Under these restrictions, equation (9.5) can be rewritten as

$$I_t^g = \beta_1 \Pi_t + \beta_2 r_t D_t + \beta_3 C_t + \beta_4 D'_t + \beta_5 (D'_t)^2 + (\delta - 1)K_{t-1} + \epsilon_t \tag{9.6}$$

where $\beta_1 \ldots \beta_5$ are parameters, the t subscript denotes the time period, and ϵ is a random disturbance term whose statistical specification is discussed in the next sub-section.

Statistical Specification

The statistical specification of ϵ_t is now considered. It is assumed that $\epsilon_t \sim N(0, \sigma_t^2)$, ϵ_t is heteroscedastic, and ϵ_t and ϵ_{t-i} are autocorrelated for all t, and particular values of i, $i \neq t$, to be determined by statistical tests. It is assumed that σ_t^2 is a function of the size of the capital stock just prior to the current period's investment flow. In particular, it is assumed that $\sigma_t^2 = aK_{t-1}^2$ for all t where a is a constant. Thus correcting for heteroscedasticity requires that all variables in equation (9.6) be deflated by K_{t-1}. The resulting equation can be written as

$$I_t^g/K_{t-1} = (\delta - 1) + \beta_1(\Pi_t/K_{t-1}) + \beta_2(r_t D_t/K_t) + \\ \beta_3(C_t/K_{t-1}) + \beta_4(D_t'/K_{t-1}) + \beta_5((D_t')^2/K_{t-1}) + V_t \quad (9.7)$$

where $V_t = \epsilon_t/K_{t-1}$ is a homoscedastic error term. Equation (9.7) not only corrects for the heteroscedasticity problem but also establishes an equation for the gross rate of accumulation (I_t^g/K_{t-1}) as a function of the gross profit rate, the rate of competition, and the debt equity ratio (contained in both rD_t/K_t and D_t'/K_t) – an index of financial fragility.[20]

Before making the explanatory variables in equation (9.7) operational, we make some further adjustments to the equation to be estimated. First, in order to preserve the non-linear relationship between the rate of accumulation and the firm's financial security, we substitute $(D_t'/K_{t-1})^2$ for $(D')^2/K_{t-1}$ in equation (9.7). Second, we recognize that both $r_t(D_t/K_{t-1})$ – the rate of autonomy costs – and D_t'/K_{t-1} are functions of the debt–equity ratio; thus a multicollinearity problem exists, particularly if D^* is in part a function of the debt–equity ratio, as is argued below. More importantly, a potential interpretation problem exists in distinguishing between the effect of the debt–equity ratio (financial fragility) and of autonomy costs on I. Given the importance of the non-linear financial security effect in our theory and given that variations in the rate of autonomy costs are heavily influenced by fluctuations in r_t, we consolidate all debt–equity effects – those related to autonomy costs and financial fragility – in the D' and $(D')^2$ terms and use

r_t as a separate variable to capture the dominant cost of autonomy effects. Finally, we assume that all rates associated with the independent variables are based on K_t rather than K_{t-1} as the scale factor. Incorporating these modifications into equation (9.7), we can rewrite the rate of accumulation of gross investment equation as

$$I_t^g/K_{t-1} = (\delta - 1) + \beta_1(\Pi_t/K_t) + \beta_2 r_t + \beta_3(C_t/K_t) + \beta_4(D'_t/K_t) + \beta_5((D'_t/K_t)^2) + V_t \tag{9.8}$$

An equation for the net rate of accumulation is derived by subtracting δ from the right side of equation (9.8).

We now construct the dependent and independent variables from existing data sources. While the gross and net rates of accumulation, *GRA* and *NRA*, and the rate of interest, r, can readily be constructed from existing data, the expected gross profit rate, *EGPR*, the rate of competition, and D'_t/K_{t-1} need further elaboration.

Under Keynesian uncertainty, we assume that the firm bases its projection of the future gross profit rate on the past performance of the gross profit rate, *GPR*. Thus $EGPR = \sum_{s=0}^{k} \gamma_s(\Pi_{t-s}/K_{t-s}) = \sum_{s=0}^{k} \gamma_s GPR_{t-s}$ where γ_ss are constants and $0 < \gamma_s < 1$. Given that measures of *GPR* are readily available, *EGPR* can be constructed.

The level of competition ($P^F - U$) determines the level of net exports, $M - X$, where M is imports and X is exports. The rate of competition can be formed by dividing $M - X$ by an appropriate output measure Q which is directly related to the level of K. An alternative, but similar, measure of the rate of competition which is standard in empirical work is the import penetration ratio, *IPR*: $M/(Q - X)$.[21] In our empirical work we employ the latter. If the firm projects the rate of competition from current and past values of the import penetration ratio, the expected import penetration ratio $EIPR = \sum_{s=0}^{m} \phi_s IPR_{t-s}$ where ϕ_s is a distributed lag coefficient and $0 < \phi_s < 1$.

The case of D'_t/K_t is complicated by the inclusion of an attitudinal variable D^* in D'. Recognizing that $D'_t/K_t = (D_t/$

K_t) $- (D_t^*/K_t) = L - L^*$ where L is the degree of leverage (debt–equity ratio) and L^* is a critical debt–equity ratio based on the manager's attitude to financial risk, we assume that L^* is determined by past values of L and by Z, a vector of variables that control the adjustment of L^* for changes in L. Thus $L^* = j(\sum_{s=1}^{l} \alpha_s L_{t-s}, Z)$ where Z may include the bankruptcy rate, the rate of hostile takeovers, the frequency of refinancing under financial duress and so on. In other words, it is hypothesized that higher debt–equity ratios, particularly those that rise above recent historical trends, which do not alter the perceived level of financial risk, as captured by Z, are gradually incorporated into the manager's perception of a reasonably safe leverage rate. In periods in which Z indicates that recent L levels are more risky, the adjustment of L^* on the basis of past values of L is less complete and slower as managers are more reluctant to accommodate to a higher L level: Z determines both l, the length of the adjustment period, and the $\alpha_s s$, the extent of the adjustment over that period. Thus the function j summarizes a behavioural process whereby management may or may not adjust to higher debt–equity ratios.

Under the above specification, L^*, $L - L^*$ is a function solely of present and past values of L where the length of the lag on L is determined by the manager's assessment of the level of financial risk which is unobservable. Thus the $L - L^*$ variable can be constructed as $(L - L^*) = L_t - \sum_{s=1}^{l} \alpha_s L_{t-s} = h(L)$ and the length of the lag, l can be estimated econometrically.

An observation on the implications of the L^* lag structure is in order. Increases in L will at first raise $L - L^*$ and reduce financial security because L^* is slow to adjust. This will result in a decline in GRA and NRA in the current period. Given the non-linear specification of the effect of $(L - L^*)$ on GRA, the gradual adjustment of L^* in subsequent periods will result initially in further declines in GRA, and then in increases in GRA as L^* rises. The extent of the recovery in GRA, once a new steady state is reached, depends on the extent of the adjustment in L^*. The extent of the recovery in GRA and thus the extent of the adjustment in L^* can be tested econometrically by calculating the overall impact of $(L-L^*)$ on GRA from the sum of estimated lag coefficients. In addition the proposed time distribution of the effects of $L-L^*$ on GRA – negative effects in the early periods and positive effects in later periods – can be econometrically tested from the estimated lag coefficients. Finally the length of the lag and thus the (un)conservative nature of the adjustment process, based on the degree of perceived risk, can also be determined in our econometric specification.

Rewriting equation (9.8) in its operational form and by taking into account the possibility of (unforeseen) gestation lags and a constant term as a result of aggregation,[22] we arrive at an equation for the gross rate of accumulation *decision*, $GRAD$:

$$GRAD_t = \beta_0 + \beta_1 EGPR_t + \beta_2 r_t + \beta_3 EIPR_t + \beta_4(h(L)) + \beta_5(h(L))^2 + V_t$$

Recognizing that GRA_t is itself a distributed gestation lag on $GRAD_t$, we can write

$$\dot{GRA}_t = \sum_{s=0}^{p} w_s GRAD_{t-s} \qquad (9.9)$$

where w_s, for $s = 0 \ldots p$, is a set of lag coefficients and $0 < w_s < 1$ for all s.

Given that a gestation lag of length p on explanatory variables which consist of distributed lags of length q results in a distributed lag of length $p + q$, the estimating equation for GRA, equation (9.9), is a distributed lag of length $p + k$ in GPR, of length $p + m$ in IPR, of length p in r and of length $p + l$ in L and L^2. Thus equations (9.8) and (9.9) can be written as

$$GRA_t = \beta_0 + \sum_{s=0}^{p+k} \beta_{1s} GRP_{t-s} + \sum_{s=0}^{p+m} \beta_{2s} IPR_{t-s} + \sum_{s=0}^{p} \beta_{3s} r_{t-s} +$$

$$\sum_{s=0}^{p+1} \beta_{4s} L_{t-s} + \sum_{s=0}^{p+1} \beta_{5s} L_{t-s}^2 + v_t \tag{9.10}$$

where β_{is} and β_0 are parameters to be estimated.

The definition and construction of GRA, NRA, r, GPR, IPR and L are discussed in the next section. The generalized least squares estimates of the parameters in equation (9.10) are derived and reported subsequent to the discussion of the data.

The Data

Our theory of accumulation is empirically tested by estimating the distributed lag equation in equation (9.10). Two equations are tested – the above equation for GRA and an analogous equation for NRA – using postwar data, both annual and quarterly, for the US manufacturing sector. The manufacturing sector is chosen because we feel that it affords the best test of the important Marxian competition effect. Alternative choices such as the more highly aggregated non-financial corporate business sector or the sectors encompassed by the measure of business fixed investment and gross private domestic investment include industries that have been either heavily regulated or for which competition, particularly foreign competition, is not a viable issue. Worse yet, there is no reasonable index of the degree of competition for these sectors. Thus we confine our analysis to the manufacturing sector. We now consider the construction from existing data of the variables contained in equation (9.10).

GRA   In order to construct a consistent GRA series where the numerator and denominator of GRA are both calculated on the same basis (establishment basis), GRA is constructed from the US Department of Commerce annual capital stock series for manufacturing from 1947 to 1986 contained in *Fixed Reproducible Tangible Wealth in the U.S., 1925–85* and various updates. Gross investment is defined as the change in the year-end constant cost gross capital stock of fixed non-residential private capital (equipment and structures) plus the constant cost valuation of total discards for all manufacturing. Gross investment in period t is divided by the constant cost valuation of the net capital stock (equipment and structures) lagged one period in order to generate an annual series (1947–86) for *GRA*. A quarterly series for *GRA* is created by estimating the best linear unbiased (*BLU*) distribution, from annual to quarterly data, of the gross investment variable using a related time series[23] – new plant and equipment expenditures by manufacturing business from the Department of Commerce survey of plant and equipment expenditure – and by dividing the resulting investment series by the series resulting from the linear distribution, from annual to quarterly, of the net capital stock.

NRA The *NRA* series, both annual and quarterly, are constructed analogously to the *GRA* series by subtracting the constant cost valuation of depreciation from gross investment.[24]

GPR Gross profits are defined as corporate manufacturing profits (net of operating expenses) before taxes (with IVA) plus corporate manufacturing net interest (interest paid minus interest received) minus federal, state and local corporate manufacturing profits tax liability where all series are in current dollars. The *GPR* is constructed by dividing gross profits by the current cost valuation of the net capital stock for corporate manufacturing.[25] The series that comprise the numerator of *GPR* are from the US Department of Commerce, NIPA, from 1947–86. The annual series on *GPR* is derived from annual data on these series, while the quarterly series is generated from quarterly data on profits and the linear distribution of the capital stock, tax liability, and net interest series.

r The real interest rate series is defined as Moody's Industrial BAA bond rate minus the expected rate of inflation for manufacturing output prices. The expected inflation rate is generated as a distributed lag on the percentage change in manufacturing prices which in turn is calculated from the GNP deflator for the price of manufacturing output.[26] This series is readily available in both annual and quarterly variants for the years 1947–86.

IPR The import penetration ratio is defined as the value

of manufacturing imports for consumption to the value of manufacturing shipments less the value of manufacturing exports, which is the percentage of the manufacturing sector's domestic market that is captured by imports. Annual import and export data were compiled from various issues of *U.S. Commodity Exports and Imports as Related to Output* (US Department of Commerce) for the years 1958–82. Manufacturing shipments data were compiled from various issues of *Current Industrial Reports* (US Department of Commerce). Given the limited time span for the import and export data, the annual *IPR* series was extended to cover the years 1947–86 by using the *BLU* forecast and backcast of the *IPR* from a forecasting and a backcasting equation based on a related time series – an economy wide *IPR* derived from NIPA data on imports, GNP and exports.[27] Finally a quarterly series for *IPR* from 1947 to 1986 is generated from the *BLU* distribution of *IPR* using a related time series from 1958–82 and the *BLU* backcasts and forecasts for the remaining quarters.[28]

L The leverage ratio employed is the debt–equity ratio.The *L* series is compiled from the debt–equity ratio for manufacturing in various issues of the *Quarterly Financial Report for Manufacturing Corporations*, 1947–86 (US Department of Commerce). The series is available on both an annual and quarterly basis. The debt component of the ratio is based on the market value of the current stock of debt, while the equity component is based on book value. To our knowledge, no current value series for manufacturing equity is available.

The quarterly series for *GRA*, *NRA*, *GPR*, *r*, *IPR* and *L* are depicted in Figures 9A. 1–6 in the appendix.

Results

Regression results for *GRA* and *NRA* equations based on annual data for 1954–86 and quarterly data for 1954:2–1986:2 are respectively reported in Tables 9.1 and 9.2,[29] which report the current period lag coefficient, the sum of lag coefficients for each variable, AR (autoregressive) and MA (moving average) coefficients, and a series of summary statistics. Annual equations report an MA(1) coefficient and quarterly equations report AR(1) or AR(1) and AR(2) coefficients. A complete set of distributed lag coefficients is available upon request. All equations are estimated using generalized least squares (GLS) with the Cochrane-Orcutt procedure to correct for serial correlation. Lag structures are estimated by a polynomial distributed lag (PDL). Reported summary statistics include R^2, the Durbin-Watson statistic (d), and the Q statistic (portmanteau test) based on 8 and 25 (Q_8, Q_{25}) lags for annual and quarterly equations.[30]

All distributed lag coefficients with the exception of the L and L^2 coefficients lie on an unrestricted second-degree polynomial in the annual equations and an unrestricted third-degree polynomial in the quarterly equations. The L and L^2 coefficients lie on unrestricted third- and fourth-degree polynomials respectively in the annual and quarterly cases.[31] In order to prevent an upward bias in the length of the lag, lag lengths were chosen on the basis of $F > 2$ associated with tests of linear restrictions, rather than the maximum $\bar{R}^2$. Annual lag lengths for *GPR*, *IPR*, *r*, *L* and L^2 are respectively: 3, 3, 1, 7 and 7. Quarterly lag lengths are respectively: 12, 12, 6, 28 and 28. In order to preserve degrees of freedom in the annual case the *r* lag is run in its unrestricted least squares form and reported under *r* and *r*(-1) (*r* lagged one period) in Table 9.1.

The results in Tables 9.1 and 9.2 provide strong empirical support for the Marxian theory of accumulation developed in Section 1. In particular the overall Marxian competition effect, which isolates the firm's response to increased competitive pressures holding other factors, particularly the profit rate, constant, is large and significant. The manufacturing sector responds to increased competition by defending its existing capital through new investment, presumably geared at cost reduction rather than output enhancement. Based on the equations in Table 9.2, a 0.01 increase in *IPR* results in a 0.015 increase, approximately, in *GRA* and *NRA*.[32]

While the results reported here cannot provide conclusive support for the behavioural mechanisms outlined in our theory, they are not inconsistent with our theory and in combination with the other results they allow us to explain the stylized facts of the postwar period (see Section 3) in a manner

*Table 9.1   Rate of accumulation equations, annual data
(1954–1986)**

Independent variable and summary statistic	Dependent variable: equation no.	
	GRA-eq. (1)	NRA-eq.(2)
Constant	−0.384	−0.483
	(−2.26)	(−2.82)
r	−3.61	−0.390
	(−1.69)	(−1.78)
r(−1)	0.052	0.073
	(0.17)	(0.244)
GPR		
Current period	0.419	0.397
	(4.27)	(4.02)
Sum of coefficients	1.28	1.24
	(3.02)	(2.89)
IPR		
Current period	1.14	0.969
	(0.90)	(0.748)
Sum of coefficients	2.41	2.10
	(2.16)	(1.86)
L		
Current period	−0.898	−0.758
	(−1.04)	(−0.872)
Sum of coefficients	1.86	1.98
	(2.27)	(2.39)
L^2		
Current period	1.02	0.855
	(1.09)	(0.902)
Sum of coefficients	−3.43	−3.48
	(−2.09)	(−2.11)
MA(1)	−0.915	−0.853
	(−2.41)	(−2.28)
R^2	0.91	0.92
d	1.81	1.82
Q_8	4.36	4.63

Note: *t statistics in parentheses.

Table 9.2 Rate of accumulation equations, quarterly data (1954:2–1986:2)*

Independent variable and summary statistic	Dependent variable: equation no.			
	GRA-eq.(3)	GRA-eq.(4)	NRA-eq.(5)	NRA-eq.(6)
Constant	−0.285	−0.304	−0.413	−0.430
	(−3.86)	(−4.13)	(−5.58)	(−5.87)
r				
Current period	−0.072	−0.074	−0.073	−0.076
	(−0.931)	(−0.924)	(−0.967)	(0.970)
Sum of coefficients	−0.213	−0.222	−0.278	−0.284
	(−1.84)	(−2.01)	(−2.38)	(−2.54)
GPR				
Current period	0.082	0.083	0.077	0.078
	(4.72)	(4.60)	(4.48)	(4.36)
Sum of coefficients	1.00	1.03	1.04	1.06
	(7.01)	(6.90)	(7.28)	(7.16)
IPR				
Current period	0.510	0.453	0.469	0.422
	(2.30)	(1.92)	(2.16)	(1.82)
Sum of coefficients	1.58	1.63	1.45	1.49
	(3.65)	(3.76)	(3.34)	(3.43)
L				
Current period	−2.77	−0.289	−0.288	−0.287
	(−1.37)	(−1.31)	(−1.44)	(−1.31)
Sum of coefficients	1.51	1.61	1.76	1.86
	(3.74)	(4.12)	(4.33)	(4.74)
L^2				
Current period	0.346	0.370	0.362	0.371
	(1.50)	(1.48)	(1.58)	(1.50)
Sum of coefficients	−2.61	−2.78	−2.93	−3.08
	(−3.55)	(−3.86)	(−3.96)	(−4.28)
$AR(1)$	0.738	0.799	0.746	0.809
	(11.18)	(7.02)	(11.65)	(8.14)
$AR(2)$	–	−0.125	–	−0.118
		(−1.28)		(−1.21)
R^2	0.97	0.97	0.97	0.97
d	1.86	2.05	1.86	2.05
Q_{25}	16.54	16.44	16.89	17.15

Note: *t statistics in parentheses.

that supports our behavioural theory: firms are coerced by competitive pressures to take on increased risks and higher levels of debt which were previously not optimal in the hope of surviving the competitive onslaught, thus increasing financial fragility in an already crisis-prone environment.

In addition, the *GPR* has an important impact on *GRA* and *NRA*. An increase of 1 per cent in *GPR* results in a 1 per cent overall increase approximately in the rate of accumulation. The profit rate acts as the traditional Marxian attractor of new investment. Higher expected profits signal profit advantages that the profit-maximizing firm in a competitive environment cannot afford to pass over if it is to improve or maintain its competitive position and thus its chance of survival.

The *GPR* result also establishes an important micro-macroeconomic linkage for the transmission of economic crisis. *Ceteris paribus*, changing macroeconomic conditions that affect microeconomic profitability can result in an accumulation crisis.

The non-linear effect of financial security on investment/accumulation is also strongly supported by our results. The overall effect of L on *GRA* can be expressed as $\partial GRA/\partial L = \hat{S}_L + 2\hat{S}_{L^2}L$, where $\hat{S}_L$ and $\hat{S}_{L^2}$ are respectively the sum of the lag coefficients for L and L^2 and $\partial NRA/\partial L$ is defined analogously. The results in Tables 9.1 and 9.2 reveal that $\partial GRA/\partial L \gtrless 0$ and $\partial NRA/\partial L \gtrless 0$ for $L \lesseqgtr 0.29$. *From the appendix it can be shown that $\partial GRA/\partial L < 0$ and $\partial NRA/\partial L < 0$ from 1965:4, the beginning of the period in which the first rapid postwar rise in L takes place.* Between 1965:4 and 1986:2, $\partial GRA/\partial L$ and $\partial NRA/\partial L$ range approximately between 0 and -1.80 and decrease steadily throughout the period as L rises. Statistical tests reveal that, in the relevant range of L, $\partial GRA/\partial L$ and $\partial NRA/\partial L$ are statistically indistinguishable from zero in the period 1954–65. Thus $\partial GRA/\partial L$ and $\partial NRA/\partial L$ are effectively zero in the early period and increasingly negative through the latter period (1966–86) when L rises dramatically: as the G–S tradeoff intensifies, the firm reduces its investment demand and the rate of accumulation. In the relevant historical period, the absolute size of the decline in investment per unit rise in L is related to the degree of debt leverage: at higher values of L,

$|\partial GRA/\partial L|$ and $|\partial NRA/\partial L|$ increase. These results establish the important linkage between financial conditions and the rate of accumulation discussed above.

This result is different from the typical Post-Keynesian treatment of debt leverage and investment demand. Our theory is based on $L\text{-}L^*$ rather than L alone. The inclusion of L^*, an attitudinal variable towards financial risk, implies that higher levels of L do not necessarily deter investment. It is only when higher levels of L are perceived as unsafe that investment is adversely affected. Our approach emphasizes the historically specific attitudes of managers towards financial risk.

We now consider the full lag distribution, not reported, associated with the L and L^2 variables. The lag structure reveals, in general, for relevant values of L ($0.24 \leq L \leq 0.55$) that $\partial GRA/\partial L$ and $\partial NRA/\partial L$ are negative in the current and early lagged periods and then positive for latter lags. While this pattern does offer some support for our hypothesis that the firm's perception of a reasonably safe level of L adjusts slowly over time in response to changes in L and that investment may recover, the support is not conclusive. First, the sign change does not occur for all levels of L. For values of $L > 0.45$ the sign change is sporadic. Second, there is a tendency in most equations for the sign of the L effect to switch back to negative towards the end of the lag period. In these instances the absolute value of the L effect is small and presumably not statistically different from zero. Given the high degree of multicollinearity in the sample data, it may be unrealistic to hope to distinguish the fine detail of the lag structure proposed by our theory from our estimation results.

With respect to the length of the L and L^2 lags and the overall effect (discussed above), the long lag length suggests that *the adjustment of L^* in response to an increase in L is very slow and* a negative overall L effect on GRA and NRA suggests that the adjustment is *incomplete*. Both these results are to be expected. A lag length of seven years, depending on the length of the gestation lag, suggests an adjustment period of between four and five and a half years. In an historical period characterized by two large increases – from 1965 to 1970 and in the

1980s – in L one would expect a conservative managerial attitude towards financial risk, particularly in the latter years when firms were compelled to take on new debt due to increasing competitive pressures. Thus L^* is likely to adjust slowly. Under the same circumstances, it is also expected that the adjustment in L^* is only partial: *ceteris paribus*, increasing financial fragility has kept management consistently uncomfortable with its degree of leverage.

The overall r effect on GRA and NRA is estimated to be negative and significant. Compared to the GPR, IPR and L effects, the magnitude of this effect is less substantial.

In general, the full lag structures, not reported here, take on the standard inverted U shape that is expected when expectational and gestational lags are combined. With the exception of the lag structure for L and L^2, discussed above, the lag distributions imply a gestation lag and an expectational lag of one and half to two years in length. Both lags seem reasonable on a priori grounds.

Finally an examination of the residuals associated with the six equations reported in Tables 9.1 and 9.2 reveals that we have avoided a problem in estimating (forecasting) investment in the 1980s that has troubled more standard investment equations (theory q, the neo-classical model) but are not endemic in our model. Other models have systematically underpredicted the strength of investment in the late 1970s and 1980s.[33] In contrast, an examination of the residuals in our equations shows that the problem of systematic underprediction is not present. Our equations tend to be as likely to generate positive residuals as they are to generate negative residuals.

The significance of the GPR, IPR, L nexus in explaining postwar accumulation is addressed in our concluding section.

3 CONCLUSION

The main objective of this chapter has been to summarize and, more importantly, empirically support a Marxian micro-founded theory of accumulation. It has been argued that the optimal investment decision depends on the level of expected profitability, the degree of competition and the degree of financial fragility. Empirical support for our theory is obtained from a polynomial distributed lag regression analysis of the determinants of the rate of accumulation in the US manufacturing sector between 1954 and 1986 (where competition is confined to the degree of international competition). Our econometric results establish a strong Marxian competition effect – increases in the intensity of competition compel the firm to undertake additional investment in order to defend its existing illiquid capital. Our results also strongly support the notion of a growth–financial security/autonomy tradeoff in the determination of the level of investment: *ceteris paribus*, perceived increases in the degree of 'unsafe' leverage lead to reductions in the rate of accumulation and thus the growth objectives of the firm. In addition, our results support the standard strong positive effect of expected profitability in Marxian theories of accumulation.

In addition, the profit rate–competition–financial security nexus allows us to explain important trends in the post-war accumulation of capital. In particular, the tendency to a strong rate of accumulation in the face of declining profit rates and increasing financial fragility is explained by this nexus.

NOTES

1. The Keynesian aspects of the theory are associated with the nature of uncertainty and the role of financial markets on investment decisions. In particular the firm's financial position under conditions of uncertain cash flows influences its investment decisions through the manager's concern for the preservation of financial security and decision-making autonomy from finance capitalists. While the incorporation of the manager–finance capitalist relationship can be argued to be consistent with Marxian analysis, the concepts of 'true' uncertainty and financial fragility are more fully developed in the works of Keynes and the Post-Keynesians, respectively. Thus we feel that it is appropriate to make reference to the Keynesian influences on our Marxian theory of investment.

2. Changes in the capital–labour relationship and their impact on profitability and investment are not a focus in the models in Crotty and Goldstein (1990a, 1990b). Their effect on investment is captured through the mark-up and is thus treated as exogenous. The important

dynamic relationship between capital–labour relations and investment decisions in one of its forms – the cyclical profit squeeze – has been analysed in Boddy and Crotty (1975) and Goldstein (1985).

3. In Marxian theory competition is a continuous process of struggle over market shares, growth rates, profits and survival; a struggle that varies in intensity over time but never permanently ceases. Since the primary objective of the Marxian firm is to reproduce itself, the concept of Marxian competition implies that firms will seek to take advantage of all new investments that will help them grow, command greater profits and protect the viability of their existing, illiquid capital assets.

   But Marxian competition has effects other than this. It generates an unstable, dangerous and above all unpredictable environment within which the firm operates. Within this environment there is no unique, optimal profit or expected profit maximizing investment decision. As explained below, we think that this Marxian competitive environment creates a distinctive effect on investment. When confronted with an intense competitive attack, a Marxian firm may face an uncertain 'invest or die' decision. Either they invest in variable cost-cutting, labour-saving new capital in the face of deteriorating markets and profits or face a short-to-intermediate-term threat of marginalization or even bankruptcy. This decision is not about whether such investment is or is not long-run profit maximizing: the firm cannot know whether it is or it is not. It is a question of staying in the 'game' or getting out. In the spirit of Marx's theory, we assume that many firms will choose to stay in the game.

4. Under 'true' or Keynesian (or Knightian) uncertainty the future is *unknowable* in principle. Neo-classical theory uses a subjective probability density function to capture the effect of 'risk'. But, as has been stressed by Post-Keynesian writers, this approach is adequate only for successive outcomes produced by a knowable and unchanging generating mechanism. The outcomes in economics are not so generated: knowledge, institutions and agents all change with each successive 'draw'.

   Keynes rejected the probability calculus and its implications for the theory of investment and of portfolio selection. He insisted that firms and wealth-holders could never obtain the information they needed to make rational decisions, yet had to make them nevertheless. As a result, firms develop psychological, sociological and institutionally-specific strategies for dealing with investment decisions under Keynesian uncertainty. Such strategies introduce instability and an historical open-endedness into the theory of investment.

   It is our belief that a satisfactory investment theory must reflect in a significant way the environment of Keynesian uncertainty within which the firm operates.

5. The optimal investment decision discussed in this chapter is derived from a static – one-period – model of investment. In Crotty and

Goldstein (1990a, 1990b) it is shown that the sequential implementation of this solution is equivalent to dynamic optimization under the assumptions invoked here.

6. In addition we assume that the output enhancing effects of I^w exceed those of I^D, implying that I^w may also be preferred to I^D on these grounds.

7. The inclusion of K in the G function along with the traditional R variable allows for the possibility of a marginal size–net revenue trade-off. Thus the sign of R_I is indeterminate.

8. The sign indeterminacy of F_I depends on the size and sign of R_I which is indeterminate. While increases in I increase financial obligations, the probability that expected gross profits do not exceed those obligations depends on the size and sign of the marginal change in gross profits. The existence of a potential size–revenue trade-off (n.7) implies that the marginal change in gross profits could be small or even negative.

9. If $P(Q)$ is the inverse demand curve and $Q(K,L)$ the production function, then these conditions hold when $P_Q < 0$, $P_{QQ} \leq 0$, $Q_K > 0$ and $Q_{KK} \leq 0$.

10. These results are shown to hold for both a uniform and a normal probability distribution of gross profits.

11. Increases in the interest rate and the price of capital both raise interest payments to creditors, while increases in the depreciation rate increase replacement investment, which in turn raises the amount of debt financing.

12. It should be noted that the costs of autonomy and the firm's level of financial fragility/robustness are not independent. On the one hand, increases in costs of autonomy are increases in the firm's financial commitments and thus are responsible for reductions in financial robustness. On the other hand, the costs of autonomy differentiate the Marxian concept of gross profits from the concept of profit of enterprise (gross profits minus interest payments) and it is in this context that they are included as a determinant of investment demand.

13. When $I^D = 0$ the only way the competitive constraint can be met is if I^D increases – a reduction in I^w cannot lower unit costs because the composition of output cannot be shifted to lower unit cost production when $K^D = 0$. Given that substantial costs of adjustment, which raise unit costs, are associated with I^D, large increments in I^D are necessary to ultimately offset the adjustment costs and thus reduce unit costs. Thus the transition to I^D establishes I^D as the dominant mode of accumulation.

14. Comparative static results are undefined for the case in which there is a discontinuous transition-induced jump in the choice variables.

15. A positive total effect is a strong condition for the resulting situation. The same results could be obtained with negative total effects of specific magnitudes.

16. The thesis that a Marxian theory of competition is required to make sense of the simultaneous occurrence of a falling rate of profit, rising

17. This equivalence requires that gestation lags are unforeseen and that all costs of adjustment with the exception of those associated with a change in the mode of accumulation are negligible.

    corporate indebtedness and a surprisingly strong rate of accumulation is not original here: Pollin (1986) has stated it quite clearly. What is original, we believe, is that we have shown that such behaviour is consistent with a rational investment strategy.

17. This equivalence requires that gestation lags are unforeseen and that all costs of adjustment with the exception of those associated with a change in the mode of accumulation are negligible.

18. The $O_{GG} < 0$ assumption is necessitated by the mathematical structure of the model, particularly the behaviour of U. It ensures that cuts in I^W are not the primary method by which firms reduce costs to meet the competition. Given that it is commonplace for actual firms to meet the competition through increases in cost-cutting investment, the $O_{GG} < 0$ assumption is particular to the structure of our model and need not be incorporated in the econometric specification.

19. We implicitly assume that K_{-1} is not equivalent to K^*_{-1}. Under Keynesian uncertainty it is realistic to assume that the adjustment to the previous period's desired capital stock is slow, and under the Marxian concept of competition, discontinuous changes in investment strategies are possible. Thus it is consistent with the core assumptions of our analysis to assume that $K_{-1} \neq K^*_{-1}$ and that I^N is based on K^*_{-1}.

20. In contrast to typical adjustments for heteroscedasticity, where both sides of the equation are divided by potential GNP or GNP, (see Clark, 1979) and the deflated K_{t-1} term remains on the right-hand side, our correction for heteroscedasticity establishes an equation for the rate of accumulation and eliminates the spurious correlation and artificial goodness of fit created by the similar time trends in K_{t-1} and I^*_t, thus establishing a more rigorous test of our theory.

21. See Pugel (1978) and Goldstein (1986a).

22. A constant term is included because the aggregated equations that we test at best approximate the sum of the equations for all firms.

23. See Chow and Lin (1971). The equation employed is $GI = 4.34 + 0.57PE$ with an $AR1$ correction ($\rho = 0.73$), estimated for 1947–86, where GI is gross investment and PE is the new plant and equipment expenditure survey series. For the above equation $R^2 = 0.97$ and the t-statistics are respectively 1.05 and 13.65.

24. In addition the form of the equation used for the BLU distribution of net investment is altered: $NI = -16.78 + 0.60PE + 0.09T - 0.04T^2$ with $AR1$ correction ($\rho = 0.71$) where NI is net investment and T is time. For this equation, $R^2 = 0.86$ and the t statistics are respectively -.3.06, 8.75, 0.18 and -3.23.

25. In the annual series, the mid-year, rather than end-year, value of the capital stock is used where mid-year values are derived as the average between two end-year values.

26. The expected rate of inflation is calculated as

$$\sum_{s=0}^{1} \alpha_s \dot{P}_{t-s}$$

where $\dot{P}$ is the actual inflation rate. The length of the lag is respectively 2 and 7 for the annual and quarterly cases. The distributions of α, are respectively (0.6, 0.3, 0.1) and (0.35, 0.25, 0.15, 0.1, 0.05, 0.04, 0.03, 0.03) in these two cases.

27. The forecasting equation used to generate the *BLU* forecasts of *IPR* is: *IPR* $= -0.013 + 0.0684IPRE + 0.0007T$ with an *AR*1 correction ($\rho = 0.67$), where *IPRE* is the economy-wide *IPR* and *T* is time. This equation is estimated for the period 1974–82 and has $R^2 = 0.94$ and respective t statistics -0.081, 1.88 and 4.86. The backcasting equation employed is: *IPR* $= 0.016 + 0.24IPRE - 0.0002T$ with no *AR* correction. The equation is estimated for the period 1958–64 and has $R^2 = 0.76$ and t statistics 1.18, 1.91 and -0.38. Separate forecasting and backcasting equations are employed to capture the distinct historical trends in the *IPR* in these two time periods.

28. The forecasting and backcasting equations are described in n.27. The distribution equation: *IPR* $= -0.018 + 0.0553IPRE + 0.0008T$ with an *AR*1 correction ($\rho = 0.74$) and $R^2 = 0.95$.

29. The restricted sample sizes, compared to data availability from 1947–86, are necessitated by lags of up to seven years, autocorrelation corrections and observations lost in the linear distribution of certain variables.

30. The Q-tests are also conducted for annual lag lengths of 5 and 10 and quarterly lag lengths of 15, 20 and 30 with the same qualitative results: the null hypothesis, no autocorrelation, cannot be rejected.

31. The degree of the polynomial is chosen by a sequential test of the significance of the coefficients on the actual *PDL* variables – linear combinations of lagged independent variables. The higher degree polynomial on L and L^* is justified by the hypothesized non-linear effect of L on the rate of accumulation. The hypothesized negative effect can be generated by positive or negative signs of the correct magnitudes on the L and L^2 lag coefficients. Thus it is possible for the hypothesis to be met by frequent sign reversals that occur simultaneously in the L and L^2 lag coefficients, implying that polynomials of higher degrees are appropriate.

32. In neo-classical theory, increased competition can never lead to an increase in cost-cutting as opposed to output-enhancing investment because all firms are cost-minimizing at all times. An increase in competition caused by new entrants lowers output-augmenting investment by existing firms because it lowers the marginal product of capital. However *industry* output-augmenting investment will rise because greater competition means a lower average price and greater industry output, *ceteris paribus*.

Our results must be distinguished from the neo-classical treatment of competition. To the extent that our *IPR* reflects changes in foreign competition, the sign on the competition variable is both the sign of

the firm and industry response to competition. In neo-classical theory, both of these responses cannot be positive.
33. See Clark (1979) and Kopcke (1985).

REFERENCES

Boddy, Raford and James. R. Crotty (1975), 'Class Conflict and Macro-Policy: The Political Business Cycle', *The Review of Radical Political Economics*, 7,(1), Spring.

Chow, G. C. and A. Lin (1971), 'Best Linear Unbiased Interpolation, Distribution and Extrapolation of Time Series by Related Series', *Review of Economics and Statistics*, 53,(4), November.

Clark, P. (1979), 'Investment in the 1970s: Theory, Performance, and Prediction', *Brookings Papers on Economic Activity*, 1.

Crotty, James R. (1990), 'Owner–Manager Conflict and Financial Theories of Investment Instability: A Critical Assessment of Keynes, Tobin and Minsky', *Journal of Post Keynesian Economics*, 12,(4), Summer.

Crotty J. and J. Goldstein (1990a), 'A Marxian Version of the Keynes–Minsky Model of Investment Instability', unpublished manuscript.

Crotty, J. and J. Goldstein (1990b), 'Marxian Competition and the Theory of Coerced Investment', unpublished manuscript.

Elster, Jon (1982), 'Marxism, Functionalism, and Game Theory: The Case for Methodological Individualism', *Theory and Society*, 11,(4), July.

Elster, Jon (1983), *Explaining Technical Change: A Case Study in the Philosophy of Science*, New York: Cambridge University Press.

Goldstein, Jonathan P. (1985), 'The Cyclical Profit Squeeze: A Marxian Microfoundation', *The Review of Radical Political Economics*, 17,(1–2), Spring–Summer.

Goldstein, Jonathan P. (1986a), 'Mark-up Variability and Flexibility: Theory and Empirical Evidence', *Journal of Business*, 59,(4), October.

Goldstein, Jonathan P. (1986b), 'The Micro-Macro Dialectic: A Concept of a Marxian Microfoundation', in P. Zarembka (ed.), *Research in Political Economy: A Research Annual*, Volume 9, Greenwich: JAI Press.

Kopcke, R. W. (1985), 'The Determinants of Investment Spending', *New England Economic Review*, July–August.

Minsky, Hyman P. (1975), *John Maynard Keynes*, New York: Columbia University Press.

Minsky, Hyman P. (1986), *Stabilizing an Unstable Economy*, New Haven, Yale University Press.

Pollin, R. (1986), 'Alternative Perspectives on the Rise of Corporate Debt Dependency: The U.S. Post-War Experience', *Review of Radical Political Economics*, **18**,(1–2), Spring–Summer.

Pugel, T. A. (1978), *International Market Linkages and U.S. Manufacturing: Prices, Profits, and Patterns*, Cambridge, Mass.: Ballinger.

Roemer, J. (1981), *Analytical Foundations of Marxian Economic Theory*, New York: Cambridge University Press.

Roemer, J. (1982), 'Methodological Individualism and Deductive Marxism', *Theory and Society*, **11**,(4), July.

APPENDIX

Figure 9A.1   Rate of accumulation for gross investment

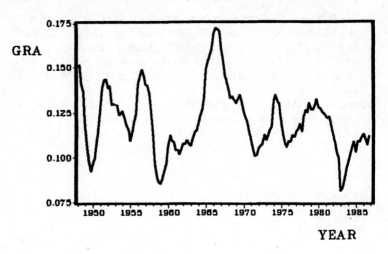

Figure 9A.2   Rate of accumulation for net investment

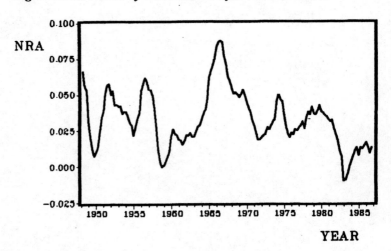

Figure 9A.3   Gross profit rate

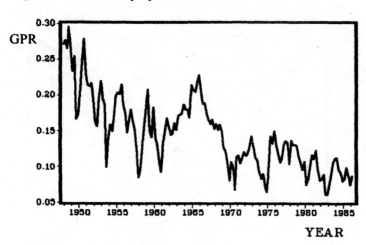

Figure 9A.4   Real interest rate

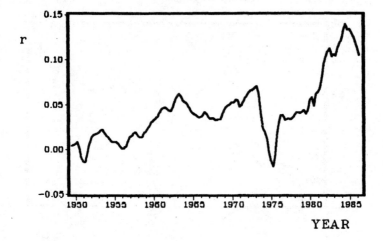

Figure 9A.5   Import–penetration ratio

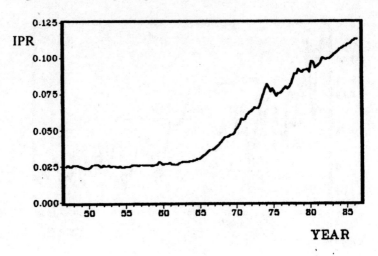

Figure 9A.6   Debt–equity ratio

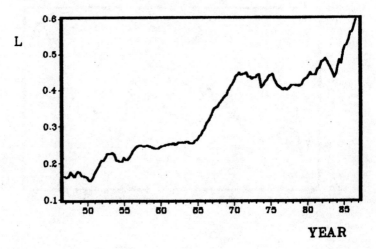

10. Technological Change, Distribution and Stability*

Gérard Duménil and Dominique Lévy

INTRODUCTION

This study provides an overall interpretation of the evolution of the US economy since the Civil War, based on the description of the historical profile of distribution and technology, and the analysis of stability phenomena. Although this analysis does not ignore the impact of the transformations of relations of production and institutions, only the major features of this evolution are mentioned in the interest of brevity. This choice of focus is in accord with our view that tendential laws (concerning technology and distribution) and the mechanisms which determine the stability of the general levels of activity and prices are two key elements in the interpretation of economic history. This perspective, although not fully original, does contrast with many other interpretations which stress the transformations of competition (competitive v. monopolistic capitalism).

What is presented here relies heavily on two other recent papers: Duménil, Glick and Lévy (1991; chapter 3 of this volume) and Duménil and Lévy (1991a) (later denoted as DGL and DL), where we derived a periodization of the evolution of the US economy in three stages, based on the observation of the transformations of distribution and technology: (1) up to the turn of the century; (2) from the early twentieth century to the aftermath of the Second World War; and (3) since the 1950s.[1] For labour cost and the productivity of labour, it is the growth of the variable which manifests a similar configuration: slow, fast and increasing, diminishing. In the earlier and later periods, labour cost and labour productivity rise simultaneously at a low rate, whereas the technical composition of capital is increased, and the productivity of capital and profit rates diminish. In the inter- mediate period, the growth of labour cost and labour productivity is accelerated, and the trends of the capital productivity and profit rate are now upward. This inter- mediate period appears as a period of restoration in which the trends are upward (but the growing heterogeneity of technology which accompanied this restoration undermined the continuation of prosperity and was dramatically mani- fested in the Great Depression).

The first and third periods, up to the turn of the century and since the 1950s, can be characterized as patterns of evolution *à la* Marx, with a constant rate of surplus-value, an increasing organic composition of capital and a falling profit rate. The intermediate period appears as exceptional from the point of view of the fundamental laws of motion of capitalism. We attribute this specificity to a revolution in organization and technology, related to the development of 'business staffs', which we describe as the first stage of a managerial revolution, which developed at the turn of the century, as a response to the long slide downward of the profit rate, in the context of a severe depression. This revolution had a profound impact on the profile of technical progress until the 1950s. The response of the system to the second episode *à la* Marx, since the 1950s, is different. No revolution in technology is apparent in the USA. Only the speed at which the economy follows this track was reduced, and this reduction was manifested in the slow- down of the growth in the labour cost and labour producti- vity.

With this first account of the evolution of the US econ- omy, we combine a second aspect: the analysis of stability. By 'stability' we mean the ability of the economic system to correct for disequilibrium by reallocating resources among industries, adjusting relative outputs and prices, and limiting the fluctuations in the general level of activity and prices. Our analysis of the stability of capitalism is based on the construction of dynamic models in which the agents act in disequilibrium and, specifically, react to the observation of disequilibrium. We show that capitalism is very stable with respect to its ability to allocate capital among industries, to determine relative prices or outputs, what we call '(in)stability in proportions', but very unstable with respect to the determination of the general level of activity and prices, what we call '(in)stability in dimension'.

There is a relationship between the two types of phenomena, tendential laws affecting distribution and technology, on the one hand, and instability in dimension, on the other, via the determination of the behaviours of economic agents, and this relation accounts for the importance of profitability. First, the value of the profit rate has a direct impact on behaviour: if the profit rate falls, the behaviour of individual firms is modified and the instability of the system is increased. Second, the historical movement of the profit rate induces the progress of management, which also materializes in modified behaviours. Even when the progress of management was able to offset the tendency for the profit rate to fall, as was the case in the intermediate period, this restoration was obtained at the expense of an increasing instability.

This inner tendency towards an increasing instability was not outwardly manifested because it was constantly checked by the development of the economy-wide institutions (state intervention: laws, regulations and economic policy). Although this progress of social control has been continuous throughout the history of US capitalism, it accelerated in the aftermath of the Great Depression and the Second World War. We identify this transformation as the second stage of the managerial revolution – at the centre, in opposition to the earlier stage concentrated at the level of the private management of firms.

Thus our general thesis concerning stability (in dimension) in capitalism combines the two notions of a *tendential instability* resulting from the progress of the private management of firms and of the simultaneous historical progress of the *social control of stability*. The outcome of these two movements is that capitalism is constantly maintained at the limit between stability and instability. Recurrent lags in the development of controls are observed for limited periods of time, since these controls are usually improved following the actual experience of instability. For brevity, we call this thesis the 'Tendential Instability Thesis'. It should be clear that we do not mean by this expression that the system was more and more unstable historically, but that it is constantly driven back to instability, in spite of the progress of controls.

From this analysis, one can derive several possible scenarios for the future. A first hypothesis is that the movement along the present pattern *à la* Marx will be maintained, with a slow technical progress. The profit rate will fall unless the growth rate of the labour cost is reduced to very low levels (in relation to the growth rate of technical progress, which is very slow). A second scenario is that a new revolution in technology, again reversing or only relaxing the presence of historical trends as in the intermediate period, is under way (in the USA or in another country) and new opportunities will be opened for the progress of labour productivity and the purchasing power of wage earners. However the signs of this restoration are not clearly evident in the series up to 1989 for the US economy. A third scenario concerns the emergence of a really new stage in the history of capitalism, with a different type of dynamics of the variables, but it is difficult to be specific in this respect. In each case it appears clear that important institutional trans-formations will probably be observed.

The study divides into three parts. Section 1 is devoted to historical tendencies. We discuss the relevance of Marx's notion of historical tendencies and interpret the transforma-tion of technology and distribution in the US economy using an explanatory scheme derived from this analysis. Section 2 addresses the issue of stability. We present a framework for the analysis of stability and make explicit our 'Tendential Instability Thesis', on which we base our view of the relation-ship between profitability and stability. Section 3 briefly sketches the general interpretation of the economic history of the US economy since the Civil War which follows from this analysis.

1   HISTORICAL TENDENCIES

We begin by discussing Marx's analysis of historical tendencies from both theoretical and factual points of view and then derive from this analysis the analytical framework which we use to interpret the history of the US economy.

The Relevance of Marx's Analysis

In this section, we first outline Marx's analysis and then discuss its factual relevance. We show that the first and third stages which we distinguish in the history of US capitalism correspond to patterns described by Marx, but that the evolution in the intermediate period does not.

Theory

Marx, in his analysis of historical tendencies in capitalism (Marx, 1894, Chapters 13 to 15), described a tendency for the rate of profit to fall (already identified in Adam Smith and David Ricardo, with different explanatory schemes). In Marx's analysis, the tendency for the rate of profit to fall is part of a broader set of historical tendencies. He actually refers to five such laws: (1) the diminishing labour value of commodities; (2) the increasing technical and organic compositions of capital; (3) the rising rate of surplus-value; (4) the falling rate of profit; and (5) the acceleration of accumulation.

This analysis must be understood in relation to the Industrial Revolution in England that Marx directly observed. Seen in this light, it is not surprising that he stressed the effects of mechanization and the development of the composition of capital. Ricardo stressed the consequences of the rising value of labour power and its consequences on the profit rate via the profit share. Marx replied that, even with a constant rate of surplus-value (or share of profits in total income), the profit rate could diminish because of the increasing organic composition of capital.

The weak point in Marx's analysis is the absence of any reference to the real wage or labour cost. This absence is felt at several points:

1. There is no analysis of the historical tendency of the real wage and of the mechanisms involved in its determination. It is well know that this deficiency resulted in endless controversies among radical economists concerning the relative or absolute impoverishment of the workers.

2. In his description of the mechanism which induces capitalists towards technological change, Marx contends that new techniques are adopted which guarantee super profits to their users when they are introduced, but are less profitable when they are generalized. It has been shown by Nobuo Okishio (Okishio, 1961) that this result cannot be obtained under the assumption of a constant real wage. (The mechanism described by Marx is compatible with the assumption of a constant share of profits, or constant rate of surplus-value.)

3. More generally, the relationship between the movement of labour cost and that of the technical composition of capital is not treated explicitly; only cursory remarks can be found in Marx's *Capital*.[2]

Facts

Abstracting from a number of well-known difficulties (for example, the difference between labour values and prices, the distinction between productive and unproductive labour, the heterogeneity of labour, the definition of the capitalist sector of the economy as opposed to self-employed and so on), Marx's five laws refer to the following variables:

1. The value of commodities is derived from their labour content, that is to the inverse of labour productivity. We denote the net national product (NNP) in constant dollars as Q, and the total number of hours worked as L. The average value of commodities is L/Q, and labour productivity is $P_L = Q/L$. A downward tendency of the first ratio is equivalent to an upward tendency of the second. The upward trend of labour productivity is well known (cf. Figure 3.7 in DGL).

2. K denotes the net stock of capital in constant dollars.

Therefore the technical composition of capital is K/L. With w denoting the wage rate deflated by the NNP deflator, and p the price of fixed capital also deflated by the NNP deflator, the organic composition of capital is $\gamma = Kp/Lw$. These two ratios display a pattern in three stages: upward, downward, upward. The technical composition of capital is presented in Figure 3.9 in DGL. The organic composition is displayed in Figure 10.1 below. The trend line in this figure is derived as in section 3 of DGL from the trends of the variables chosen as 'basic'.

3. With Π denoting total profits deflated with the NNP deflator, the rate of surplus-value is $\tau = \Pi/Lw$. The profit share is $\pi = \Pi/Q$, and the two variables are linked by the relation: $\pi = \tau/(1+\tau)$. The two ratios move in the same direction (upward, according to Marx). The profit share is presented in Figure 3.10 of DGL and the rate of surplus-value in Figure 10.2 of the present chapter. As above, the trend lines have been reconstructed as in DGL. The productivity of capital, $P_k = Q/Kp$, is defined as the ratio of NNP in current dollars to the net stock of capital also in current dollars. Since $\gamma = (1 + \tau)/P_K$, an increasing organic composition of capital is approximately equivalent to a diminishing capital productivity under the assumption of a nearly constant rate of surplus-value τ. These properties explain the similarities between Figures 10.1 in this chapter and 4 in DGL.

4. The profit rate is $r = \Pi/Kp$. One has $r = \tau/\gamma$, and not $r = \tau/(1 + \gamma)$ as in Marx's analysis, since only the stock of fixed capital is considered. Using the productivity of capital, one can also write $r = \pi P_K$. With the assumptions of the constancy of the profit share, the profit rate reproduces the movements of capital productivity and the inverse of the organic composition of capital. The profile of the profit rate has been discussed in DGL, where it has been shown that it is actually similar to that of P_K (cf. Figures 3.4 and 3.8 in DGL).

5. In Marx's analysis, the acceleration of accumulation seems to refer to the increase in the share of profits devoted to accumulation.

Consider first the period 1869–1900. Globally the factual relevance of Marx's analysis is remarkable for the last decades of the nineteenth century. The main series very convincingly support Marx's vision : diminishing value of commodities, increasing organic composition of capital and falling profit rate. A first difference between Marx's description and our observations is that the share of profits, or rate of surplus-value, is constant or even diminishing in the nineteenth century. It is not possible, however, to be conclusive in this matter because of the huge oscillation in the share of profits observed during this period and the absence of an adjustment for unproductive workers (cf. Moseley, 1988). Another problem concerns the acceleration of accumulation: if one considers the share of net investment in net profits, this rate has actually been rather constant during this first period. Again the absence of separation of the strictly capitalist section of the economy from the rest of the productive system does not allow an outright rejection of Marx's insights.

The same series show clearly that the pattern of evolution

Figure 10.1   The organic composition of capital (1869–1989)

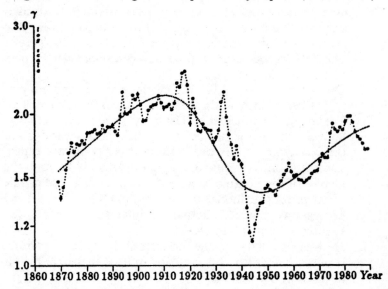

described by Marx was interrupted in the early twentieth century by the rise in the profit rate and productivity of capital (or the declining compositions of capital) for a period of about 40 years. This interruption would naturally lead to the conclusion that the explanatory power of Marx's analysis was limited to a particular stage of development of capitalism. However the observation that a similar pattern is again apparent since the 1950s questions this interpretation. Another view that is plausible is that the intermediate stage is presented as a revolution – limited in duration – interrupting a set of basic inherent tendencies. We favour this last interpretation, which stresses the combination of a law of motion and a revolution.

Concerning the first and third stages, all the components of Marx's analysis are not necessarily relevant, but the basic insights are clearly remarkable:

1. The disconnection between the movement of the rate of surplus-value or the profit share (approximately constant)

Figure 10.2   The rate of surplus-value (1869–1989)

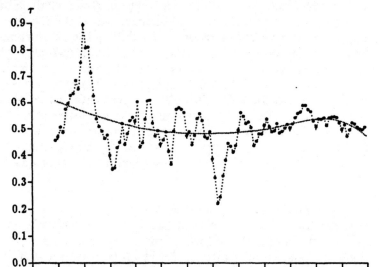

and that of the profit rate (diminishing), since the productivity of capital manifests a clear trend downward.
2. The view that the progress of labour productivity is a function of the increasing technical composition of capital.
3. The notion that this dependency poses a threat to the profitability of capital.

The core of this analysis is a specific view of the relationships among the variables involved in the description of technological change. It is the purpose of the following to investigate more thoroughly the exact relations implied in this pattern, and to illustrate its explanatory power.

A Marxist Framework of Analysis

In what follows we will present three explanatory schemes based on Marx's analysis of historical tendencies, which differ in the number of variables treated as endogenous or exogenous (among labour cost, technical composition, labour productivity and technical progress).

A first choice concerns the interpretation which is given of Marx's analysis of technological change, that is the relationship between his first and second laws, linking the diminishing value of commodities (that is, the rise of labour productivity) and the increasing composition of capital. Depending on the exact specification of this relationship, as an *ex post* or *ex ante* mechanism, two or three variables will be treated as exogenous. In a more ambitious interpretation, it is possible to relate the profiles of labour cost and technical progress to that of the profit rate, through feedback mechanisms, and to articulate all variables in a coherent set of interrelations. This project is also discussed.

The *ex post* function of technological change
One interpretation of the relationship between Marx's first and second laws is the following: the progress of labour productivity was paid for historically by an increasing technical composition of capital. We denote this relation as the *ex post*

function of technological change. The two variables involved are $P_L = Q/L$, the productivity of labour, and K/L, the technical composition of capital:

$$P_L = f\left(\frac{K}{L}\right) \tag{10.1}$$

in which f is an increasing function of its argument. This function may depend on time, and this dependency defines a type of 'exogenous' technical progress, in the sense that this progress is not explained by the variables under consideration.[3]

As shown in Figure 10.3, this relation is solidly grounded in the empirical evidence. It is not surprising to notice that a break can be observed in the intermediate years, during which labour productivity is increased, whereas the technical composition of capital remains constant or diminishes slightly.

We specify equation (10.1) as:

$$lnP_L = lnA(t) + \alpha(t)ln\frac{K}{L} \tag{10.2}$$

This formalism expresses the idea that the progress of labour productivity has two distinct origins: (1) the rise of the technical composition of capital (an expression of 'mechanization') and (2) exogenous technical progress (or technical progress in the strict sense, as used in the remainder of this chapter). The interpretation of Marx's view of technological change which follows from this analysis is that the first mechanism is far more important than the second.

We adopt for $A(t)$ a model similar to that introduced in the second section of DGL:

$$ln \, A(t) = a + bt + c\frac{exp\frac{t-\bar{t}}{\Delta} - 1}{exp\frac{t-\bar{t}}{\Delta} + 1} \tag{10.3}$$

and for $\alpha(t)$: $\alpha_0 + \alpha_1 t$.

Figure 10.3   Labour productivity v. technical composition of capital (1869–1989)

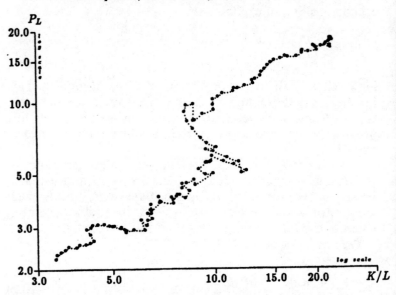

The results of the regression are presented in the two first lines of Table 10.1.[4] The results displayed in the first line demonstrate that α's dependence on time cannot be maintained, since parameter α_1 is not significant. The results for α constant are presented in the second line. The slope of the

Table 10.1   The trend exogenous technical progress ($\ln A(t)$) (1869–1989)

	a	b	c	α_0	α_1	T	Δ	R^2
(1) *Ex post* Function	1.47 ($t=3.0$)	0.00682 ($t=2.7$)	0.824 ($t=1.2$)	0.253 ($t=3.4$)	−0.00247 ($t=0.7$)	43.0 ($t=6.3$)	16.6 ($t=2.1$)	0.997
(2) *Ex post* Function	1.23 ($t=7.3$)	0.00500 ($t=2.6$)	0.507 ($t=6.7$)	0.245 ($t=2.7$)		37.3 ($t=32.2$)	12.4 ($t=6.9$)	0.997
(3) *Ex ante* Function	1.08 ($t=25.5$)	0.00333 ($t=2.8$)	0.518 ($t=7.4$)	0.334		36.6 ($t=46.2$)	11.8 ($t=8.5$)	0.994

asymptotes corresponds to an annual growth rate of technical progress of only 0.5 per cent. The maximum growth rate, in 1937 ($\bar{t}$), is equal to 2.5 per cent ($b + c/2\Delta$).

The profile of $A(t)$ is displayed in Figure 10.4 ($\bigcirc$). One can recognize in this figure the usual configuration in three stages: slow, fast, slow.

In DGL, the profit rate has been expressed as a function of three 'basic' variables, the productivity of labour P_L, the productivity of capital P_K (with numerator and denominator in current dollars) and labour cost w: $r = P_K (1 - w/P_L)$. The function of technical progress above suggests that r should be expressed in a different manner:

$$r = \frac{Q - wL}{pK} = \frac{Q/L - w}{pK/L} = \frac{A(t)(K/L)^\alpha - w}{pK/L} \qquad (10.4)$$

With this interpretation of Marx's analysis, the movements of the profit rate are still explained by those of three exogenous variables, but different from those selected in DGL: the technical composition of capital, the labour cost and time (exogenous progress), to which one should add the relative price of fixed capital whose variation was limited historically.

The *ex ante* function of technological change
The analysis in DGL also revealed two other striking historical patterns:

1. The profit share in total income is approximately constant and this invariance reaffirms the correlation between the productivity of labour and labour cost. The scatter diagram of the logarithm of the two variables is displayed in Figure 10.5. A nearly perfect straight line is observed. This corresponds to one of the most puzzling laws of motion of US capitalism since the Civil War.
2. The technical composition of capital is also well correlated to the labour cost (cf. Figures 6 and 9 in DGL) in the first and third stages.

In order to account for these two relationships, one need only slightly modify Marx's idea that the progress of labour productivity has been paid for historically by increasing the technical composition of capital: at each stage of development, the progress of labour productivity can be obtained by an increasing technical composition of capital. This statement defines an *ex ante* function of technical change whose formal expression is identical to that presented in equations (10.1) or (10.2). Labour productivity and the technical composition of capital are not considered here only for the values which have been observed historically: the relation defines a set of technological combinations at each given point in time. The actual combination is assumed to be the one which maximizes the profit rate.

The maximization of the profit rate as in equation (10.4) allows for the determination of the optimal productive combination characterized by its productivity of labour and technical composition of capital, $\left(\dfrac{Q}{L}\right)^*$ and $\left(\dfrac{K}{L}\right)^*$:

Figure 10.4   *Two measures of technical progress ex post model (○) and ex ante model (●) (1869–1989)*

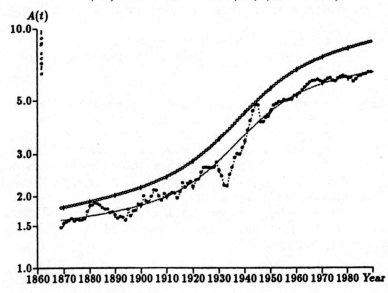

$$\left(\frac{Q}{L}\right)^* = \frac{w}{1 - \alpha} \tag{10.5}$$

$$\left(\frac{K}{L}\right)^* = \left(\frac{w}{A(1 - \alpha)}\right)^{\frac{1}{\alpha}} \tag{10.6}$$

A priori, both parameters A and α may have varied historically, and this is easy to verify, since they can be computed from the values of Q/L and K/L actually observed:

$$\alpha(t) = \frac{Q/L - w}{Q/L} \quad \text{and} \quad ln\,A(t) = ln\frac{Q}{L} - \alpha ln\frac{K}{L}$$

In the regression of α on time, the trend is not significant. (The t score is 1.30). For this reason we will consider α as constant (as in the *ex post* function). It can be estimated as the average value of π over the period, that is 0.334. This constancy is another expression of that of the profit share ($\pi = \alpha$) or of the correlation between labour cost and labour productivity, $w = (1 - \alpha)P_L$, (cf. equation 10.5). On the

Figure 10.5   Labour productivity v. labour cost (1869–1989)

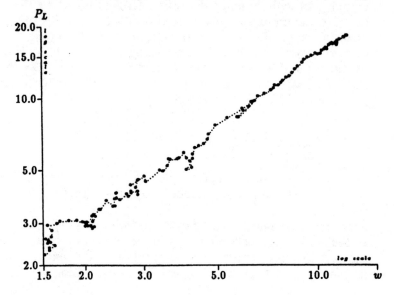

contrary, A varied historically, as shown in Figure 10.4 (●). The pattern obtained is very similar to that resulting from the *ex post* function (○). We again use the model defined in equation (10.3) to determine the trend of this variable. The results are presented in the third line of Table 10.1 (see the dotted line in Figure 10.4). The slope of the asymptotes corresponds to an annual growth rate of technical progress of 0.3 per cent, even smaller than for the *ex post* model. The maximum growth is unchanged.

Using equation 10.6, one can see that the direction of variation of K/L depends on the degree of exogenous technical progress. When technical progress is slow, that is when $A(t)$ grows more slowly than labour cost, as during the first and third periods, the substitution effect is dominant and the technical composition of capital varies with labour cost. When technical progress is strong, as was the case during the intermediate period, the technical composition of capital diminishes.

With this *ex ante* interpretation, only two exogenous variables are now considered: the labour cost and technical progress. They explain the technical composition of capital, labour productivity and the profit rate. Again Marx's thesis refers to the limitation of technical progress. Thus the movement of the profit rate appears even more clearly as the outcome of a conflict between the two exogenous variables. With the function of technological change as in equation (10.2), the rate of growth of the profit rate, labour cost and technical progress are linked by the relation:

$$\rho(r) = \frac{1}{\alpha}\rho(A) - \frac{1 - \alpha}{\alpha}\rho(w)$$

Exogenous technical progress alleviates the pressure on the profit rate resulting from an increasing labour cost.

Feedback mechanisms: labour cost and technical progress
In the analysis of technological change and profitability with the *ex ante* model, two variables are still treated as exogenous: labour cost and technical progress. This observation does not

mean, however, that the movements of these variables cannot be explained, related to one another or through feedback mechanisms, linked to the evolution of the variables that they determine (although we believe that they cannot be made endogenous in the strict sense of the term, as in a model). On the contrary, we believe that they should be interpreted as components of a specific historical pattern of events.

Consider first labour cost. The series depicted in DGL suggests the existence of a relationship between the acceleration of labour cost (cf.Figure 3.6 in DGL) in the intermediate period and that of technical progress and, consequently, the corresponding rise of the profit rate, which occurred about ten years before.[5] It is puzzling that the maximum value of the trend profit rate was attained in 1948 and the maximum growth rate of labour cost in 1947 (Figures 3.6 and 3.8 of DGL). By way of response, it is possible to introduce, at least as a research hypothesis, the notion of an impact of technical progress on the movement of wages, via the profit rate.

In this line of argument, technical progress is defined by $A(t)$, but never by P_L, for which the causality runs from labour cost to labour productivity, and not the reverse (cf.equation (10.5)). Our analysis, in this respect, is quite different from the common point of view in the literature which emphasizes the determination of labour cost by labour productivity.

With a declining profit rate the resistance of capitalists to rising wages is strong. Technical progress in the intermediate period, and the corresponding restoration of the profit rate, was an inducement for capitalists to accept higher wages. Technical progress created the historical possibility of an increasing labour cost.

The same sort of mechanism may be at work with respect to the present stagnation of the purchasing power of wages, in relation to the falling profitability of capital since the late 1960s. The feedback mechanism evoked here suggests a causal relationship running from the falling profit rate to stagnating wages. One may even surmise that, if there were a rise in technical progress similar to that which occurred at the turn of the century, real wages might again increase in the future. In the absence of such a rise in technical progress, rising wages would pull the profit rate further downward, and enterprises would be expected to resist strongly any such pressure from the workers.

Now consider technical progress. Although it is not possible fully to endogenize its movement, we believe that there is also a type of feedback mechanism at work from the decline of the profit rate in the first stage to the revolution of technology which was manifested during the intermediate period. This revolution, as already suggested, responded to the slide of the profit rate in the nineteenth century and the ensuing depression. Concerning the present situation of capitalism, the question is now posed of a similar feedback, from low levels of profitability to a new surge of technical progress. It is not obvious, however, that history will repeat itself in this respect.

At the centre of this third interpretation, in which two feedback mechanisms are considered, still lies the same distinction of three stages, with two patterns *à la* Marx, interrupted by a period of restoration, but we now contend that:

1. The first episode *à la* Marx produced both a first revolution in technology (technical progress) and the acceleration in the growth of the purchasing power of workers.
2. The second pattern *à la* Marx put an end to the acceleration of the labour cost and labour productivity, which returned to growth rates similar to those observed in the ninettenth century. (In the present circumstances, the profit rate is low, as was the case in the late nineteenth century, and the situation is difficult to manage.)

2 PROFITABILITY AND STABILITY

Already, underlying the analysis in the previous section, is the notion that historical tendencies and, in particular, the movement of the profit rate are important. In this section we provide a justification for this role conferred on these tendencies. The crucial idea is that profitability is a determinant of stability.

In order to make explicit this relationship between profitability and stability, it is necessary to make an important detour through the analysis of stability, but we begin by briefly summarizing the few principles which are strictly required for the understanding of the argument developed in Section 3.

The analysis of stability is then developed in three phases. We introduce the general framework: the various terms considered, the treatment of disequilibrium and the models of adjustment behaviours. The main results are then summarized. We distinguish between stability in proportions and in dimension and discuss the condition for stability in dimension. We present our first thesis concerning stability in capitalism: it is very stable in proportions, but unstable in dimension. However these phases abstract from the historical aspects of these phenomena, which are left for the third phase, which makes explicit the relationship between profitability and stability and presents our second thesis concerning stability, which we call the 'tendential instability thesis'.

How Does Profitability Matter?

We believe that profitability is a crucial variable in the evolution of capitalism in several respects. As already noted above, the simultaneous increase of the profit rate (in relation to an autonomous wave of technical progress) and of the growth rate of labour cost, in the intermediate period, suggests the existence of a feedback from the movement of profitability on wages. This, in itself, would be sufficient justification to contend that profitability makes a difference, since its trend conditioned the evolution of the purchasing power of workers. In a similar manner, a lengthy decline of the profit rate in the nineteenth century has been evoked as a possible trigger for a revolution in technology, and this achievement is no less important. It is also clear that the variations of the profit rate have an impact on the division of profits. One share of profits is transferred to the state (federal, state and local) through taxation (cf.DGL, Figure 3.2). Another share is destined for accumulation through various channels.

Without denying the importance of these mechanisms or

others, we will insist here on the fact that profitability is related to the stability of the general level of activity, that is to business fluctuations. Marx himself linked low levels of profitability to the occurrence of crises: '[A fall in the rate of profit] promotes overproduction, speculation and crises, and leads to the existence of excess capital alongside a surplus population' (Marx, 1894, Chapter XV, p. 350). The idea of a relationship between profitability and the determination of the general level of activity, through demand mechanisms, is rather common in the literature of Marxist–Keynesian inspiration, to which we devote the appendix of this chapter.

In order to make explicit the relationship between profitability and crises, it is necessary to develop a theoretical interpretation of business fluctuations. We believe that the investigation of the mechanisms which ensure the correction of disequilibrium in the economy and prevent them from becoming cumulative, that is stability analysis, is crucial in the interpretation of business fluctuations. The overall correction of disequilibrium in a private economy actually results from the individual reactions of each agent to the disequilibria that he/she confronts (for example, the reaction of firms to disequilibrium between supply and demand). However this outcome is not automatic: individual reactions to disequilibrium do not result, under every circumstance, in the overall stability of the system. In other words, stability is conditional. A crisis corresponds to a situation in which this transformation of individual corrections into an overall stabilization process fails.

This approach to business fluctuations in terms of stability is not common in the economic literature. In the formation of economic theory much attention has been paid to equilibrium phenomena, while far less research has been devoted to the analysis of stability. It was clear, however, that Adam Smith's famous allusion to the 'invisible hand', which is supposed to ensure the coordination of the actions of private agents through market mechanisms, directly referred to the stability of equilibrium.

Obviously the stability of the general level of activity depends on a complex network of relationships and mechanisms (monetary, real and institutional) and cannot be reduced to any single factor (see below). However, within each institutional context, the profit rate is a crucial determinant of stability (see the 'Tendential Instability Thesis', below) via its impact on firm behaviour. More precisely, it is important to distinguish between two types of relationships between profitability and stability:

1. The profit rate is one of the parameters to be considered by management, at each stage of its historical development. Thus the variations in the profit rate are reflected in firm behaviour which, in turn, has an impact on stability.
2. The notion of technical progress is more common in the literature than that of the progress of management, but we believe that the progressive development of management is no less important. (Actually, the two processes are tightly related and should be considered simultaneously.) A falling profit rate stimulates the progress of management (in the same manner as it induces technical progress) and thus has an impact on stability.

Finally the stability of the system depends on two types of conflicting forces:

1. The actual fall in the profit rate and the continuous progress of management induced by the tendency for the profit rate to fall provoke similar transformations of firm behaviour in directions which are destabilizing from the point of view of the general level of activity.
2. This evolution towards an increasing instability stimulates the progress of institutions which control the overall stability of the system. They are progressively developed as a response to the manifestations of instability: overheatings, recessions and depressions.

We term this analysis the 'Tendential Instability Thesis'. We do not mean by this expression that instability has been increasing throughout the history of capitalism,[6] but that capitalism is constantly driven back to the stability frontier in spite of the constant improvement of the social controls of stability.

This analysis of the history of US capitalism stresses the importance of specific types of institutions, those in charge of the social control of stability.

A Framework for the Analysis of Stability

Here we will very briefly summarize the main aspects of our analysis of stability in capitalism, as developed by earlier studies.[7] This analysis is based on the construction and investigation of the properties of a set of dynamic models, developed along the same principles. We begin by distinguishing between three 'terms': short term, long term and the term of historical tendencies. Next we introduce the modelling of behaviours in terms of adjustment, which we call 'disequilibrium microeconomics'. A first example of adjustment is presented in the context of the decision to produce and we end with a discussion of money and credit.

The notation and equations are borrowed from Duménil and Lévy (1990b). We abstract here from any historical considerations, which will be developed in the next section.

Temporal frameworks

In our analysis of the dynamics of capitalist economies we distinguish between the short term, the long term and historical tendencies (or the very long term). The general idea in the distinction between these time periods is that the various variables considered have different speeds of adjustment. For example, output can be adjusted faster that the capital stock, or technology can only be modified as capital is renewed and therefore changes at a slower rate than the capital stock. In the analysis of a specific term one uses this difference of adjustment speed to assume that some variables are constant (those considered in longer terms) or that some equilibrations have already been realized (concerning variables involved in shorter terms).

The first distinction, between the long term and historical tendencies is fundamental in the works of the classics. The *long term* refers to the formation of prices of production as a result of the mobility of capitals led by profitability differentials. Classical economists developed this analysis assuming that distribution and technology are given. It is obvious that distribution and technology are continuously transformed, and that prices of production vary historically. But classical economists believed that these transformations do not prevent the gravitation of prices of production around this comparatively slowly moving target. The term of *historical tendencies* is that of the variation of the real wage or labour cost, and technological change. The issue in the analysis of this very long term is not that of the gravitation around a target, but the definition of a continuous movement of the variables. Our analyses in DGL and DL deal with historical tendencies.

The distinction between the long term and short term is common in the literature. The *short term* refers to mechanisms which can be analysed assuming that the capital stocks are constant (and that distribution and technology are also given). Since the stocks of capital are constant in the short term, the variation of outputs implies changes in capacity utilization rates. This variable is crucial in the investigation of short-term phenomena.

Disequilibrium microeconomics

By 'disequilibrium microeconomics', we refer to the behaviour of economic agents (decision to produce, to fix prices, to allocate capital and so on) within disequilibrium. 'Disequilibrium' can refer to the following situations:

1. The commodity markets do not clear. This is equivalent to saying that involuntary stocks of inventories of finished goods exist. Since firms, because of the constant variations of demand, tend to maintain a certain volume of inventories ('normal' inventories) this means that inventories are larger or smaller than this volume.
2. The second disequilibrium concerns capacity utilization rates. Firms tend to use their productive capacities at a certain level (also called 'normal'). The actual capacity utilization rates may differ from this normal level.
3. The profit rates on the various investments of a capitalist, or on his/her opportunities to invest, are not equal.

4.   The general level of prices is not constant. This disequilibrium is not directly felt as such by individual agents, but perceived at a macroeconomic level by monetary authorities.

Obviously other disequilibria could also be considered, concerning, for example, debts, the labour market, international trade and finance, and so on.

The behaviour of economic agents is described in terms of adjustment. Agents observe disequilibria and react to these observations by modifying their behaviours. For example, in the analysis of the formation of prices of production by classical economists, capitalists observe profitability differentials and move some fraction of their capital in response. The degree of the reaction to the disequilibrium is crucial. The same accumulation of inventories or the same difference of profitability can entail reactions of quite different amplitudes. In the modelling of behaviours, this sensitivity of economic agents will be represented by parameters which we call 'reaction coefficients'. With this approach, equilibrium is always presented as the possible outcome of a dynamic mechanism (the 'gravitation' of classical economists) and not postulated *ex ante*.

The decision to produce

We now give a first example of adjustment, corresponding to the decision to produce. The general idea is that firms will react to the disequilibrium between supply and demand by increasing or diminishing their output.

In the short term, the stock of capital and technology, and therefore the productive capacities, are given. Thus the decision to produce is, in fact, equivalent to the decision to use productive capacities at a certain level: that is, the choice of a capacity utilization rate. We assume that firms decide on the use of their productive capacities on the basis of their capacity utilization rate at the previous period and the disequilibrium on their inventories (that is, the difference between supply and demand). If, for example, inventories are large, then the capacity utilization rate will be diminished.

We denote u_t the capacity utilization rate in period t, and $\bar{u}$, the normal value of this rate. In a similar manner, s defines the ratio of inventories to productive capacities and $\bar{s}$ the normal value of this ratio. With this notation, the decision to use productive capacities in period $t + 1$ can be modelled by the following equation:

$$u_{t+1} = \bar{u} + \sigma(u_t - \bar{u}) - \epsilon(s_t - \bar{s}) \tag{10.7}$$

In this equation $u_t - \bar{u}$ and $s_t - \bar{s}$ represent the two disequilibria, on productive capacities and inventories observed in t. Excessive stockpiling $(s_t - \bar{s}) > 0$, for example, induces firms to diminish their output. Parameters σ and ϵ are two reaction coefficients.

Money

We believe that monetary mechanisms are crucial in the analysis of the dynamics of capitalism. The loop Production → Income → Demand → Production is perturbated by credit and the issuance of money.

The modelling of monetary mechanisms is complex, and we will only consider here loans granted to firms by the banking system for the purpose of investment, which we believe is critical to the analysis of business fluctuations. The capital aspect one must capture in describing credit mechanisms is that a high level of activity stimulates the demand for loans from enterprises, but inflation causes the banking system to call in these loans (and conversely).

We denote ΔL_{t+1}, the variation of the net stock of loans outstanding for investment, and consider the ratio of these loans to the value, K_t, of the stock of fixed capital in current dollars. This ratio is modelled as an increasing function of the level of utilization of capacity and a decreasing function of the rate of variation of the general price level, denoted j_t:

$$\frac{\Delta L_{t+1}}{K_t} = \omega(u_t - \bar{u}) - \varphi j_t \tag{10.8}$$

in which $u_t - \bar{u}$ and j_t measure the two disequilibria considered in the negotation between the firm and the bank, and ω and φ are two reaction coefficients.

Results

We present below the main results of our stability analysis. First we introduce the distinction between proportions and dimension, as well as our thesis concerning stability in proportions and instability in dimension. Next we examine the condition for stability in dimension. We end with a brief analysis of business fluctuations.

Proportions and dimension

The description of behaviours supplemented by a number of accounting relations defines a dynamic model, from which the values of the variables in one period can be deducted from their values at the previous period. The problem is, then, to analyse the equilibria of this model and their stability.

Our models always possess an equilibrium position corresponding to the normal functioning of the economy. Other equilibria can also exist, depending on the exact modelling of behaviours, but we will abstract here from these equilibria, and focus on the issue of the stability of normal equilibrium. The main results obtained concerning stability are the following:

1. Equilibrium can be stable.
2. This stability is subject to certain conditions regarding the value of reaction coefficients.
3. Two types of stability can be distinguished, with different properties:
    (a) stability in proportions; that is stability with respect to the relative values of the variables (relative stocks of capital in each industry, relative prices and outputs);
    (b) stability in dimension; that is, stability with respect to the absolute values of the variables (general level of activity, general price level).

The conditions for stability in proportions are easily satisfied, whereas the conditions for stability in dimension are easily violated. This property corresponds to our first thesis about the stability of capitalism: capitalism is very stable with respect to proportions and very unstable with respect to dimension.

This distinction between proportions and dimension is not explicit in the literature, but it plays a crucial role in economic theory. In the Walrasian tradition, the problem of dimension is treated in a trivial manner. By adopting the point of view of macroeconomics, Keynes abstracts from proportions and focuses on dimension. Classical economists, in their analysis of the formation of prices of production, treat a problem of proportions and overlook the issue of dimension.

Note that our thesis about stability in proportions and instability in dimension sheds some light on the traditional debate concerning private interest and state intervention:

1. Individual interest ensures stability in proportions and, thereby, guarantees a certain form of efficiency in the system. (Capitals are allocated rather properly, commodities are usually available on the market in appropriate amounts for the customers who have the capability to pay.)
2. Individual interest at the level of individual firms is also responsible for the instability of the general level of activity. In combination with the management of monetary relations, individual behaviours may be responsible for the instability in dimension of the system. For this reason monetary relations were subjected to specific institutional regulations.

The condition for stability in dimension

We now present more explicitly a few results concerning stability in dimension and its relation to the analysis of business fluctuations. Since we abstract from all phenomena relative to proportions, it is possible to keep in mind the image of a single-commodity economy.

Stability in dimension refers to the stability of the loop

Production → Income → Demand → Production, in which credit mechanisms and the issuance of money (see above) are articulated. The crucial elements in this loop are: (1) the decision to produce, which commands the volume of output, but also income distribution; and (2) the decision to invest and borrow for investment (since we assume here that the decision to spend from a realized income is straightforward).

Instability in dimension is due to these decisions to produce and to invest. The decision to produce implies that a high level of demand in comparison to output, that is inventories below normal, will result in a stimulation of activity (high activity → high activity). A temporal problem is involved in the analysis of the effects of the decision to invest. Investment is stabilizing, or countercyclical, from the point of view of the long term. Firms decide to invest more or less in relation to their deficient or excessive capacity utilization rate in the present, to adjust this rate for the future (high activity → lower activity). In the short term, however, this behaviour is procyclical, since a large capacity utilization rate provokes an immediate reaction which stimulates demand and, thus, activity in the economy; that is it tends to increase the capacity utilization rate (high activity → high activity). The converse is obviously true for a low capacity utilization rate.

The loop Production → Income → Demand → Production is difficult to stabilize because of this dependency between short- and long-term phenomena. It is controlled through the management of monetary institutions:

1.   Firms are generally rationed concerning the financing of their investment plans for the future. They make decisions under a capital or financing constraint. This point of view has always been part of the classical perspective. It is essential to the notion of capital mobility.
2.   This capital constraint is imposed by the monetary system – who holds the privilege to issue money.

The exact form of the condition for stability in dimension depends on the model, but some basic patterns recur. For example, in a very simple form of the model (a short-term model with fixed prices), the condition is:

$$\theta < 1 \text{ with } \theta = \sigma + \epsilon\frac{\omega}{\varphi} \tag{10.9}$$

In this equation, θ is a synthetic parameter, and σ, ϵ, ω and φ are the reaction coefficients which were introduced in equations (10.6) and (10.7).

If θ is larger than 1, stability in dimension is no longer ensured; σ and ϵ correspond to the effect of demand on production or supply (cf. equation 10.7. The ratio ω/φ accounts for the effect of the level of activity on the formation of demand, via credit relations (cf. equation 10.8). It is easy to recognize the pro- and countercyclical effects of credit relations, corresponding respectively to ω in the numerator and φ in the denominator.

Business fluctuations

With this model it is possible to account for business fluctuations. Consider, for example, the business cycle as described by Marx for the nineteenth century: 'If we consider the turnover cycle in which modern industry moves – inactivity, growing animation, prosperity, overproduction, crash, stagnation, inactivity, etc.,' – (Marx, 1894, Chapter 22, p. 482). The cycle can be described as a succession of periods in which condition (10.8) is satisfied and then violated. When condition (10.8) is satisfied, the model converges towards an equilibrium (what Marx calls 'prosperity'). When the condition is violated, the outcome is different: 'overproduction', 'stagnation', and so on.

In order to describe exactly what happens when the stability of normal equilibrium is not ensured, it is necessary to be more specific concerning the description of behaviours at a distance from equilibrium (and to take non-linearities into account). Other equilibria can exist and be stable. We refer to two such equilibria as *overheating* ($u > \bar{u}$ and $s < \bar{s}$) and *stagnation* ($u < \bar{u}$ and $s > \bar{s}$), and interpret the business cycle as a succession of switches between the three equilibria (see, for example, Duménil and Lévy, 1987b).

Marx's description corresponds to the sequence: Stagnation – Balanced Growth – Overheating – Stagnation. The passage from balanced growth to overheating results from the violation of what we called the 'capital constraint', manifested in the rise of ω/φ in equation (10.8). The switch from overheating to stagnation is easily initiated by an economic shock and may develop into the cumulative contraction of the level of activity (the 'Crash') due to the combined effects of ϵ and ω.

In this interpretation of the business cycle, θ fluctuates around 1, sometimes above and sometimes below, but remains in a vicinity of 1. This is a general feature of business fluctuations (independently of their exact form which varied historically). It is the mathematical expression of the general thesis of the instability of capitalism with respect to dimension. In what follows we will provide an historical interpretation of this property, and introduce the corresponding notion of 'stability frontier'.

The Tendential Instability Thesis: Tendential Instability and Increased Social Controls

It is from the 'Tendential Instability Thesis' that we derive our view of the relationship between profitability and more generally historical tendencies. We begin by introducing the central idea in this analysis, which opposes the growing instability due to the transformation of firm management to the corresponding development of the social control of stability. Next we discuss more thoroughly the role conferred on the transformation of management in relation to the above analysis of stability and the tendency for the profit rate to fall. For brevity, the evolution of the institutional framework in charge of the control of stability will not receive a similar discussion. Finally we restate the role conferred on profitability in this analysis in relation to the periodization in three stages established in DGL.

Destabilizing behaviours, increasing social controls of stability and the stability frontier

Our general analysis, the 'Tendential Instability Thesis', can be summarized in three points:

1. The historical transformation of internal management creates in the economy an historical tendency towards an increasing instability.
2. The institutional framework (laws, regulations, policies) in charge of the social control of stability is developed in response to this growing instability.
3. Because of the combined effects of these two types of forces, stabilizing and destabilizing, the system is constantly maintained in the vicinity of the condition for stability which we call the 'stability frontier'.

The first of the three elements above provides an explanation for the paradoxical observation that, in spite of the growing social control of stability, capitalist economies are constantly close to overheatings, recessions or depressions.

There is in a capitalist system a tendency towards 'tighter' management, which ultimately increases instability in dimension. This increased instability results periodically in the multiplication of overheatings, recessions or depressions. Confronted with these manifestations of instability, the control of stability is progressively improved at the centre. These innovations do not usually anticipate the difficulties, but follow the experience of macroeconomic disequilibrium. Thus, in the history of capitalism, stability is constantly checked and then re-established in new configurations in which the individual contribution to the overall instability is increased, as well as the social control of stability.

These mechanisms can be easily understood using the model presented above:

1. Firm behaviour is represented by equations such as (10.7) and (10.8): the form of these equations is important, as well as the value of the reaction coefficients such as σ, ϵ and ω. These coefficients are involved in the condition for stability (cf. equation 10.9). Assuming that ϵ and ω increase, this accounts for the first statement that the transformation of firm behaviour may have an impact on stability.

2. The reaction of the institutional framework in charge of the social control of stability is represented by coefficient φ in equation (10.8). As shown by equation (10.9) the rise of φ may counteract the increase of ε and ω. But the transformation of this coefficient implies the progress of a complex set of institutions (in particular the banking system and its functionings).
3. The notion of a stability frontier refers to the fact that θ is constantly maintained in the vicinity of 1, whereas the values of ε and ω, on the one hand, and φ, on the other hand, are constantly increasing.

Management, instability and profitability

We now discuss why changes in management have historically increased instability. In our opinion the evolution of management should be approached using a distinction similar to that which is used in the analysis of technological change, which considers both the impact of prices (in particular labour cost) on the choice of the optimal combination (substitution) and technical progress. Applied to the analysis of management, this distinction opposes the two following mechanisms:

1. In a given state of knowledge, the choice of optimal behaviours (optimal reaction coefficients) depends on 'price' variables such as the cost of holding inventories or unused capacities, the cost of changing the level of activity and so on, and the profit rate. The profit rate, when it is actually falling, changes firm arbitration between present and future returns, implying the simultaneous rise of ε (for the short term) and ω (for the long term).
2. Management procedures have been the object of a constant progress throughout the history of capitalism. New procedures and practices have increased efficiency from the point of view of individual firms. Consider first the decision to produce in the short term. The profit rate will benefit from any improvement in the ability of the firm to maintain itself with lower levels of inventories (to minimize $\bar{s}$) or to use more intensively its productive capacities

(to maximize $\bar{u}$), provided that the firm preserves the capability to supply the good, possibly with the delay considered as normal in the course of business in the industry. This implies a modification of coefficients σ and ϵ, in the direction of a faster response to the evidence of disequilibrium. This is equivalent to saying that ϵ must be larger.[8] Similar outcomes are obtained for the decision to invest. The improvement of management leads firms strictly to control the use and growth of their productive capacities. This is equivalent to the increase in the coefficient ω.

The development of capitalism has been accompanied by a progressive deepening in the layers of management and a growing specialization of tasks. The individual capitalist in charge of the financing of the activity, the conception and organization of production, the supervision of the workers, the purchase of materials and the commercialization of goods, the control of inventories and liquidities and so on has been progressively compartmentalized and the object of specific business staffs. This evolution is not recent and was already well identified by Marx:

> Joint-stock companies in general (developed with the credit system) have the tendency to separate this function of managerial work more and more from the possession of capital, whether one's own or borrowed; [...] since on the other hand the mere manager, who does not possess capital under any title, neither by loan nor in any other way, takes care of all real functions that fall to the functioning capitalist as such, there remains only the functionary, and the capitalist vanishes from the production process as someone superfluous. (Marx, 1894, Chapter 23, p. 512)

Profitability and stability: a summing up

It is important to stress here the exact nature of the relationship between profitability and stability in relation to the periodization in three stages which was established earlier in DGL.

Along a trajectory *à la* Marx, as in the first and third periods, both mechanisms discussed above work in the same direction. The falling profit rate implies directly a tighter management, as well as the progress of management and, consequently, a tendency towards an increasing instability in two respects. During these periods technical progress was not sufficient to offset the tendency. From this observation one can surmise that the progress in management was also slow. Therefore its contribution to the growing instability of the system must have remained limited in comparison to the straightforward impact of diminishing profit rates.

During the intermediate period a revolution in technology and organization occurred. One can hypothesize that this revolution was also manifested in the overall management of firms (not only in the workshop). However, during this period, the two mechanisms were working in opposite directions, since the profit rate was actually restored. We have no evidence on which to base a contention that one mechanism was dominant. Still one can notice that two major crises occurred in this intermediate period (1921 and 1929).

Consider now the social control of stability. It is well known that the succession of the New Deal and the Second World War coincided with a major revolution in this evolution. This observation introduces a second element of periodization in two stages, which is actually quite traditional, between the two periods prior to and after the Second World War. We see this transition as an acceleration in the permanent historical tendency towards increasing central control.

In this interpretation, the profitability factor plays a central role, since it is the historical stimulus, directly, to the transformation of management and, indirectly, to the social control of stability. This analysis also sheds some light on the notion of a minimal profit rate, which could be defined as the smallest profit rate tolerable from the point of view of stability in a given institutional context. This notion is obviously relative.

3   HISTORY

In this section, we will briefly illustrate the explanatory power of the analysis presented in this study with respect to the interpretation of the history of the US economy since the Civil War, also using the descriptions provided in DGL and DL. We combine the description of historical tendencies and the analysis of stability, as well as the corresponding periodizations. This section divides into four, the first three parts corresponding to the three stages which we distinguish in the history of the US economy (before the turn of the century, between the turn of the century and the 1950s and since the 1950s). We end with a brief discussion of plausible scenarios for the future.

The First Historical Pattern *à la* Marx and the First Stage of the Managerial Revolution

We interpret the last decades of the nineteenth century as a typical period *à la* Marx. Recall that this is the period that Marx himself observed, which he called modern industry. In this first stage, real wages were slowly increasing and technology was correspondingly modified, with a continuous substitution of fixed capital for labour. Technical progress in the strict sense existed, but it was not sufficient to offset the tendency for the profit rate to fall. We can hypothesize that management was also progressing slowly. What we know from business fluctuations reveals that the general level of activity was not very stable, and the institutional social control of stability was archaic.

Obviously this evolution could not be maintained forever, and capitalism moved towards a deadlock. This situation culminated in the depression at the turn of the century, with unemployment rates skyrocketing to levels similar to those which would be reached in the 1930s (18.4 per cent in 1894 and 25.2 per cent in 1933). The US economy, to which the world economy could obviously not be reduced, provided in those years a good illustration that there were some grounds to Lenin's thesis concerning imperialism as the 'last stage of capitalism'.

The outcome of this situation was not the proletarian revolution but the acceleration of the progress of managers and, more generally, business staffs. The importance of this movement is such that we believe that it should be characterized as the first stage of a managerial revolution. The result of this transformation was the overwhelming empire of organization, in the workshop and outside, and its main achievement was the surge of technical progress. However a complete justification of the role conferred upon business staffs in this interpretation oversteps the limits of the present study.

Strength and Fragility of the Intermediate Stage and the Second Stage of the Managerial Revolution

The profile of the variables in this intermediate period, which lasted approximately until the 1950s, was in many respects quite specific. The productivity of capital and profit rate rose, and the growth in labour cost and labour productivity was accelerated. This period was obviously a period of restoration. However it was also undermined by a number of inherent weaknesses:

1. The rate of return on investment was increasing in a totally unusual manner. It resulted in the 1920s in a sharp upward movement in the financial markets, which, although not deprived of real foundations, was difficult to control.
2. Important and unusual risks were also associated with the accelerated rate of technical progress. As is shown in DL, technology became progressively more and more heterogeneous and considerable fractions of the stock of capital had to be discarded ahead of schedule in relation to the rise in labour cost. The threat came from the possible acceleration of such discards on the occurrence of a recession and the ensuing transformation of this recession into a depression.
3. The implementation of the institutional framework in charge of the social control of stability was progressing very slowly, in comparison with the destabilizing transformation of firm behaviour and the two specific threats introduced above. The development of capitalism was

accompanied by the growth of private centralized institutions, such as the financial market and the banking system, with inappropriate regulations and deficient state intervention.

These three features explain the dramatic character of the Great Depression: the speculation on the financial market, the exceptional extension and duration of the devalorization of capital, and the inability of the state to intervene effectively. With this interpretation, a double historical function is conferred upon the Great Depression: (1) considerable fractions of the capital stock rendered obsolete by the rise of labour cost were discarded; and (2) the institutional framework in charge of the social control of stability was thoroughly transformed by the combined experiences of the New Deal and the Second World War. This second effect of the depression so profoundly transformed the working of the system that one can refer to this transformation as the second stage of the managerial revolution, affecting mainly state agencies, instead of private enterprises.

The US economy emerged from the Second World War under exceptionally favourable conditions, culminating in the advantages of the two revolutions in technology and control of stability, and freed from the burden of obsolete vintages of capital. This juncture accounts for the prosperous character of the postwar years.

In this study, as well as in DGL and DL, the US economy has been considered in isolation, abstracting from the rest of the world. We can, however, hypothesize that the US economy was the first to undertake these transformations, in particular, to escape from the historical pattern *à la* Marx, at the turn of the century, anticipating the movement in the rest of the developed countries by several decades. After the First World War, its industry became progressively dominant in the world economy. It was deeply affected by the Great Depression, but the depression can be interpreted as a specific stage in this transformation. Finally the US economy emerged from the Second World War in the position of world leader.

The Second Pattern à la Marx

In the analysis of the period following the Second World War, we will distinguish two sub-periods as suggested in DGL: (1) the two glorious decades of the 1950s and the 1960s, in which the growth rates of labour productivity and labour cost remained high, although decelerating; and (2) the famous 'productivity slowdown' since the 1970s, a period in which these two rates of growth are low (and still decelerating).

Up to the late 1960s: the benefits of two revolutions

It is important to understand that all the dividends of the intermediate stage had been harvested in the 1950s. This means simultaneously that the performance of the US economy in the areas of technological change and distribution were very high, and that a new stage was initiated with new features à la Marx. The situation was, indeed, still very favourable, but the progressive erosion of this advantageous position was already under way. This situation was manifested in a different manner in the 1950s and 1960s.

The 1950s: high performance and instability   In spite of the beginning of the deceleration in the progress of technology and labour cost, the 1950s must be described as a very prosperous period. This feature has not always been acknowledged because of the even higher records obtained in the 1960s in some respects.

The profitability of capital was very high, but the benefit of this restoration had been transferred to the state through taxation (cf. DGL, Figure 3.2). Considering exclusively the effects of the transformation of firm management, the inherent instability in the economy was high. The progress of the social control of stability benefited from the transformation, manifested in the new stabilization policy, which we characterize as the second stage of the managerial revolution (at the centre). However this transformation was never consolidated and policies oscillated constantly between conflicting objectives (stimulation of the economy, retirement of the public debt and so on). Globally the period can be described as a period of constant fluctuation in the general level of activity, from high to low utilization rates, but without depression or cumulative inflation.

The 1960s: the Keynesian reprieve   At the beginning of the 1960s, it became clear to President John F. Kennedy's advisers that the economy had never fully recovered from the 1958 recession. They initiated an unprecedented effort to pull the economy upwards towards high levels of utilization of capacity, combining demand and fiscal policies. Thus the decline corresponding to the beginning of the second pattern *à la* Marx was at first hidden by the effects of policies in the 1960s,[9] and the rate of growth of wages was maintained.

This policy was successful until the end of the 1960s, when it became clear that the low value of the profit rate could no longer be explained by the effects of the fluctuations in the general level of activity. (Again we abstract here from the international dimension of these phenomena.) This is when it was acknowledged that the trend of the profit was downward (see references in the appendix to DGL) and that the rate of growth of labour productivity was diminishing. Simultaneously inflation continued to ratchet upward.

Post 1970s: the slow down, stagflation and the new stability

Beginning in the 1970s, the tensions over income distribution, associated with the falling profit rate (even after taxes), were followed by the reduction of the growth rate of labour cost and the increasing difficulty in financing state expenses. In relation to the very slow progress of labour cost, labour productivity also entered a phase of stagnation.

This period can again be divided into two sub-periods corresponding to (1) the return to technological and distribution trends (after the deviation in the 1960s) characterized by new instability and stagflation; and (2) a possible restoration of stability since 1983.

The 1970s: the return to the trend and the 'crisis'   The new pattern of evolution *à la* Marx was, in many respects, similar to that observed in the last decades of the nineteenth century. However the situation in the 1970s was specific in at least two respects (with opposite effects):

1. Not only were the trends in technology and distribution downward, but the variables abruptly returned to this trend, after what was called above the 'Keynesian reprieve'.
2. The benefits of the second stage of the managerial revolution (the increased ability to manage stability in dimension) were now felt. Thus history did not repeat itself in every respect and the 'crisis' seems to have been less severe than at the turn of the century.

Instead of a depression, the economy entered a stage of latent 'crisis', as a new policy was implemented emphasizing monetary policy. A new instability was observed, in relation to the diminished profitability of capital, with recurrent recessions of unusual amplitude (in 1970, 1974, 1980, 1981–2). The experience of the low levels of profitability by firms led to the adoption of new responses with respect to investment and prices. These adjustments were reflected in the rise of unemployment and a new type of inflation resistant to low levels of activity (called 'stagflation').

This episode had several important effects, in particular (1) the alleviation of the burden of debts and, probably, the discard of obsolete fractions of the capital stock of enterprises; and (2) the sharp decrease in the growth rate of labour cost and its reduction to levels 'compatible' with the pattern *à la* Marx.

Parenthetically one may notice that this analysis sheds some light on the effects of Keynesian policies in the 1960s. These policies pulled the economy towards very high capacity utilization rates and very low rates of unemployment. This movement certainly contributed to the continuation of the rise in labour cost, whereas technical progress in the strict sense was already slowing down. However it seems clear that this rise cannot be interpreted as the cause of the difficulties still faced by the US economy, since the return to the trend has been realized.

The 1980s: back to the trend and the new stability It is always difficult to identify new trends in recent developments. For this reason we will base our interpretation on several hypotheses, and only present a few tentative comments on the 1980s or, more precisely, the period 1983–9. In order to understand the specificity of this last episode it is important to distinguish between the analysis of the historical trends of technology and distribution, and the social management of stability: (1) technology and the profit rate are back to the trend, and the movement along the pattern *à la* Marx is slow; (2) after the latent crisis in the 1970s and early 1980s, the progress accomplished in the social management of stability was able to check the increased instability. As a result the general level of activity and prices were stabilized.

This analysis is based on three hypotheses concerning the interpretation of recent series: (1) the capacity utilization rate returns to normal and the phase of stagflation is terminated (a quite optimistic description[10]); (2) no inflexion upward of technical progress in the strict sense is evident; and (3) no accelerations of labour cost and labour productivity are under way. The thorough discussion of these three hypotheses oversteps the limits of the present study and would require a specific investigation.

The second point above (the restoration of stability) must be related to the remark made in Section 2 above, concerning the relative character of a 'minimum' profit rate. Once again this limit has been lifted as a result of the progress of policies.

Three Scenarios for the Future

This analysis does not suggest any easy remedy for the present difficulties of capitalism. The economy emerged from the latent crisis of the 1970s in a situation similar to that reached after an open crisis. Recovery was evident in the release of the inflationary pressure, and a certain restoration of stability. However the constraint associated with the pattern *à la* Marx has not been relaxed: the economy continues to follow the same track at a very slow pace (slow growth of wages and labour productivity, and slowly diminishing capital productivity and profit rate).

Beginning with this situation several scenarios can be devised for the future:

1. If the movement along the trajectory *à la* Marx continues, the difficulty will be to maintain stability and to manage social conflicts in the long term, in a situation of stronger oppositions over distribution. Note that, if the rate of growth of the labour cost is controlled (in relation to the limited rate of technical progress), the profit rate may be stabilized, and this would define a new pattern.
2. The most favourable event would be the repetition of a revolution similar to that recorded at the turn of the century. This new progress could correspond to significantly different mechanisms, for example an increased 'socialization' of technical progress, instead of the transformation of private management, and be followed by new acceleration of the growth rate of wages. Concerning the US economy, to which this study is devoted, no such restoration is clearly apparent in the series up to 1989.
3. A third scenario would be the emergence of a new stage in which a type of social coordination would be achieved between technical progress in the strict sense, labour cost, and the control of stability, with a prominent role conferred upon technical progress. The growth of labour cost would be fully endogenized and dependent on technical progress, but not necessarily stagnating. One may wonder, however, whether these new relationships could be obtained without a third stage in the managerial revolution.

As for the question of the emergence of a new industrial paradigm in Japan, for example, corresponding to one of the last two scenarios above, it clearly lies beyond the limits of the present study, and must be left for further research.

NOTES

*   We thank Mark Glick for his aid in the translation of this text into English.
1. In DGL, we derived a slightly different periodization: from the Civil

War to the First World War, from the First World War to the 1950s, and since the 1950s. In DL. we develop our analysis of technical change by considering the vintage technology, that is the technology which is characteristic of each new vintage of fixed capital. With this approach to technological change, the beginning of the transformation of technology can be dated as early as the turn of the century. This is the date that we use here for the transition between the two first periods.

2. In Volume I (Marx, 1867, Chapter 15 (2), 515–17), for example, Marx elaborates on Ricardo's analysis in chapter XXXI of *The Principles*, 'On Machinery'. He quotes Ricardo: 'Machinery and labor are in constant competition, and the former can frequently not be employed until labor rises' (Ricardo, 1817, 270). Following Ricardo and Marx, the criterion used by capitalists for the introduction of a new machinery is that of the reduction of the value, or more rigorously the cost, of the commodity: the machine will be used only if this cost is comparatively lower and this might be the case only for higher wages. This is equivalent to saying that the capitalists maximize their profits. An even more rigorous formulation would be to refer to the profit rate.

3. Obviously, 'exogenous', or 'endogenous' must always be understood in relation to a specific framework of analysis, and never as an intrinsic characterization of a variable.

4. As in the remainder of this chapter, we do not present the values of the Durbin-Watson test which are usually smaller than 2. The series are serially correlated since they reflect business fluctuations, and no other variable is available to account for this dependence.

5. It is clear that further investigation will be needed to clarify the difficult issue of the determination of wages. Several competing explanations could be proposed: did enterprises confront an increased difficulty in recruiting workers at the turn of the century (in relation to the controls on immigration and the limitation of the work week)? Did political conditions (the situation of the labour movement on a world basis) account for the acceleration of the growth in labour cost? Should this acceleration be related to the growing heterogeneity of technology or increase of business staffs? Or should these factors be considered in combination?

6. This issue is controversial. See, for example, Romer (1989) and Balke and Gordon (1989).

7. Duménil and Lévy (1987a, 1987b, 1987c, 1989a, 1990b and 1991b).

8. See Duménil and Lévy (1990a) where the determination of these coefficients is analysed. We also show that the improvement of the information of firms will produce a similar effect.

9. The average rate of growth of the profit rate over the period 1946–68 is positive, whereas the trend determined in DGL, Figure 3.8 is downward.

10. Figures recently released suggest that 'stagflation' might still be a good characterization of the economic situation in 1990.

REFERENCES

Aglietta, M. (1979), *A Theory of Capitalist Regulation*, London: New Left Books.

Balke, N. S. and R. G. Gordon (1989), 'The estimation of prewar gross national product: Methodology and new evidence', *Journal of Political Economy*, **97**,(1), 38–92.

Baran, P. and P. Sweezy (1966), *The Monopoly Capital*, New York and London: Monthly Review Press.

Devine, J. (1983), 'Underconsumption, overinvestment, and the origins of the Great Depression', *Review of Radical Political Economics*, **15**, (2), 1–29.

Duménil, G., M. Glick and D. Lévy (1991), 'Stages in the Development of US Capitalism: Trends in Profitability and Technology since the Civil War', Chapter 3 of this volume.

Duménil, G. and D. Lévy (1987a), 'The dynamics of competition: A restoration of the classical analysis', Cambridge Journal of Economics, **11**,(2), 133–64.

Duménil, G. and D. Lévy (1987b), 'The macroeconomics of disequilibrium', *Journal of Economic Behavior and Organization*, **8**, 377–95.

Duménil, G. and D. Lévy (1987c), 'La concurrence capitaliste: Un processus dynamique', 127–54, in J. P. Fitoussi and P. A. Muet (eds), *Macrodynamique et déséquilibres*, Paris: Economica.

Duménil, G. and D. Lévy (1988), 'Theory and facts, what can we learn from a century of history of the U.S. economy?' Barcelona: Colloque international sur la théorie de la Régulation.

Duménil, G. and D. Lévy (1989a), 'The analytics of the competitive process in a fixed capital environment', *The Manchester School*, **LVII**,(1), 34–57.

Duménil, G. and D. Lévy (1989b), 'Les Régulationnistes pouvaient-ils apprendre davantage des classiques?: Une analyse critique de quatre modèles'. Forthcoming in *Economie et société*.

Duménil, G. and D. Lévy (1989c), *The Regulation School in Light of One Century of the U.S. Economy*, Paris: CEPREMAP, LAREA-CEDRA.

Duménil, G. and D. Lévy (1990a), 'The rationality of adjustment behavior in a model of monopolistic competition', 224–42, in R. E. Quandt and D. Triska (eds), *Optimal Decisions in Markets and Planned Economies*, Boulder, San Francisco, and London: Westview Press.

Duménil, G. and D. Lévy (1990b), 'Stability in capitalism: Are long-term positions the problem?', paper presented at the workshop on

Convergence to Long-period Positions, Siena, 5–7 April 1990. Forthcoming in *Political Economy*.

Duménil, G. and D. Lévy (1991a), 'Investment and technological change since the Civil War in the U.S.: A vintage model', Paris: CEPREMAP, 9120.

Duménil, G. and D. Lévy, (1991b), 'Micro adjustment toward long-term equilibrium', *Journal of Economic Theory*, 53, (2), 369–95.

Keynes, J. M. (1936), *The General Theory of Employment, Interest and Money*, London, Melbourne, Toronto: Macmillan (1967).

Lipietz, A. (1979), *Crise et inflation: Pourquoi?*, Paris: Maspero.

Marx, K. (1867), *Capital, Volume I*, New York: First Vintage Book Edition (1981).

Marx, K. (1894), *Capital, Volume III*, New York: First Vintage Book Edition (1981).

Moseley, F. (1988), 'The rate of surplus value, the organic composition of capital, and the general rate of profit in the U.S. economy, 1947–1967: A critique and update of Wolff's estimates', *American Economic Review*, 78,(1), 298–303.

Moulton, H. G. (1935), *Income and Economic Progress*, Washington, DC: Brookings Institution.

Okishio, N. (1961), 'Technical change and the rate of profit', *Kobe University Economic Review*, 7, 86–99.

Ricardo, D. (1817), *The Principles of Political Economy and Taxation*, London: Dent and Son Ltd (1960).

Romer, C. D. (1989), 'The prewar business cycle reconsidered: New estimates of gross national product, 1869–1908', *Journal of Political Economy*, 97,(1), 1–37.

APPENDIX: PROFITABILITY AND STABILITY IN THE LITERATURE OF MARXIST INSPIRATION

We will first discuss two justifications for the importance of profitability common in the Marxist and Keynesian literature. Both refer to the occurrence of crises in relation to the formation of demand: excess profitability leads to a lack of demand for consumption goods, and deficient profitability leads to a lack of demand for investment goods. These two mechanisms are first considered separately, and then we discuss the relationship between disproportions and profitability in the explanation of crises.

Demand for Consumption Goods

The view that crises arise from a deficient demand for consumption goods (underconsumption) in relation to the excessive profitability of capital has always been a popular interpretation of business fluctuations. In the 1930s, it was denoted as the man-on-the-street interpretation of the Great Depression. It was given a theoretical foundation at the Brookings Institution, in particular, in the work of Harold Moulton (Moulton, 1935). It is also a common explanation in the Marxist literature (cf., for example, Baran and Sweezy, 1966, or Devine, 1983) and was revived, in France, by the Regulation School (Aglietta, 1979).

Since the argument hinges on the formation of demand (consumption) in relation to income distribution, the crucial variable here is not the profit rate but the share of gross profits in GNP.

The basic idea can be stated very simply in a Keynesian framework of analysis. The equality between the product and demand can be written $Q = I + C$, with an obvious notation. I is assumed constant and C is proportional to the product: $C = cQ$. The thesis under consideration implies that c is a decreasing function of the profit share π: $c = c(\pi)$. With this model the product itself is a diminishing function of π: $Q = I/(1-c(\pi))$.

Following this underconsumptionist interpretation of crises, the expectation is that the profit share increases before the occurrence of crises. In particular this should be the case for the Great Depression to which this analysis has been mostly applied. It is easy to test for the factual relevance of this analysis. As shown in Figure 10A.1, the share of gross profits in GNP was not exceptionally large or increasing in the 1920s.[1] The share of consumption was not exceptionally low either (cf. Duménil and Lévy, 1989c, Figure 3). The same is true for the crisis in the late nineteenth century or in the 1970s. As already noted, the profit share (net or gross) was very constant historically and its short-term variations *reflect*, and do not explain, business cycle fluctuations.

Demand for Investment Goods

Another traditional interpretation of the importance of profitability is the idea that the profit rate motivates investment.

Figure 10A.1   The share of gross profits in GNP (1869–1989)

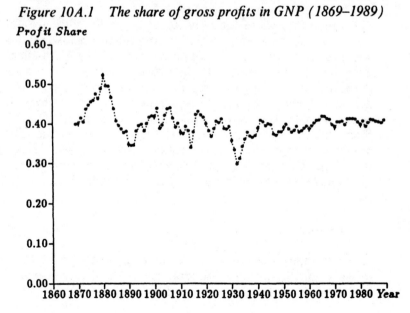

Capitalists invest because they are attracted by a return on their investment that they judge sufficient. This mechanism is common in the literature. It was at the centre of Keynes's theory of investment (the comparison between the marginal efficiency of capital, that is the expected profit rate, and the rate of interest): 'Now it is obvious that the actual rate of current investment will be pushed to the point where there is no longer any class of capital-asset of which the marginal efficiency exceeds the current rate of interest' (Keynes, 1936, p.136).

This view can be stated with the same formalism as above. Investment is an increasing function of the profit rate $I = I(r)$ and c is constant. Thus the product is an increasing function of r: $Q = I(r)/(1-c)$.

We reject this relationship as a general mechanism in the functionings of capitalism. Investment is limited in the general case by a capital constraint, except during recessions (and the 'recent' period of stagflation, but the discussion of these specific circumstances oversteps the limits of the present study; see Duménil and Lévy, 1988). A deficient investment is not the cause, but the consequence of recessions.

These two views of the importance of profitability are not exclusive and they can be easily combined. Following this interpretation, capitalist economies confront a permanent dilemma. If wages increase rapidly *vis-à-vis* technical progress, there will be a strong demand for consumption goods and a deficient demand for investment goods. On the contrary, if wages increase only slowly, and the profit share is inflated, there will be a deficient demand for consumption goods. The notion of an optimum rate of profit (that which maximizes Q, with I and c, both functions of r), or, at least, a tolerable range of variation of the profit rate, is actually implied in this analysis.

Disproportions

Another interpretation of crises in relation to profitability refers to the old notion of disproportions that Marx criticized in Ricardo's analysis. This thesis has been revived, for example, by Alain Lipietz (Lipietz, 1979), in relation to the effects of technological change.

Technological change may result in the transformation of the proportions among industries and, in particular, in the relative size of industries producing investment and consumption goods. If technological change is too rapid, it might, following this interpretation, outrun capital mobility. We refuted this view in Duménil and Lévy (1989b).

Note

1. Since the issue is that of demand, the consideration of the share of gross profits in GNP is more adequate than the share of net profits in NNP, as in Figure 3.10 of DGL.

11. A Negative Social Wage and the Reproduction Crisis of the 1980s

John A. Miller

The social wage was once an uncontroversial topic. Political economists had only to count the growing benefits bestowed upon working people by welfare state spending. Not so today. Political economists no longer agree either about the distributional impact of the social wage or about its effect on the accumulation process. Some maintain that the net social wage – or the social wage after taxes – is positive, and that it grew with the expansion of the welfare state in the postwar period and ultimately became one of the chief causes of the unravelling of the postwar boom (Bowles and Gintis, 1982). Others argue that working people pay out more in taxes than they receive back in benefits from state spending – or that the net social wage is negative – and that this shortfall got larger in the 1970s and 1980s (Shaikh and Tonak, 1987). For these political economists, the net social wage was not an impediment to the continuation of the postwar boom but a prop that helped to sustain it.

This chapter assesses the empirical evidence about the net social wage and asks if that evidence best supports a net social wage that is negative or positive, growing or diminishing. It also asks what that evidence implies about the distributional effect of welfare state spending and taxing policies and about the role these policies played in sustaining the postwar boom or bringing that boom to a close. In addition the author offers his own estimates of the social

284

wage spending, the tax burden of the working population and the net social wage, and concludes by arguing that a negative net social wage helped to push the US economy into a 'reproduction crisis' in the 1980s.

1 THE SOCIAL WAGE DEBATE

The social wage theorists argue that workers receive two types of wages: money wages that they earn as workers and social services from the state that they earn as citizens. Together these two wages, the money wage and social spending, constitute the societal wage of citizen-workers in the USA.

According to the social wage theorists (Bowles and Gintis, 1982; Bowles, Gordon and Weisskopf, 1984), the social wage of citizens, not the money wage of workers, has been the major arena of working-class gain in the postwar US economy. For instance, in 'The Crisis of Liberal Democratic Capitalism' Bowles and Gintis wrote that 'the major distributional gains made by workers were not achieved in their direct confrontation with capital over the bargaining table, but in the state' (Bowles and Gintis, 1982, p. 70). Bowles and Gintis's article offers quantitative evidence to support their contention (Bowles and Gintis, 1982, p. 73). (See Table 11.1 taken from their article.) By their calculation, social wage expenditures increased five times more quickly than take-home earnings over the postwar period. They conclude that these state policies increased the societal wage bill and, therefore, 'squeezed' profits and 'made a significant contribution to the slowdown' of the late 1970s and 1980s (Bowles and Gintis, 1982, p. 77).

Just as workers must work to receive wages, workers as citizens pay taxes to receive their social wage. So what becomes important in tracing the distributional gains of the working class through state policy is not social wage expenditures alone, but the difference between those expenditures and the taxes workers pay to the state – or what I call the net social wage. To demonstrate that working-class gains in the postwar

Table 11.1   Bowles and Gintis's citizen wage (1948–1977)

Year	Gross average weekly earnings[a] (1)	Estimated weekly direct taxes on earnings[b] (2)	Spendable average weekly earnings[c] (3)	Estimated weekly social welfare expenditures[d] (4)
1948	68	1	67	14
1950	74	2	72	16
1955	84	5	79	19
1965	101	10	91	32
1972	104	10	94	71
1977	104	10	94	71
Average annual rate of growth, 1948–77	1.5%	7.9%	1.2%	5.6%
Increase, 1948–77	36	9	27	57

Notes
[a]Gross average weekly earnings of production and non-supervisory workers, in 1967 dollars.
[b]Estimated weekly direct taxation (including employee contributions by social insurance) for production or non-supervisory workers, in 1967 dollars.
[c]Spendable average weekly earnings of production or non-supervisory workers, in 1967 dollars, for a worker with three dependants.
[d]Estimated weekly social welfare expenditures under public programmes per family of four, 1967 dollars.

Source: Sam Bowles and Herbert Gintis (1982), 'The Crisis of Liberal Democratic Capitalism: The Case of the United States' *Politics and Society*, **11**, (1), 51–93.

period have come through state policies, Bowles and Gintis show that workers' net social wage has increased, and increased more quickly than gross wages (Bowles and Gintis, 1982, p. 73). (Again, see Table 11.1.) By their estimation, taxes on workers, which they measure as the difference between gross wages and spendable income (as measured in the *Hand-*

book of Labor Statistics) are less than the social wage expenditures. Furthermore the difference between these taxes and social wage expenditures, Bowles and Gintis's estimate of the net social wage, grows throughout the postwar period. This difference constitutes the redistributive effect of state policies that has made a 'significant' contribution to the slow-down of the postwar boom in Bowles and Gintis's analysis'.

In 1987, Shaikh and Tonak, two orthodox Marxist political economists, challenged these findings (Shaikh and Tonak, 1987). In 'The Welfare State and The Myth of The Social Wage', they estimated the net social wage, or what they call the net transfer, for the period 1952 to 1985 (Shaikh and Tonak, 1987, p. 184). With the exception of the recession years of the 1970s and early 1980s, they found the net social wage to be negative. According to their calculations, for most of the postwar period workers paid out more in taxes to the state than they received back from the state in benefits from social spending. In their calculations, the net social wage became highly negative both in absolute terms and as a percentage of employee compensation (see Table 11.2 and Figure 11.1).

Shaikh and Tonak draw two conclusions from this evidence. First, the growth of the 'so-called welfare state' has caused a net reduction in workers' wages, not an addition (Shaikh and Tonak, 1987, p. 183); and second, as a result, the cause of the slow-down of the postwar boom cannot be found in the redistributive policies of the state (as the social wage theorists claim). As more orthodox Marxists, they argue instead that increasing capital costs brought on a decline in profitability of private production, which in turn caused the economic slump (Shaikh, 1987).

What accounts for the dramatic difference in these authors' results? A direct reply is difficult. The authors analyse the social wage from two quite different theoretical perspectives. In addition they used quite different methods to estimate the net social wage. And, unfortunately, their methods are not directly comparable because, as Shaikh and Tonak point out, Bowles and Gintis do not provide 'a consistent methodology and comprehensive framework' for calculating the net social wage (Shaikh and Tonak, 1987, p. 185).

Table 11.2   Shaikh and Tonak's net transfer (1952–1985)

Years	Exp. and benefits received by labour	Taxes paid by labour	Net Transfer
1952	21.01	34.58	− 13.57
1953	22.75	36.31	13.58
1954	26.85	34.89	− 8.04
1955	28.82	38.56	− 9.74
1956	32.69	43.68	− 10.99
1957	37.08	47.68	− 10.27
1958	43.29	47.84	− 4.55
1959	45.79	53.68	− 7.89
1960	49.21	59.96	− 10.75
1961	55.67	62.27	− 6.60
1962	59.39	68.43	− 9.04
1963	63.14	74.28	− 11.14
1964	68.01	74.52	− 6.51
1965	75.02	80.74	− 5.72
1966	85.84	97.21	− 11.37
1967	99.36	108.52	− 9.16
1968	111.75	125.15	− 13.40
1969	124.72	147.68	− 22.96
1970	144.97	151.48	− 6.51
1971	166.21	157.06	9.15
1972	183.22	184.74	− 1.52
1973	207.39	211.25	− 3.86
1974	241.83	237.21	4.62
1975	289.12	241.70	47.42
1976	310.98	277.57	53.41
1977	336.59	315.86	20.53
1978	367.93	362.21	5.72
1979	404.81	413.94	− 9.13
1980	468.92	457.18	11.74
1981	504.37	520.44	− 16.07
1982	548.14	561.18	− 13.04
1983	591.40	581.09	10.31
1984	598.51	646.10	− 47.59
1985	467.83	705.27	− 237.44

Source: A. Shaikh and A. Tonak (1987), 'The Welfare State and The Myth of the Social Wage', in Cherry *et al.* (eds), *The Imperiled Economy,* New York: Monthly Review Press.

In fact, as Shaikh and Tonak point out in their critique, Bowles and Gintis make two fundamental mistakes when they apply their estimates of social wage spending and taxes on workers to family income. Both mistakes inflate the net social wage. On one hand, Bowles and Gintis overestimate the benefits of social spending for workers by overstating the size of the average family. On the other hand, they underestimate taxes paid by workers by understating the number of workers per household (Shaikh and Tonak, 1987, p. 185).

This chapter asks if either team of authors provides a 'fair test' of the social wage concept as articulated (if not measured) by Bowles and Gintis and the other social

Figure 11.1   Shaikh and Tonak's net wage

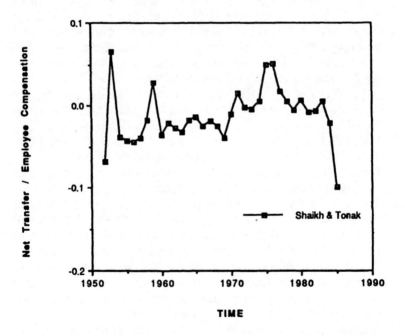

Source: A. Shaikh and A. Tonak (1987), 'The Welfare State and The Myth of the Social Wage', in Cherry *et al.* (eds), *The Imperiled Economy*, New York: Monthly Review Press.

wage theorists. The chapter then presents two alternative measures of the net social wage, both based on demand-side Marxist theories. And both produce a negative net social wage.

2   MAKING SENSE OF BOWLES AND GINTIS'S CALCULATIONS

To evaluate Bowles and Gintis's evidence that the net social wage is positive and growing, I translated their estimate of the weekly net social wage for each working family to an annual estimate of the net social wage for the entire working population. The translation has two advantages over Bowles and Gintis's original estimates. First, it avoids Bowles and Gintis's miscalculation of the number of workers (or taxpayers) per family and of the number of dependants (or beneficiaries) per working family. Second, it allows us to look more closely and more critically at Bowles and Gintis's modelling of workers' tax burden and social welfare spending.

Bowles and Gintis's treatment of the taxes paid by the working population is more problematic than their estimate of social wage spending. In fact, Bowles and Gintis never directly measure taxes paid out by workers to the state (see Table 11.1). Instead they offer a rough estimate of workers' tax burden: the difference between gross weekly earnings and weekly spendable earnings as presented in the *Handbook of Labor Statistics*. At best this measure captures only the direct tax burden of workers and ignores the indirect tax burden of other taxes (like the sales tax) that reduce the real income of the working population. But even as a measure of the direct tax burden of labour their estimate is flawed. The Bureau of Labor Statistics calculates average spendable earnings by subtracting federal income taxes withheld and federal social security taxes paid by workers from gross earnings. The Bureau has actually stopped calculating spendable earnings because the concept failed to subtract state income taxes from gross income and, therefore, no longer gives even an accurate measure of workers' weekly take-home pay.

Bowles and Gintis's use of the difference between gross and spendable earnings as a measure of the tax burden of labour is even more unsatisfactory than the Bureau's use of spendable earnings as an estimate of take-home pay. Taking the difference between gross and spendable earnings as labour's tax suggests a highly doubtful division of the taxes burden between labour and capital, or class incidence of taxes (Miller, 1986). By Bowles and Gintis's calculations, labour assumes only the burden of federal personal income taxes and employees' contribution to social security – the difference between gross and spendable earnings. The burden of all other taxes – from state income taxes to corporate income taxes to property taxes to employers' contribution to social security – falls on capital.

The results of applying Bowles and Gintis's class incidence of taxes are also highly problematic. For instance, in Bowles and Gintis's world labour's and capital's shares of total taxes were almost constant over the postwar period and labour's share of the tax burden never exceeds 42 per cent! (See Figure 11.2). In fact, a few years later, Bowles suggested something quite at odds with this result in his work with Gordon and Weisskopf. These authors maintain that 'capitalists have been able since the Korean War to reduce more or less continuously their share of the overall tax burden' (Bowles, Gordon and Weisskopf, 1986, p. 146). And Bowles, Gordon and Weisskopf's class incidence of taxes suggests that labour's tax share would range between 60 per cent and 75 per cent of total taxes in the postwar period.

On the expenditure side, Bowles and Gintis count as social wage expenditures the social welfare expenditures identified by the Historical Statistics of the United States (HSUS). The HSUS includes not only the usual social welfare expenditures, from public assistance to social security, but also veterans' benefits, military retirement and military disability. This measure grows continuously over the postwar period (see Table 11.3). Subtracting their estimate of labour's tax produces Bowles and Gintis's net social wage (corrected for their miscalculation of the average family size). That net social wage is negative in the 1950s, slightly positive in the 1960s and then more highly positive with the expansion of social security in the 1970s and early 1980s.

Even with these corrections, Bowles and Gintis's results are unsatisfactory. The tax analysis is not credible. And their social wage includes military spending. Given these shortcomings, I turned away from the Bowles and Gintis estimates of the net social wage and towards Shaikh and Tonak's calculation of the net social wage and assessed the credibility of their calculations as a test of the social wage concept.

3   SHAIKH AND TONAK'S NEGATIVE NET SOCIAL WAGE: IS IT GENUINE?

Is Shaikh and Tonak's negative net social wage as much a product of miscalculation as Bowles and Gintis's positive net social wage? Have Shaikh and Tonak systematically understated the benefits of social spending or overestimated the tax

Figure 11.2   Bowles and Gintis's tax analysis

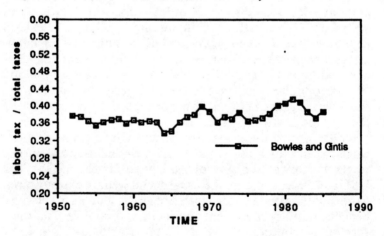

Sources: US Department of Commerce Bureau of Economic Analysis (1976), National Income and Product Accounts, 1929–1976; and *The Survey of Current Business* (July 1984, July 1987, July 1988), Washington DC: US Government Printing Office.

Table 11.3   Bowles and Gintis's net social wage

Year	Social wage exp.	$ Billions Labour's tax	Net social wage
1952	25.58	33.93	−8.35
1953	27.05	35.26	−8.21
1954	29.55	32.65	−3.10
1955	32.64	35.66	−3.02
1956	35.13	39.67	−4.54
1957	39.35	42.63	−3.28
1958	45.46	42.27	3.19
1959	49.82	46.41	3.41
1960	52.29	51.13	1.16
1961	58.24	52.36	5.88
1962	62.66	56.85	5.81
1963	66.77	60.97	5.80
1964	71.49	58.56	12.93
1965	77.18	64.41	12.77
1966	88.00	76.39	11.61
1967	99.71	84.96	14.75
1968	113.84	99.36	14.48
1969	127.15	117.72	9.43
1970	145.89	116.70	29.19
1971	171.91	116.32	55.59
1972	191.36	137.16	54.20
1973	213.94	152.07	61.87
1974	239.40	174.27	65.13
1975	290.06	171.24	118.82
1976	332.00	197.03	134.97
1977	361.55	223.84	137.71
1978	394.60	259.24	135.36
1979	430.70	305.96	124.74
1980	492.53	339.54	152.99
1981	550.55	395.95	154.60
1982	594.88	408.80	186.08
1983	643.44	408.20	235.24
1984	671.97	436.30	235.67
1985	730.40	488.60	241.80

Sources: As Figure 11.2.

burden of workers and thereby produced a positive net social wage?

Underlying Shaikh and Tonak's estimates of the net social wage is a vision of the state altering workers' wages by 'sleight of hand' (Shaikh, 1979). With one hand the state provides services that add to the wages of workers (health care and so on) and with the other hand the state takes taxes away from workers, reducing their wages. What is important, of course, is the overall effect of the movement of the two hands of the state – or the net social wage.

The Hand That Taketh Away

Let us begin by looking more closely at the second hand of the state, the revenue hand, How do Shaikh and Tonak estimate what the state pinches from workers' wallets?

Shaikh and Tonak use three steps to calculate the tax on labour. First they assign taxes to either capital or labour (see Table 11.4). For instance, Shaikh and Tonak count as direct taxes on workers all social security taxes or payroll taxes, and shares of personal income taxes, property taxes on homes and non-taxes (like motor-vehicle licences) based on labour's share of personal income (see Table 11.4). The remainder of taxes, which do not fall directly on labour, they assign to capital. Second, from the National Income and Product Accounts, they estimate the revenues raised by those taxes that fall directly on labour. Finally, to get their estimate of the private wage, they subtract the revenues raised by direct taxes on labour from the total compensation of employees.

We need to look closely at the first and third steps because they make it possible for Shaikh and Tonak to overstate the tax on labour and thereby underestimate the net social wage. I began with this question: do Shaikh and Tonak divide taxes between capital and labour in a way that is consistent with their earlier work estimating the rate of surplus-value in the US economy (or are they now assigning a larger share of the tax burden to labour)?

Their estimate of labour's tax is, in fact, greater than Shaikh's 1978 estimate of labour's direct tax (Shaikh, 1978).

Table 11.4 The class incidence of three Marxist theories

Tax	O'Connor	Shaikh and Tonak	Miller
Personal income tax	Personal income: capital and labour	Personal income: capital and labour	Personal income: capital and labour
Estate and gift tax	Capital	Capital	Capital
Corporate income tax	Consumption: capital and labour	Capital	Half capital and half consumption: capital and labour
Indirect Business Taxes			
Property tax	Consumption	Capital Some owner-occupied homes on labour	Half capital and half consumption: capital and labour
Sales tax	Consumption: capital and labour	Capital	Consumption: capital and labour
Social security tax	Labour	Labour	Employee's share on labour employer's share on consumption: capital and labour
Other taxes and non-taxes	Personal income: capital and labour	Personal income: capital and labour	Personal income: capital and labour

What they have added to labour's tax is labour's share of the property tax on owner-occupied homes. This change, however, was included in Tonak's 1987 estimates of labour's direct tax (Tonak, 1987). Furthermore this change does not significantly alter their results.

Since Shaikh and Tonak had not significantly altered their analysis of the class burden of taxes to calculate the social wage, I moved on to the next question: what taxes do Shaikh and Tonak include in their measure of direct taxes on labour that Bowles and Gintis leave out? Are these appropriate additions or have these additions arbitrarily turned Shaikh and Tonak's net social wage negative?

Shaikh and Tonak's tax measure differs from Bowles and Gintis's indirect measure of workers' taxes in a couple of ways. First, Bowles and Gintis use gross wages as their estimate of private wages before tax. Shaikh and Tonak's method, on the other hand, uses total employee compensation as its estimate of private before-tax wages. Total employee compensation is larger than gross wages by employers' contribution to social insurance. In effect, Shaikh and Tonak have added employers' contribution to social insurance to labour's tax. In addition, Shaikh and Tonak's labour tax includes a portion of the property tax and a share of the state income tax and non-taxes (as described above).

But these changes help to produce a more accurate measure of labour's direct tax burden. For instance, much of the public finance literature suggests that the burden of employers' contribution to social insurance is borne by labour in the form of lower wages (Pechman, 1985). All of the public finance literature would place at least some part of the burden of the property tax and other taxes and non-taxes on labour (Pechman, 1985). But, most importantly, even when part of the burden of these taxes is added to labour's tax, Shaikh and Tonak's estimate of taxes on labour remains rather modest. By their calculation, labour's share of total taxes ranged from 38 per cent in 1952 to 55 per cent in 1985 (see Figure 11.3).

In conclusion, my investigation reveals no apparent exaggeration of the tax burden of labour in Shaikh and Tonak's estimate that would by itself produce a negative net social

wage. If Shaikh and Tonak's negative net social wage is not
genuine, it must be because of their treatment of social spending, not taxes.

The Hand That Giveth

What about the other hand of the state, the one that provides
state services? Have Shaikh and Tonak underestimated the
expenditures that comprise the social wage and in that way
produced a negative social wage? Are some of Bowles and
Gintis's social wage expenditures excluded in Shaikh and
Tonak's estimates of the benefits of state spending for
workers?

Shaikh and Tonak use a two-step process similar to their
calculation of labour's tax to estimate the benefits of state
spending for labour. First, from the National Income and
Product Accounts, they identify those social welfare expenditures that benefit workers exclusively (such as social security).
Second, they add into the social wage other types of social

Figure 11.3 Shaikh and Tonak's labour tax

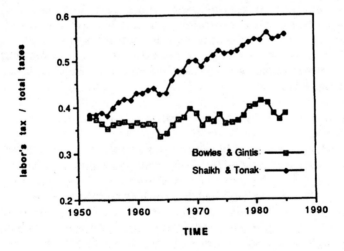

Sources: As Figure 11.2.

spending (such as education) weighted by labour's share of personal income.

This method is similar to that employed by Bowles and Gintis to estimate from social wage expenditures. There are, however, a few substantial differences. For instance, Bowles and Gintis include some state spending that Shaikh and Tonak exclude (veteran benefits, military retirement and military disability). Shaikh and Tonak count these as part of the cost of war and not the social wage. In addition, Shaikh and Tonak count under the social wage labour's share of several expenditures that Bowles and Gintis ignore: state spending for energy, natural resources, postal services and transport. In total, Shaikh and Tonak's categories account for the larger portion of state spending. For instance, in 1964, Shaikh and Tonak's social wage was derived from 48 per cent of the state spending, while Bowles and Gintis's was based on 40 per cent of the government budget.

What would happen if we added the veterans' expenditures (counted in Bowles and Gintis's social wage) to Shaikh and Tonak's estimates of the social wage? For 1964, this means that Shaikh and Tonak's social wage would now be derived from 52 per cent of the public budget. Of course adding these expenditures raises the social wage. It also makes the net social wage positive throughout the 1970s. For the rest of the postwar period, however, the net social wage is negative or almost neutral. The treatment of veterans' programmes, therefore, makes a significant difference in the calculation of the social wage.

Making the Net Social Wage Positive

Producing an unambiguously positive net social wage for the postwar period requires both excluding employers' contribution to social insurance from Shaikh and Tonak's labour tax and adding veterans' benefits to their social wage. With both these changes made, Shaikh and Tonak's net social wage would be positive after the mid-1950s and grow in absolute terms throughout the period (see Table 11.5). These results come closer to fitting Bowles and Gintis's description of a positive and growing net social wage that ultimately squeezes profits and contributes to the slowing of growth in the late 1970s. But, even with these adjustments, that fit remains problematic. The net social wage grows most quickly and reaches its highest point as a percentage of both wages and state spending in the mid-1970s as the economy slows, not before the slump.

More importantly, the adjustments necessary to create a positive net social wage are quite troublesome. First, on the revenue side, labour's share of total taxes once the employers' share of social security taxes is excluded would never exceed 40 per cent in the postwar period. On the expenditure side, the social wage would include military expenditures, not usually counted as social spending or part of the social wage equation.

In short, I was able to produce a positive net social wage only by making unrealistic adjustments to Shaikh and Tonak's analysis. Shaikh and Tonak's negative net social wage is not due to miscalculation or to an arbitrary modelling of state expenditures or taxes.

4 INDIRECT TAXES AND A NEGATIVE NET SOCIAL WAGE

If miscalculation did not produce a negative net social wage, what did? Perhaps the orthodox approach to crisis theory and state intervention that underlies Shaikh and Tonak's work leads them to their result? To test this proposition, I estimated the net social wage using a neo-Marxist demand-side model that assigns a much more crucial role to state policies than do the orthodox theorists like Shaikh and Tonak. Does this model produce a positive net social wage under an acceptable set of assumptions about the net burden of state spending and taxing policies?

James O'Connor's *The Fiscal Crisis of the State* (1973) is perhaps the best known neo-Marxist work that assigns the state an important and decisive role in the accumulation process. In this study, government spending and taxing policies sustain the accumulation process by socializing the cost of

Table 11.5   *Shaikh and Tonak's net social wage adjusted for labour's tax, less employer's contribution to social insurance and social wage expenditures, plus veterans' programme*

	$Billion	
Year	S and T net social wage	Adjusted S and T net social wage
1952	− 13.57	− 2.35
1953	− 13.58	− 2.76
1954	− 8.04	3.06
1955	− 9.74	2.41
1956	− 10.99	2.07
1957	− 10.60	3.76
1958	− 4.55	10.25
1959	− 7.89	8.67
1960	− 10.75	7.62
1961	− 6.60	12.79
1962	− 9.04	12.02
1963	− 11.14	11.80
1964	− 6.51	17.16
1965	− 5.72	18.93
1966	− 11.37	17.86
1967	− 9.16	22.88
1968	− 13.40	21.72
1969	− 22.96	17.09
1970	− 6.51	37.33
1971	9.15	58.17
1972	− 1.52	55.14
1973	− 3.86	64.56
1974	4.62	82.42
1975	47.42	133.66
1976	33.41	131.09
1977	20.53	127.81
1978	5.72	127.19
1979	− 9.13	128.22
1980	11.74	161.46
1981	− 16.07	154.19
1982	− 13.04	185.57
1983	10.31	227.98
1984	− 47.59	188.74
1985	− 237.44	14.31

Sources: As Figure 11.2.

reproducing labour and capital, augmenting aggregate demand and legitimizing the system. While state policies might enhance private profitability and forestall an economic crisis, they at the same time induce the fiscal crisis of the public sector: 'the tendency for government expenditures to outrace revenues' (O'Connor, 1973, p. 2).

In O'Connor's demand-side model, what is the net impact of state taxing and spending policies on workers? Is the net social wage negative or positive? I addressed these questions by looking first at O'Connor's analysis of state revenues, and then at his analysis of state spending.

On the revenue side, O'Connor's analysis is substantially different from that of the orthodox theorists. When O'Connor calculates labour's tax he takes into account both direct taxes and indirect taxes. The burden of direct taxes (like the personal income tax) falls directly on workers' wages. The burden of indirect taxes (like the sales tax or the corporate income tax) is shifted to workers in the form of either lower wages or higher prices. In fact O'Connor places special emphasis on the indirect taxes, for he argues that the monopoly power of large corporations has allowed them to shift the burden of many taxes onto the working class, consumers and small business (see Table 11.4). The result is what he calls the 'tax exploitation of the working class': a systematic increase in the tax burden of labour and the near pardoning of monopoly capital from taxation (O'Connor, 1973, p. 205).

As a result, O'Connor labour's tax far exceeds the tax burden Shaikh and Tonak assign to labour (see Figure 11.4). Using O'Connor's tax exploitation assumptions, labour's share of taxes range, from two-thirds to three-quarters of the total tax burden. Under Shaikh and Tonak's assumptions, labour's share of total taxes fell between 38 per cent and 55 per cent. This change alone, which dramatically increases the tax burden of labour, renders the net social wage highly negative throughout the postwar period (Table 11.6).

On the expenditure side, O'Connor identifies two types of expenditures that need to be included in his approximation of the social wage (see Table 11.7). The first, called social consumption, consists of state expenditures that promote accumulation by socializing the cost of reproducing labour (for example, social security, which reduces the cost of private retirement plans). The second consists of those social expenses that legitimize the system through welfare programs (see the starred items, which include veteran programmes). O'Connor's social wage spending exceeds Shaikh and Tonak's estimates. Nonetheless the net social wage remains negative throughout the period. Substituting O'Connor's social consumption for Shaikh and Tonak's estimate of social wage spending (and still using O'Connor's estimate of labour's tax) produces an even more negative social wage (see Table 11.8). When welfare expenditure (including veterans' benefits) are added to O'Connor's social wage it is less negative but still persistently negative and large throughout the period.

Thus a negative net social wage is just as much a part of O'Connor's neo-Marxist analysis of postwar accumulation as

Figure 11.4   O'Connor's labour tax/total taxes

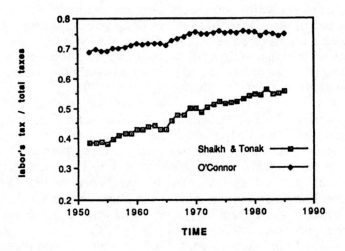

Sources: As Figure 11.2.

Table 11.6 *O'Connor's tax exploitation and the net social wage*

	$Billion	
Year	S and T net social wage	O'Connor's tax net social wage
1952	− 13.57	− 41.10
1953	− 13.58	− 43.22
1954	− 8.04	− 35.31
1955	− 9.74	− 41.18
1956	− 10.99	− 44.02
1957	− 10.60	− 44.59
1958	− 4.55	− 37.66
1959	− 7.89	− 46.40
1960	− 10.75	− 51.13
1961	− 6.60	− 47.63
1962	− 9.04	− 52.94
1963	− 11.14	− 57.98
1964	− 6.51	− 56.98
1965	− 5.72	− 59.10
1966	− 11.37	− 68.29
1967	− 9.16	− 68.02
1968	− 13.40	− 82.71
1969	− 22.96	− 97.35
1970	− 6.51	− 83.54
1971	9.15	− 75.08
1972	− 1.52	− 92.67
1973	− 3.86	− 103.43
1974	4.62	− 104.31
1975	47.42	− 65.00
1976	33.41	− 96.02
1977	20.53	− 119.50
1978	5.72	− 148.62
1979	− 9.13	− 174.98
1980	11.74	− 165.37
1981	− 16.07	− 205.93
1982	− 13.04	− 205.79
1983	10.31	− 202.26
1984	− 47.59	− 274.29
1985	− 237.44	− 478.29

Sources: As Figure 11.2.

of Shaikh and Tonak's orthodox analysis. In neither model is the net impact of state spending and taxing policies on labour positive. A negative net social wage is not merely the product of Shaikh and Tonak's orthodox approach to crisis theory.

That O'Connor's model produces a negative net social wage should not be surprising. The revenue side of O'Connor's analysis almost pre-ordains this result. In fact, when the implications of O'Connor's concept of tax exploitation are recognized, it is clear that the state budget almost always works on behalf of capital and at the expense of labour in his theory (see Miller, 1986). In part, this is why O'Connor assigns to state spending and taxing policies such a crucial role in the accumulation process. Of course, for the very same reasons, Shaikh and Tonak argue that state policies cannot be the main suspect in an investigation of the cause of the collapse of the postwar boom.

5   INDIRECT TAXES AND REPRODUCTION EXPENDITURES

The best way to assess the direct impact of state spending and taxing policies on workers is to look at their effect on the reproduction of labour over the long term. That requires accounting for both direct and indirect taxes on the revenue side and examining the effect of the social wage on the reproduction of labour over the long term.

In an earlier critique of O'Connor's work, I suggest that his notion of tax exploitation eliminates the class struggle over the state budget (see Miller, 1986). No matter what taxes are enacted, labour almost always bears their burden in O'Connor's world and, as a result, state spending is all but cost-free to capital. In my analysis, monopoly capital cannot as freely avoid the burden of financing the state as in O'Connor's work. For instance, in my framework the entire burden of corporate taxes and property taxes is not passed forward in the form of high prices (see Table 11.4). As a result, labour ends up assuming part of the burden of each of these taxes. My analysis assigns to labour a share of the tax burden that falls

Table 11.7   O'Connor's taxonomy of government expenditures

Social capital expenditures (accumulation expenditures)

Social investment consists of expenditures for: (1) natural resources and agriculture; (2) transport for commercial use; (3) urban renewal; (4) economic development assistance; (5) higher education and other non-elementary or secondary school education; (6) capital's share of utilities, sanitation, fire, water, sewerage, postal services and non-nuclear energy determined by the ratio of non-labour income to personal income; and (7) other.

Social consumption consists of expenditures for: (1) elementary and secondary education; (2) housing other than urban renewal; (3) health and hospital; (4) recreation and cultural activities; (5) old age survivors and disability insurance; (6) labour training and services; (7) labour's share of utilities, sanitation, fire, water, sewerage, postal services and non-nuclear energy determined by the ratio of labour income to personal income; (8) transport for non-commercial use; and (9) other.

Social expenses (legitimization expenditures)

Social expenses consist of expenditures for: (1) national defence and internation relations; (2) space research and technology; (3)* veteran benefits and services; (4) nuclear energy; (5)* medicare, medicaid, public assistance and other social welfare; (6)* unemployment insurance; (7) net interest paid; (8) civilian safety less fire; (9) financial administration including regulation; and (10) other.

*included in O'Connor's social wage expenditures.
O'Connor's social wage = social consumption + social expenses for welfare.

Source: James O'Connor (1973), *The Fiscal Crisis of the State*, New York: St. Martin's Press.

Table 11.8 O'Connor's social wage expenditures and net social wage ($billions)

Year	S&T social wage exp.	O'Connor's social wage	S&T net social wage	O'Connor's net social wage
1952	21.01	29.43	− 13.57	− 32.68
1953	22.73	31.30	− 13.58	− 34.65
1954	26.85	35.07	− 8.040	− 27.09
1955	28.82	37.64	− 9.74	− 32.36
1956	32.69	41.58	− 10.99	− 35.13
1957	37.08	46.46	− 10.60	− 35.21
1958	43.29	53.76	− 4.55	− 27.19
1959	45.79	56.06	− 7.89	− 36.13
1960	49.21	59.82	− 10.75	− 40.52
1961	55.67	66.99	− 6.60	− 36.31
1962	59.39	70.60	− 9.04	41.73
1963	63.14	75.17	− 11.14	− 45.95
1964	68.01	79.62	− 6.51	− 45.37
1965	75.02	87.21	− 5.720	46.91
1966	85.84	97.13	− 11.37	− 57.00
1967	99.36	111.32	− 9.16	− 56.06
1968	111.75	125.32	− 13.40	69.14
1969	124.72	138.79	− 22.96	− 83.28
1970	144.97	160.91	− 6.51	67.60
1971	166.21	186.11	9.15	− 55.18
1972	183.22	203.56	− 1.52	− 72.33
1973	207.39	229.86	− 3.86	− 80.96
1974	241.83	268.42	4.62	− 77.72
1975	289.12	319.83	47.42	− 34.29
1976	310.98	343.24	33.41	− 63.76
1977	336.39	363.65	20.53	− 92.24
1978	367.93	401.53	5.72	− 115.02
1979	404.81	443.19	9.13	− 136.60
1980	468.92	511.91	11.74	− 122.38
1981	504.37	568.59	− 16.07	− 141.71
1982	548.14	616.53	− 13.04	− 137.40
1983	591.40	659.58	10.31	− 134.08
1984	598.51	680.83	− 47.59	− 191.97
1985	467.83	726.27	− 237.44	− 219.85

Sources: As Figure 11.2.

between the poles represented by Shaikh and Tonak, on the one hand, and O'Connor on the other hand. For instance, in my analysis, labour's share of total taxes varies between 57 per cent and 66 per cent (see Figure 11.5).

Using my assumptions of tax incidence, I still derive a negative net social wage over the postwar period. This result holds true regardless of whether I employ Shaikh and Tonak's or O'Connor's method of calculating social wage spending (see Table 11.9). I want to emphasize three things about these results. First, in all three cases, the net social wage is least negative in the mid-1970s – *after* the slow-down of the accumulation process. Second, my revenue calculation relies only on a rather modest estimate of the indirect tax burden of labour. Third, even with this modest estimate of the indirect tax burden of labour, the net impact of state expenditures that go to reproduce labour is negative throughout the period and getting more negative in absolute and relative terms in the 1980s.

6   CONCLUSION: THE SIGNIFICANCE OF A NEGATIVE NET SOCIAL WAGE

My investigation suggests that Shaikh and Tonak's finding of a negative social wage is genuine and not merely the product of their method of calculation or their theoretical framework. In fact, using two other Marxist models, my calculation produced a net social wage more negative than the results reported by Shaikh and Tonak.

Does a negative net social wage mean that the social wage is an invalid concept, or that the 'citizen's wage' has not been an important arena of working-class gains in the postwar period? These are not easy questions to answer. For the present author, the social wage remains an important concept, even if the net social wage is negative. The impact of state policies on workers needs to be assessed carefully, even if that impact is negative. This is no less true today than it was earlier in the postwar period. A decade-long attack by conservatives has not managed to repeal the welfare state. And the distributional effect of the welfare state, or what remains of it, still needs to be assessed.

Analytically the magnitude of the net social wage and whether it is increasing or decreasing is just as important as its sign. The crucial issue for assessing the effect of the modern welfare state on the working population is this: did the changes in state policies in the 1980s leave the state taking more or less from labour than it did earlier in the postwar period?

While it might be difficult to speak of a negative net social wage as an arena of working-class gain, the lot of the working population does improve when the net social wage becomes less negative. After all, the welfare state did not create the capitalist state, it merely expanded it. Undoubtedly the capita

Figure 11.5   Miller's labour tax/total taxes

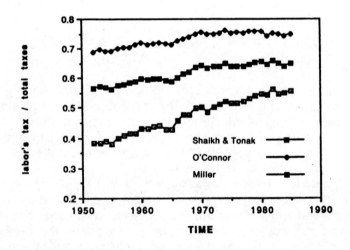

Source: As Figure 11.2.

Table 11.9 *Miller's labour tax and the net social wage*
(*$billions*)

Year	Miller's labour tax S&T labour exp. net social wage	Miller's labour tax O'Connor's soc. cons. net social wage	Miller's labour tax O'Connor's soc. wage net social wage
1952	− 30.02	− 31.33	− 21.60
1953	− 31.46	− 32.39	− 22.89
1954	− 24.24	− 26.79	− 16.02
1955	− 28.04	− 29.56	− 19.22
1956	− 30.27	− 32.16	− 21.38
1957	− 30.38	− 32.56	− 21.00
1958	− 24.00	− 27.89	− 13.53
1959	− 30.23	− 33.12	− 19.96
1960	− 34.31	− 37.22	− 23.70
1961	− 30.32	− 34.89	− 19.00
1962	− 34.26	− 38.05	− 23.05
1963	− 37.59	− 40.93	− 25.56
1964	− 35.24	− 39.05	− 23.63
1965	− 35.65	− 39.47	− 23.46
1966	− 41.99	− 48.63	− 30.70
1967	− 40.61	− 52.87	− 28.65
1968	− 51.18	− 65.63	− 37.61
1969	− 63.65	− 81.77	− 49.58
1970	− 49.86	− 74.13	− 33.92
1971	− 38.02	− 66.43	− 18.12
1972	− 51.78	− 85.00	− 31.44
1973	− 56.16	− 90.95	− 33.69
1974	− 53.47	− 98.70	− 26.88
1975	− 11.93	− 78.65	− 18.78
1976	− 34.37	− 105.05	− 2.11
1977	− 50.83	− 125.42	− 23.57
1978	− 72.89	− 149.62	− 39.29
1979	− 93.62	− 177.23	− 55.24
1980	− 80.88	− 187.20	− 37.89
1981	− 113.56	− 214.64	− 49.34
1982	− 110.69	− 233.71	− 42.30
1983	− 96.49	− 235.73	− 28.31
1984	− 153.71	− 280.40	− 71.39
1985	− 351.54	− 314.76	− 93.10

Sources: As Figure 11.2.

list state from its onset, long before the welfare state, pursued pro-capitalist policies. The relevant question is: did the welfare state lessen that pro-capitalist distributive bias?

My preliminary investigation of the social wage prior to the Second World War is inconclusive. Only in the calculations using O'Connor's theoretical categories, which assign the largest tax burden for labour, was the net social wage negative in all three selected years: 1922, 1936 and 1940 (see Table 11.10). Shaikh and Tonak's framework produces a positive net social wage in the three selected years and my own calculations show a positive net social wage in 1922 and in 1936. These tentative results, however, do suggest that it is not so much the growth of the welfare state, which had already begun in this period, that turns the net social wage negative as the growth of the 'warfare state' (assuming that these two elements of the modern capitalist state can be separated). The permanent arms economy and the expansion of the personal income tax to fall on most income earners, not just the relatively well-to-do, turned the net social wage negative early in the postwar period. In the 1980s, the Bush and Reagan governments administered another dose of the same bitter medicine that first made the net social wage negative: more public spending on military production and greater reliance on a personal income tax that is no longer progressive. This time the result has been to turn the net social wage highly negative (according to all three of my calculations).

Does a negative net social wage mean that the social wage did not make a 'significant contribution' to the slow-down of the postwar boom? In all three sets of calculations – in Shaikh and Tonak's model, in O'Connor's model and in my calculations – the net social wage became less negative in the 1960s and 1970s (and actually became positive in the mid- and late 1970s in Shaikh and Tonak's calculations). While this overall trend might suggest that a less negative social wage contributed to slowing the postwar boom, these data also present some problems for the social wage theorists. First, the improvement of the negative net social wage does not so much precede the slow-down of the boom as actually coincide with it. As Shaikh and Tonak emphasize, this pattern shows that

Table 11.10   *Rough estimates of the social wage for selected earlier years ($billions)*

Years	Shaikh & Tonak's net social wage	O'Connor's net social wage	Miller's net social wage
1922	1.05	−0.76	0.49
1936	4.46	−1.17	0.65
1940	4.93	−3.82	−1.07

Sources: US Bureau of the Census (1975), *Historical Statistics of the United States*, Washington DC: US Government Printing Office; US Department of Commerce Bureau of Economic Analysis (1976), *National Income and Product Accounts, 1929–1976*, Washington DC: US Government Printing Office.

the state intervenes most in the crisis and not before it (Shaikh and Tonak, 1987). Second, the significance of the change in the net social wage for the accumulation process is not clear. This needs to be established.

A negative social wage, however, does have important implications for the accumulation process that should not be overlooked. For instance, for the 1980s the highly negative net social wage describes state tax policies that took relatively more from labour and state spending policies that provided relatively fewer of the benefits necessary to sustain a labour force capable of producing surplus and reproducing itself. While shoving more of the burden of financing the state onto labour might be a victory for capital in the short term, these policies work against even capital's long-term interest. In fact these 'hyper-capitalist' policies ultimately compromise the accumulation process (Amott and Krieger, 1982) by endangering the reproduction of an able-bodied and skilled work force (see Miller, 1987).

Surely the 'labour shortage' in the 1980s – a shortage of highly productive workers willing to settle for modest wages – was symptomatic of the unsustainable character of these policies over the long haul (Amott and Miller, 1988). While *Businessweek* (1987) decried 'the decline of America's work force' and the *Wall Street Journal* lamented the fact that so many people are 'unemployable', surely workers were unemployable in large part because pro-capital state policies rendered them so.

In addition to its effect on the accumulation process, a negative net social wage offers a partial explanation of working-class resistance to the general expansion of the state and the appeal of the tax revolt. The distributive effect of state spending and taxing policy has been pro-capital, not pro-labour. The negative net social wage also helps to explain why workers at the same time remain willing to pay taxes for programmes which work to their benefit. This type of increase in state spending is much more likely to be pro-worker, even if much of the financing of the burden of that spending falls on labour.

REFERENCES

Amott, Teresa and Joel Krieger (1982), 'Thatcher and Reagan: State Theory and the "Hyper-Capitalist" Regime', *New Political Science*, Spring, 9–35.

Amott, Teresa and John Miller (1988), 'Square Pegs for Round Holes: The Truth Behind The Labor Shortage', *Dollars and Sense*, (134), March.

Bowles, Sam and Herbert Gintis (1982), 'The Crisis of Liberal Democratic Capitalism: The Case of the United States', *Politics and Society*, 11,(1), 51–93.

Bowles, Sam, David Gordon and Thomas Weisskopf (1984), *Beyond the Wasteland*, Garden City, NY: Anchor Press/Doubleday.

Bowles, Sam, David Gordon and Thomas Weisskopf (1986), 'Power and Profits: The Social Structure of Accumulation and the Profitability of the Postwar U.S. Economy, *Review of Radical Political Economics*, **18**, (1&2), 132–67.

Businessweek, 10 August 1987, 'The Coming Labor Shortage: Help Wanted', (3011), 48–53.

Miller, John A. (1986), 'The Fiscal Crisis of the State Reconsidered: Two Views of the State and the Accumulation of Capital in the Postwar Economy', *Review of Radical Political Economics*, **18**, (1&2), 132–67.

Miller, John A. (1987), 'State Spending and Taxing Policies in the 1980s: A Crisis of Reproduction', in Cherry *et al.* (eds), *The Imperiled Economy*.

O'Connor, James (1973), *The Fiscal Crisis of the State*, New York: St. Martin's Press.

Pechman, Joseph (1985), *Who Pays Taxes?*, Washington, DC: The Brookings Institution.

Shaikh, Anwar (1978), 'National Income Accounts and Marxist Categories', presented at the Summer Conference of the Union of Radical Political Economics.

Shaikh, Anwar, April 1979, personal communication.

Shaikh, Anwar (1987), 'The Falling Rate of Profit and the Economic Crisis in the US', in Cherry *et al.* (eds), *The Imperiled Economy*, New York: Monthly Review Press.

Shaikh, Anwar and Ahmet Tonak (1987), 'The Welfare State and The Myth of the Social Wage', in Cherry *et al.* (eds), *The Imperiled Economy*, New York: Monthly Review Press.

Tonak, Ahmet (1987), 'The U.S. Welfare State and The Working Class', *Review of Radical Political Economics*.

US Bureau of the Census (1975), *The Historical Statistics of the United States, Colonial Times to 1970*, Washington, DC: US Government Printing Office.

US Department of Commerce Bureau of Economic Analysis (1976), *The National Income and Product Accounts of the United States, 1929–1976*, Washington, DC: US Government Printing Office.

US Department of Commerce Bureau of Economic Analysis (July 1982, July 1984, July 1987), *The Survey of Current Business*, Washington, DC: US Government Printing Office.

Name Index

315

Subject Index